Fresh Woods and Pastures New

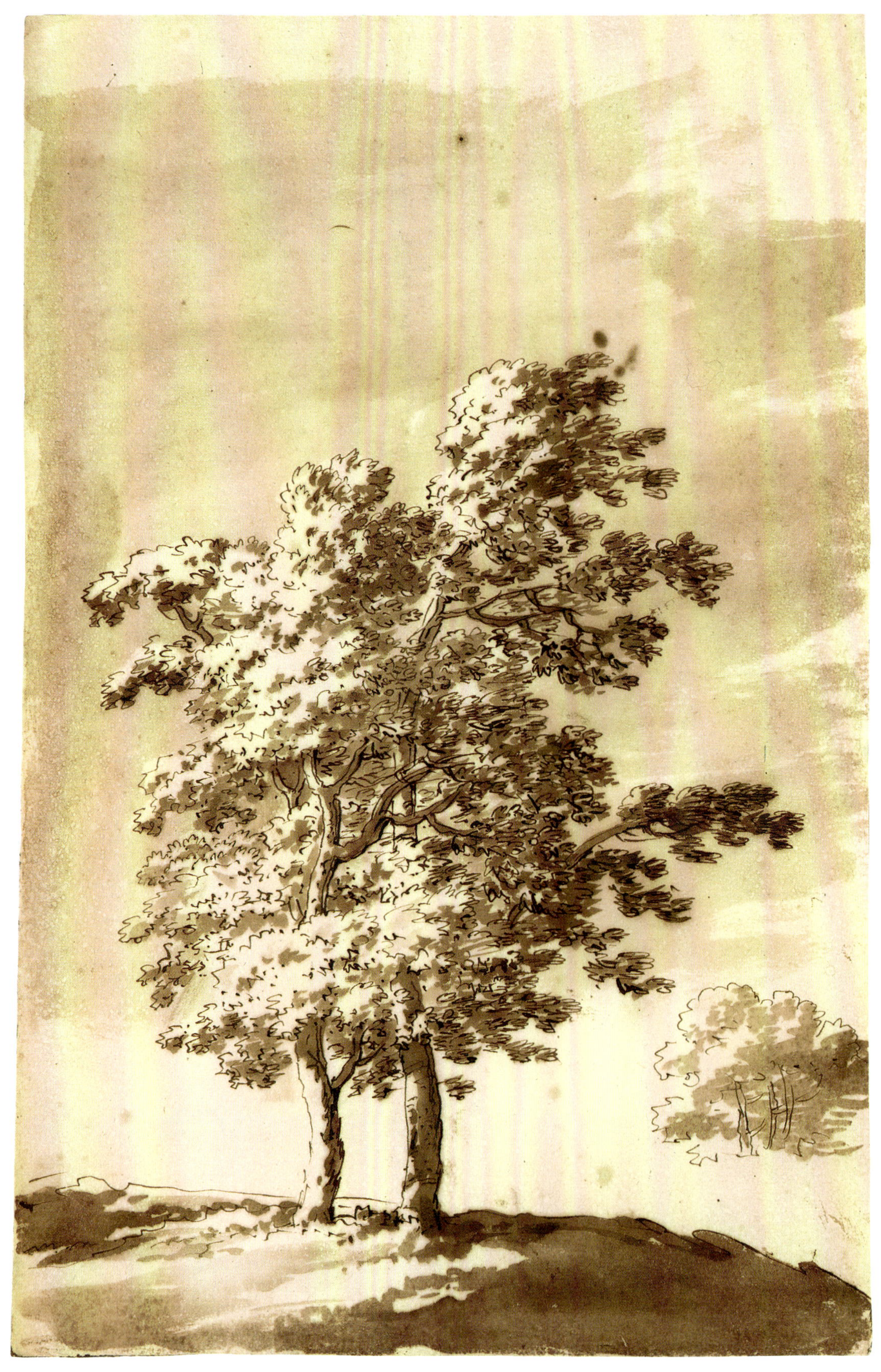

PM
4
PM
4
4
PM
4
PM

Fresh Woods and Pastures New

SEVENTEENTH-CENTURY DUTCH LANDSCAPE DRAWINGS FROM THE PECK COLLECTION

Franklin W. Robinson
and
Sheldon Peck

with contributions by
Theo Laurentius
and
Dan Kushel

1999

This catalogue accompanies an exhibition organized by the Ackland Art Museum at The University of North Carolina at Chapel Hill, curated by Franklin W. Robinson, the Herbert F. Johnson Museum of Art at Cornell University, and presented at:

ACKLAND ART MUSEUM
The University of North Carolina at Chapel Hill
Chapel Hill, North Carolina
October 3, 1999 through January 2, 2000

HERBERT F. JOHNSON MUSEUM OF ART
Cornell University
Ithaca, New York
January 29 through March 26, 2000

WORCESTER ART MUSEUM
Worcester, Massachusetts
December 16, 2000 through February 25, 2001

This exhibition and publication are funded in part by the William Hayes Ackland Trust.

Library of Congress Catalogue Card Number: 99-63183
ISBN: 0-9653805-7-2

COVER: Rembrandt van Rijn, *Canal and boats with a distant view of Amsterdam.* Cat. no. 22 (enlarged detail)

FRONTISPIECE: Jacob van der Ulft, *Two trees on a hill.* Cat. no. 31

Published by:
Ackland Art Museum
The University of North Carolina at Chapel Hill
Campus Box 3400
Chapel Hill, NC 27599-3400
http://www.ackland.org

Contents

Director's Foreword

ONE OF THE SPECIAL PLEASURES of association with a university art museum is the opportunity to collaborate with alumni whose affections for their alma mater include a bond with the campus museum. Alumni-collectors inspire students and the university community by sharing their art, expertise, and resources. Such individuals are especially precious to the Ackland Art Museum, which, at the comparatively young age of forty years, is blessed with a small, yet expanding family of alumni nurturing the arts at the University of North Carolina at Chapel Hill.

Sheldon Peck and his late brother Harvey – each a UNC-CH alumnus with two degrees – founded a collection of old master drawings that continues to grow with the participation of Sheldon's wife Leena. We are grateful to the Pecks for sharing a portion of their outstanding collection and for generously supporting the creation of this exhibition and catalogue. It is also essential to recognize Sheldon Peck's curatorial vision and scholarship evident in his essay and his contributions to the catalogue entries.

Franklin W. Robinson, the Richard J. Schwartz Director of the Herbert F. Johnson Museum of Art at Cornell University, has brought wisdom and expertise to the enterprise of curating this project. We are grateful to Theo Laurentius for sharing his comprehensive knowledge of paper in seventeenth-century Holland, and to Dan Kushel for exposing elusive watermarks through his pioneering use of low-level x-radiography.

We thank Joseph Gilbert and his colleagues for the thoughtful design of this publication. The fidelity of the catalogue reproductions is the contribution of Martin Senn, whose skill capturing the images in digital format we gratefully acknowledge.

Others who have contributed to the exhibition and catalogue include James A. Welu, director of the Worcester Art Museum, Worcester, Massachusetts, and at the Ackland Art Museum: Anne Douglas, registrar; Lyn Koehnline, conservator; and Timothy Riggs, assistant director for collections. Ami Kadar, administrative assistant at the Herbert F. Johnson Museum of Art, has also advanced the project.

– GERALD D. BOLAS, *Director*
Ackland Art Museum

Collectors' Foreword

One fall evening in 1977, I was in the Pullman-shaped drawings study at the Fogg Museum in Cambridge for the first session of a series of seminars titled, "Connoisseurship in Old Master Drawings." Konrad Oberhuber, the exuberant, young Harvard professor who organized the series, asked the handful of participants to try to pick out the Rembrandt from five unsigned drawings before us. Everyone leaned in closely, and soon eye movement was the predominant activity.

For me, this was a daunting assignment. As a lifelong science major, I never earlier had any reason to contemplate artwork so intensely. All the drawings were small by modern standards. They wore scars of age, such as tiny blotches or faded ink or darkened paper. Yet, all spoke to my visual sense and they piqued my deepest curiosity.

Finally, a woman (an artist-collector, as I learned later) in the group pointed to the "quick, brown lines" of a slight landscape and guessed correctly the Rembrandt. Konrad then explained why he was certain that this unsigned drawing was the work of the master. The small drawing was traditionally described as a winter landscape. A few brilliantly placed strokes in the foreground delineated a fence and road, diagonally receding to a sunlit farmstead seen after a fresh snowfall, he noted. Beyond the technical details, Konrad conveyed with convincing comparatives and excited gestures the drawing's remarkable clarity and unity of conception, as signs pointing to the inventive genius of the great master himself, not at all the work of a pupil or imitator. I looked and listened and swiftly became hooked.

At Konrad Oberhuber's suggestion, my first purchase was a work of art in the form of a book: Jakob Rosenberg's classic *On Quality in Art*. I have read and reread sections of this penetrating primer on connoisseurship many times since then. It enriches my view at every reading.

As a neophyte enthusiast of old master drawings with a particular attraction to Netherlandish works, I gladly received advice from the experienced on how to get started in the field. I was told, "It will take time." "You have to look at a lot of drawings." "Visit the great museums, sit in their print and drawing study rooms, and go through their boxes." "Get to know the dealers and auction-house specialists; they can help you." These directions indeed helped.

I enlisted the support of my brother Harvey, and, as usual, his collaboration was invaluable. We formed an intellectual partnership. A perfectionist by nature, he more than anyone set our standard to seek works only of high quality. Our first acquisition (Cat. no. 23) was made in the spring of 1978 with generous advice and encouragement from Konrad Oberhuber. At my brother's untimely death in 1981, the collection consisted of twelve Dutch and Flemish drawings, four of which are in this exhibition.

Since then, my wife Leena and I have enjoyed augmenting the collection as time, funds, opportunities, and inclinations have permitted. We both find great appeal in the visual and scholarly aspects of old European drawings and in the exotic "hunt" for rare and beautiful works.

This is the first exhibition organized from our collection of old master drawings. Public exhibition is a completely new experience for most of the seventeenth-century Dutch landscapes in this catalogue and show. Twenty-five have no history of exhibition anywhere. Only three of the remaining fifteen works had ever visited America in earlier shows.

Any personal endeavor spanning over twenty years, such as our specialized pursuit of art, is advanced with vital contributions from many friends, old and new. This exhibition provides us an opportunity to acknowledge and thank them for their important role in our growth and maturation in the challenging field of old master drawings.

Everyone has mentors, those who have given freely and memorably of time and expertise, early and often. We are thankful to have had several over these years. Key among them have been Konrad Oberhuber, Egbert Haverkamp-Begemann and Marjorie Cohn. Elmar Seibel is another who has steadfastly given us precious guidance and friendship for over two decades.

The idea of an exhibition for some of our drawings was seeded a few years ago by Sarah Schroth during her tenure as curator of the Ackland Art Museum at the University of North Carolina at Chapel Hill, my alma mater. From the beginning, Gerald Bolas, the Ackland's dynamic director, encouraged and supported us in this direction. Innis Shoemaker and Charles Millard, earlier directors of the Ackland Art Museum, laid the foundation of cordiality essential for such an undertaking. Franklin Robinson, noted Dutch scholar and director of the Herbert F. Johnson Museum of Art at Cornell University, inspired the focused nature of this landscape exhibition and catalogue and brought the ideas to fruition. Dutch art historian James Welu, director of the Worcester Art Museum, has graced this project with his full enthusiasm. Theo Laurentius has helped stimulate the expanded scientific consideration of our drawings with his innovative x-ray studies of seventeenth-century paper. The radiographic expertise of Dan Kushel, professor in the well-known art conservation department at Buffalo State College, was essential in delivering this special technical dimension, as was the digitized magic of Martin Senn. We appreciate the masterful skills in book design applied by Joseph Gilbert and his associates.

Many other friends have enriched our knowledge of European art, the art market, and our drawings. Some are museum professionals or independent scholars, some are from the world of art commerce, and some are fellow-collectors. All have been extraordinarily helpful and generous. They are Clifford Ackley, Noël Annesley, Boudewijn Bakker, Hans-Ulrich Beck, François Borne, Craigen Bowen, Elizabeth Chapin, Hugo Chapman, David Chernin, William Cottingham, Alice Davies, Charles Dumas, Dorothy Edinburg, Jeroen Giltaij, George Goldner, George Gordon, Naomi and Roger Gordon, René Harte, Jeffrey Horvitz, Beverly Jacoby, Rachel Kaminsky, Elina Kataja, Martin Royalton-Kisch, Lyn Koehnline, Frans Laurentius, Elizabeth Llewellyn, Elaine and Paul Marks, Barbara Matilsky, Gabriele Ouellette, Jan Peeters, Robert Putman, Timothy Riggs, William Robinson, Marianne Roelofs, Marcel Roethlisberger, Johan Bosch van Rosenthal, Gregory Rubinstein, Francis Russell, Simon Schama, Peter Schatborn, Wolfgang Schulz, Marjorie Shelley, Seymour Slive, Carol Ann Small, David Stang, Miriam Stewart, Werner Sumowski, John van de Ven, Patricia Ward, and Nicolette and Harold Wernick.

Our professional coworkers have been particularly supportive during the busy incubation time for this exhibition. Janice Wytrwal, Nessie D'Ambrosio, and Ivan Orup deserve special acknowledgment in this regard.

We joyfully honor the memory of four models of excellence: János Scholz, Harvey Peck, Sylvia Peck, and Max Peck. Each was an exemplar of exceptional taste and style, leaving impressions that we shall forever treasure.

– Sheldon Peck and Leena Peck
February 1999

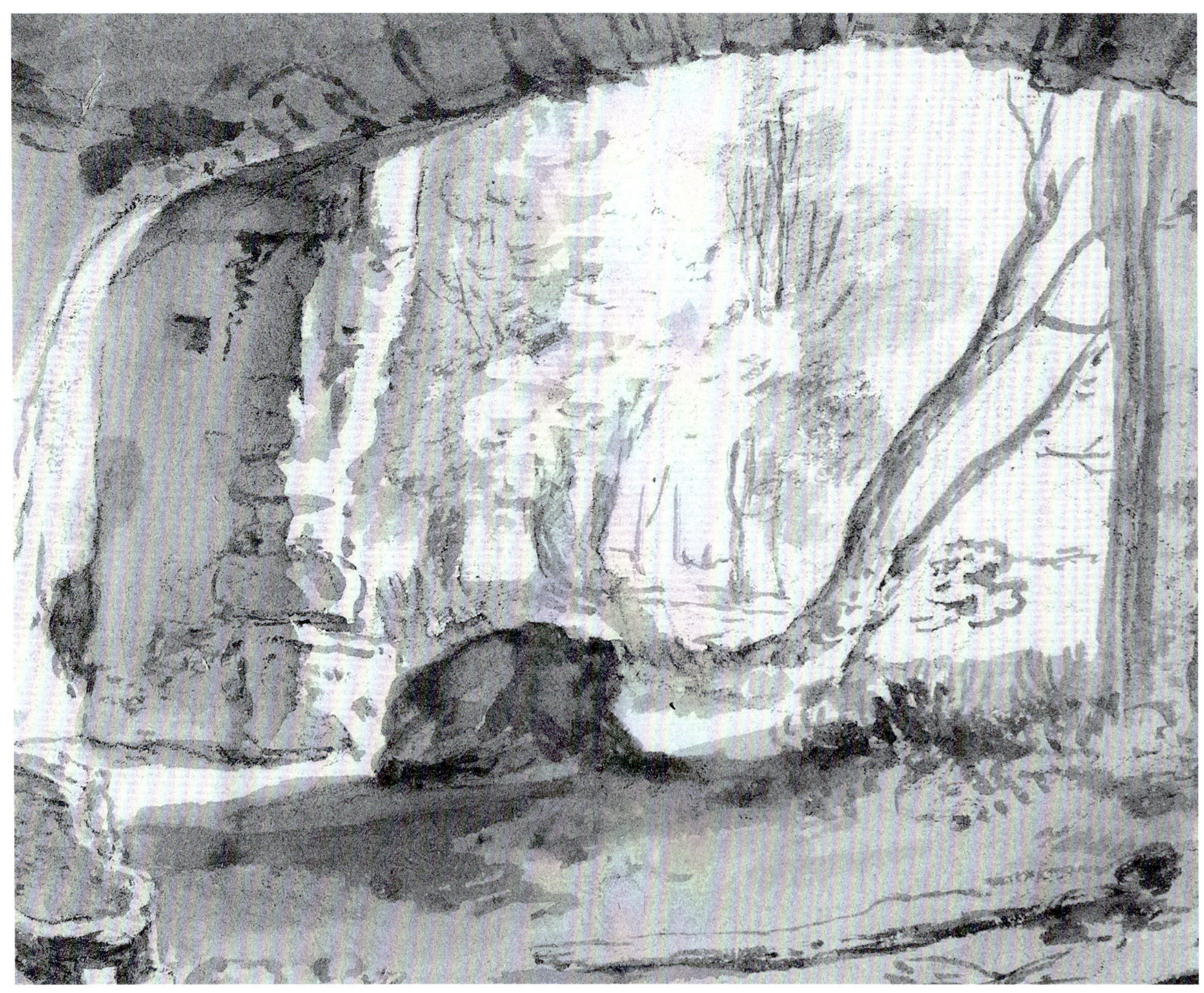

Enlarged detail, Cat. no. 3, Bartholomeus Breenbergh

Fresh Woods and Pastures New

SEVENTEENTH-CENTURY DUTCH LANDSCAPE DRAWINGS FROM THE PECK COLLECTION

Introduction

THIS SELECTION of drawings from the collection of Leena and Sheldon Peck provides an excellent introduction to seventeenth-century Dutch art in general, as well as to the special nature of Dutch drawings in particular.

Dutch society in the seventeenth century was unusually dynamic. The country had just achieved independence from the Spanish after a war lasting eighty years, off and on, and Dutch access to the North Sea allowed them to establish a worldwide network of trading posts and colonies. Amsterdam became not only a major shipping center and commodity market but also a haven for European capital. Along with this prosperity there was an atmosphere of relative tolerance that encouraged creative expression. Although the political leadership of the Netherlands was in the hands of Protestants, they barely formed a majority in Holland, the most powerful of the seven provinces that made up the country. Roman Catholics continued to practice their religion, if in secret, and other Christian sects, often exiled, like the Socinians, found a home in the Netherlands, or United Provinces, as they were called. Jews, particularly from Portugal and Spain, were a prosperous and intellectually vital part of the life of Amsterdam and other Dutch cities.

Artistic expression was stimulated by an atmosphere of intellectual experimentation, especially in the sciences. The Dutch development of the microscope, for example, was important for the study of the insect world, and many artists focused on this subject, with its emphasis on precise observation. Christiaen Huygens, the creator of the wave theory of light, had a brother, Constantijn, who was a gifted landscape draftsman, and Jan van der Heyden, a prolific painter of urban scenes, was a key figure in the development of street lighting and firefighting equipment.

In other words, art and everyday life were inextricably intertwined; the dominance of a mercantile middle class, politically and economically, reinforced this connection. The members of this class became the artists' major patrons, not the church or the nobility, and they wanted, for the most part, straightforward portraits of themselves, their possessions, and the world around them. Many patrons meant many subjects for paintings, usually familiar and recognizable, and rarely esoteric allegories and the like, in spite of the emblematic references that even the most everyday subject often conveyed.

It is in this context – Dutch self-confidence and pride in the world around them – that the drawings in this exhibition should be viewed.

The Idea of "Finish"

Dutch drawings in particular have a special character. An exhibition such as this represents a voyage of discovery not only of new, almost unknown, but gifted artists, as well as the major masters, but also of a new conception of drawing itself, its function, its economics, its quantity, even its size.

To be sure, artists of the time continued to make drawings as casual notations or first thoughts for works in other media; for example, in the Peck collection a sheet by Adriaen van de Velde is a careful preparatory study for a painting. However, there was an extraordinary growth in the production of drawings as finished products, ends in themselves, and sold as such, a phenomenon that resulted in a great increase in the sheer number of these works. There are many examples of these so-called "picture drawings" or "paper paintings" and related sheets: a long series of drawings documenting the damage done to the cathedral and other buildings in Utrecht in a storm in 1674; the documentation of *kunstkamers*, encyclopedic collections with everything from exotic seashells to unicorn horns; watercolors of tulips for sale catalogues; and many portraits, often to mark such special occasions as a wedding or graduation from the university. Certain artists seem to have made their living doing nothing but portrait drawings, including four members of the Vaillant family, while others concentrate on butterflies, bumblebees and other insects, often executed, expensively, in watercolor on vellum. Sometimes the drawings have a scientific purpose, since the line between artist and scientist was not hard and fast; careful observation was essential to both professions. Even the most modest, unpretentious subjects – flowers, pigs, peasants drinking or dancing – were given careful, elegant expression in sheets clearly made for sale.

This phenomenon of the drawing as finished product is especially apparent in the Peck collection. The three drawings by Allart van Everdingen in this exhibition are fascinating examples of this aspect of the time. Although the artist was a fairly prolific painter, he was an extraordinarily energetic draftsman, and these drawings, often highly finished and brightly colored, were clearly an important source of income for him. What is extraordinary about them is their small size; the winter landscape with skaters is less than four inches wide. Even so, it was of great enough interest to inspire a copy of the same size in the eighteenth century. Pieter Molyn, who is represented by two superb sheets in this exhibition, and Jan van Goyen, with four works made over four decades, produced hundreds of drawings that survive, and Willem van de Velde and Roelant Roghman were hardly less productive. George Keyes has called the Dutch "inveterate cataloguers of their world," and Roghman is especially interesting for his series of several hundred drawings of castles. The pen and wash drawing by Hendrik Hondius, which shows a ruined castle near Rotterdam, is very much in this tradition of topographical documentation of sites both exotic and domestic, both dramatic and intimate, whether in Brazil, Rome, or Amsterdam. In other cases, such as that of Willem Romeyn, the number of surviving sheets, their highly finished quality, and the very similar subjects – peasant life in and around Rome – suggest that they were popular with collectors and were put in their *kunstboeken*, which were stored in large cabinets called *kunstkasten*.

Another special aspect of seventeenth-century Dutch drawings also has to do with this concept of "finish," and a related phenomenon, the blurring of the boundaries between drawings, prints, and paintings. Willem van de Velde the Elder, for example, made pen paintings, seascapes in black paint on a white background on panel that convey the immediacy and spontaneity of drawings and the size and weight, as it were, of paintings. The monotype, a seventeenth-century invention, is a fusion of drawing and print; the drawing is literally made into a print, with all the freedom and uniqueness of the former and the structure and permanence of the latter. Rembrandt's work is perhaps the best example of this mixing of the media; his etchings can become a kind of public shorthand, with one part of a plate highly worked, "finished," and another only sketched in, with "mistakes" (such as a second left hand) left uncorrected, or a sheet of studies that is so informal that we have to turn the plate in different directions to read each sketch. The oil sketch, again a blurring of media and of the concept of "finish," is another specialty of Rembrandt and the Dutch, especially Adriaen van de Venne, whose energetic little peasant scenes are often decorated with Dutch sayings. This mixture is made explicit in trompe l'oeil paintings where, for example, engravings or drawings are painted as if they were pinned or pasted to a board or a wall.

In the Peck collection, a work such as the later Molyn was clearly regarded as finished; the artist has drawn a border around the whole composition, as well as signing and dating it. Willem van de Velde's seemingly casual record of a few ships in a calm sea may have had a pendant, now in an English private collection; presumably, the two works would have been conceived and sold as a pair, an arrangement usually reserved for paintings and sculpture. Even modest views of cottages and villages may have been intended as pendants; the two drawings here by Guillam Du Bois, or rather, their very similar equivalents, are related to two paintings that were also clearly a pair.

The Development of Style

This exhibition also offers us the opportunity to study the development of style in this period. We can see such development over the decades in the work of a single artist, for example, in Bartholomeus Breenbergh, from a modest sketch of an Italian road to a haunting scene inside a vault from the last year of his life, or in Jan van Goyen, as we see him grow from a fairly stiff presentation of a village scene, proceeding step by step into the background, in the 1620s, to his remarkable mature style, with its open, allusive shorthand, flooded with light, or in Herman Saftleven, whose earlier, tight intensity opens up and becomes broader and more assured fifteen years later, in the mid-1640s. It is equally instructive to compare works from early in the century to those executed at its end. The Hondius, for example, has a clarity and precision of pen line which tends to make every detail separate and distinct; this is very different from the atmospheric impression, later on, of an almost melting landscape and figures in Adriaen van de Velde, or the buildings and trees stunned with light, their contours only sketchily defined, in Jacob van der Ulft. In addition, as Lawrence O. Goedde has pointed out, although Dutch landscape paintings and drawings often respond to specific sites, they still tend to conform to one or another formal convention or pattern; their seemingly artless, relaxed informality is paralleled by the Attic or Senecan rhetoric popular with many contemporary writers.

In this context, the two greatest landscapists of the Dutch seventeenth century, Rembrandt and Jacob van Ruisdael, take an almost modest place within this group. It is not that their drawings are less important or less powerful than their paintings; their sheets have a remarkable freshness and immediacy of vision. Rather, we see in this collection as a whole the great truth about drawings, that the second-rank painter can make brilliant, imaginative, totally original drawings; there is an immediacy about this medium, so personal and spontaneous, that makes it a great leveler among artists. For example, Michiel Carrée's paintings are fairly conventional repetitions of the Italian landscape formula established by Nicolaes Berchem and his generation of Dutch painters, but his drawings have a wonderfully chaotic mixture of Dutch windmill, Italian natural bridge, and Rhine landscape that gives him a special place among Dutch draftsmen. Similarly, Willem Romeyn's paintings rarely achieve the quiet dignity and strength of his pen and wash drawings, with peasants and their animals caught in the late afternoon Italian sunlight.

Italy and the Dutch Arcadia

The title of this catalogue, "Fresh woods and pastures new," is taken from the last line of Milton's great pastoral poem, "Lycidas." The English and Continental traditions of Arcadian literature merged with a love of Italy to create a unique blend of the familiar and the exotic in Dutch art: happy, half-dressed peasants among their domestic animals playing the flute or caressing each other, with a hilly, Italianate landscape stretching into the background. The dream of Italy as a timeless, picturesque world of ease and beauty finds expression, in different forms, in several of the drawings in this exhibition. For example, all three drawings by Breenbergh are set in the Italian countryside, but they range from a quick sketch of a particular scene, made on the spot, to a dramatic set piece of a spectacular cliff to a haunting and mysterious view inside a vault, surely not a specific place but rather an almost emblematic evocation of the emotional, even spiritual overtones of enclosure and openness, deep shadow and sunlight.

Dutch artists' responses to Italy can range from the precise archaeological study by Cornelis Vroom to the Arcadian quiet of Willem Romeyn, who notes every rag and tatter of the peasant's clothes and the donkey's bundles and baskets, as well as the more dynamic, sun-splashed wash drawings of Jacob van der Ulft, an artist deeply enamored of Italy who probably never went there. One of the most remarkable of these responses is Adriaen van de Velde's beautiful study of a hut. This scene, so explicitly Dutch, is nevertheless profoundly indebted to the landscapes, and the paintings, Adriaen saw during his long sojourn in Rome in the 1650s.

Part of the charm of Italy for Dutch visitors was the presence everywhere of ancient ruins, with daily life continuing among them. Dutch artists were fascinated by their own, domestic ruins, more recent though they were. Added to their interest in the picturesque, and in documenting the visible world, was a pride in their own history, in this country which was so newly independent. This is probably the context for two of the most impressive drawings in this exhibition by Jan Lievens and Hendrik Hondius. Lawrence O. Goedde has quoted Constantijn Huygens's commendation of "the pleasure of ruins however grey or formless they may be," and he and other writers have discussed the term "schilderachtig," referring to the old and broken, as in ancient Roman or medieval Dutch ruins but also the modest, slightly timeworn farmyard that we see in Rembrandt's drawing here.

Dutch Art Today

One of the most interesting phenomena of contemporary taste is the popularity of Dutch baroque art. Exhibitions and publications about the Golden Age abound, and they are not limited to Rembrandt and Vermeer. Dutch drawings are especially popular with collectors; at this time, there are more than 3,000 in American public and private collections. Why has this happened?

One reason might be the similarity between seventeenth-century Dutch and twentieth-century American society: republican, urban, mercantile, middle class, stable. Also, Dutch paintings are immediately recognizable in subject, craftsmanlike, largely secular, relatively small, and intended for private homes; in addition, there are many different subjects and styles, with numerous individual personalities, and, until recently, they have been relatively unencumbered by theory and iconography. Another source of their popularity is their availability in the market; surely, never before had such a small country produced so many drawings. Whatever the reasons – the fact that the seventeenth is often called the first modern century, or sheer number and availability – Dutch art strikes a chord in the American psyche, and it is this spirit that infuses the Peck collection and brings us back to it again and again.

Beyond the immediate reasons for its popularity in America, why is Dutch art relevant to us today? It is truly a part of everyday life, an intense examination of the world around us, in a sense, a discovery of that world as something worth studying and recording, and celebrating. Vermeer's street in Delft, Cornelis Saftleven's pigeons, Adriaen van de Velde's hut, Rembrandt's backyard of a farm – these are all things worth looking at. To a degree, this is a function of history: the Netherlands was a new country, like ours, discovering itself and, in fact, making itself. Its language was new (in European terms), its cities were new, and newly populous, its religion, its definition as a separate political entity, its independence as such, and its global empire, were all new. Even the land itself was in the process of being reclaimed from the sea, the lakes, and the swamps. In pursuing these connections between our two republics, it is worth remembering that the Dutch golden age lasted less than a hundred years; by the last quarter of the seventeenth century, the Netherlands had lost its hegemony to England and France.

There are still other lessons that Dutch art and society offer us: its openness to all religions, its interest in science, from entomology to geometry, the end of the medieval guild and the beginning of modern industrial practice, and its fascination with new cities and old ruins, its faith in the future as well as its interest in the past. Above all, the Dutch artist seems to be saying, "I see; therefore, I am, and everything I see is of value." This collection is testimony to this fascination with the visible, this ability to take the everyday world and reveal its beauty, a lesson for which later centuries remain grateful.

THIS WRITER would like to thank the three photographic libraries he used in preparing this catalogue: the Frick Library, the Witt Library at the University of London, and, above all, the Rijksbureau voor Kunsthistorische Documentatie, one of the great resources in this field. I am also grateful to Gerald Bolas, director of the Ackland Art Museum of the University of North Carolina at Chapel Hill, for his energetic support of this project, and to Theo Laurentius, for his perceptive essay in this volume, as well as Ami Kadar, who has typed the many drafts of my essay and entries.

Above all, I want to thank the collectors for their patience, kindness, and hospitality. They have been the model of the truly scholarly collector, providing voluminous files on each of the drawings and many ideas on a whole range of relevant issues. It has been a great pleasure working with them.

– FRANKLIN W. ROBINSON

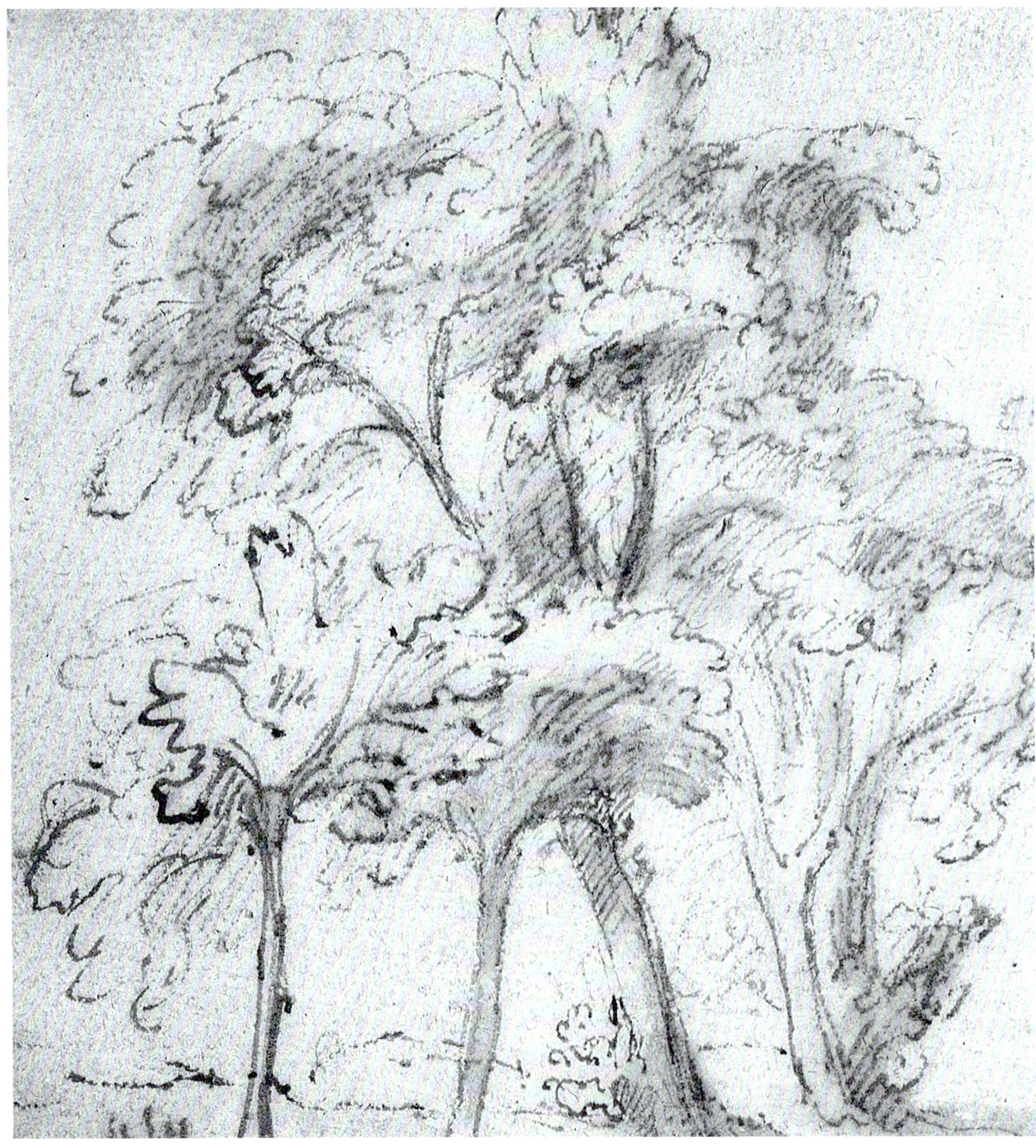

Enlarged detail, Cat. no. 10, Abraham Furnerius

Is that Drawing Right?

NOTES ON AUTHENTICITY AND CONNOISSEURSHIP

DUTCH ARTISTS of the seventeenth century were uncannily skilled at creating simple depictions of the truths of nature. It is this penetrating fidelity that first attracted my devotion to their drawings. The landscapes featured in this exhibition preserve timeless images of natural beauty from the labyrinthine ground cover of Lievens (Cat. no. 18) to the grassy polder of Rembrandt (Cat. no. 22), from the wind-swept homestead of Pieter Molyn (Cat. no. 20) to the windless sea of Willem van de Velde the Younger (Cat. no. 35), and from the summer idyll of Michiel Carrée (Cat. no. 4) to the winter frolic of Allart van Everdingen (Cat. no. 8). They record firsthand some quaint images the artists of the day found highly appealing, such as the avian roof-trappings of Cornelis Saftleven (Cat. no. 28) and the carefully rigged donkey-trappings of Willem Romeyn (Cat. no. 25). After years of receiving my most studious gazes, the forty masterworks presented here continue to elicit pleasure, learning, and awe – the ultimate paybacks from art. Yet, at another level, these 300- to 400-year-old sketches from the vision and imagination of gifted artists often have become the objects of my scientific curiosity and scrutiny.

The doctor's perspective may have something to do with this analytical focus. My wife Leena and I are professionally and academically involved as orthodontic specialists. In clinical medicine, patient problems are best identified and addressed by asking questions, the right questions. In 1902, Rudyard Kipling succinctly framed the salient queries in a verse accompanying his story "The Elephant's Child" (with my respects for Dr. Richard Asher, whose brilliant essay[1] on this subject was published thirty years ago):

> I keep six honest serving men
> (They taught me all I knew);
> Their names are What and Why and When
> And How and Where and Who.

What follows is a multifaceted exploration of old European drawings. First is a rather basic introduction to some esoterica about the nature of old master drawings, the attribution problems they present, and the experts who are skilled at resolving these problems. Then, the drawing "style" of artists is discussed, emphasizing, as connoisseurs do, the thought-out strokes and passages of a composition. Finally, I attempt to introduce and illustrate some aspects of a concept of graphic stroke analysis that has informed my "eye" over years of purposeful study. It is based on scientific studies noting subtle, remarkable consistencies in the way individuals execute writing and drawing strokes. These findings, coming from outside the community of art scholars, will be freshly applied to provide some new graphic clues to the draftman's nonvolitional style and to his identity. Thus, in this essay, I shall be exercising several of Kipling's serving men. In the process, I hope the boundaries of seeing may be extended for many other enthusiasts of the drawn image.

The Special Problems of Old Drawings

Until the nineteenth century, drawings made by European artists were seldom signed, annotated, or dated. Drawing with ink or chalk on paper was a method artists used to develop or test out their ideas, to practice their sketching skills, or simply to dawdle pleasurably, despite the high cost of paper. Drawings were considered peripheral to the artist's principal task of painting enduring, and usually signed, color pictures on canvas or wood panels. For the most part, then, signatures or inscribed identification was considered unnecessary for these personal experiments on paper – an innocent omission often contributing to uncertainties in attribution a few centuries later.

Compounding this question of artist's identity is the scarcity of old master drawings, even in earlier times. At least two influences, one psychological and the other methodological, may be responsible for the rareness of drawings from many European masters. Artistic insecurity probably provoked many of the old masters to suppress or destroy their drawings, so as not to detract from their more consequential oeuvre of paintings and sculpture. Michelangelo near death is said to have ordered the burning of his drawings and clay models.[2] The size of the surviving corpus of his drawings, albeit an issue of current controversy,[3, 4] appears to be unusually small. The other influence is the common use of erasable tablets (*tafeleten*, in Dutch) as an affordable alternative to expensive paper.[5] The *tafelet* was a stiff laminate of paper sheets, specially coated to facilitate metalpoint sketches and to make them easily erasable. The *tafelet* method, promoting efficient reuse of drawing and writing paper, surely helps account for the dearth of existing preliminary studies and experimental sketches by some well-known artists of the time. The complete absence today of authenticated drawings by great Dutch masters such as Johannes Vermeer, Frans Hals and Jan Steen could be the result of willful destruction and economical erasures during their lifetimes.

Anonymity and scarceness make the study of most old European drawings at once interesting and complicated. However, what compels us to want to attach a draftsman's name firmly to a drawing? Why care about the attribution of old master drawings? Why study authenticity?

To admire a sketch for its esthetic charm or visual strength is quite satisfying, even when its artist is unknown. Nevertheless, most conscientious curators, serious students, and collectors of old master drawings would study an anonymous work with the hope of attaching, at least provisionally, a nationality or school or an artist's name to it. Later on, someone may ask, "Is that drawing *right?*" "Right" in this sense means: Is the way in which the drawing was handled – composed and executed – consistent with the known styles of the period and the artist believed to have created it? In other words, "Is that drawing authentic?" Establishing a sound basis for the authenticity of old artwork is significant at several levels. The most compelling motives driving this pursuit, I believe, are scholarly curiosity and the search for historical truth. Also important are the financial interests of dealers, museums, art donors and tax collectors; a work of art usually has greater market value if it is incontrovertibly right.

The Connoisseur's Knack

Analysis of an artist's style has been a cornerstone in the traditional scholarly approach to find the right attributions for old drawings and to determine intrinsic values of quality. To evaluate a draftsman's individual style, the connoisseur may study closely the artist's choice of materials and subject matter, the compositional structure, the modeling of figures and faces, and the treatment of space and light, for example. The cerebral processing of this visual information coincides with what connoisseurs call their "good eye" or visual intuition, a sense enhanced (or biased) by certain aptitudes, education, experiences, and memories. Great connoisseurs (and great artists) expectably abound with visual intuition. They cultivate their skills through years of detailed observation of original works of art. Their "good eye" might be called their knack, which with years and title often earned earlier connoisseurs considerable privilege, wealth, respect and fear.[6] Today, most art experts are either professional scholars (university-based, museum-based, or independent), in the trade (dealers and auction-house specialists), or amateurs (an earlier designation for collectors, many of whom were accomplished artists themselves, who embraced particularly the collecting of drawings and prints as an intellectual avocation and an ante-photographic resource for images).

These days, only a few powerful dealer-connoisseurs remain, their numbers having been greatly diminished by a democratization of the art sales process over the last half-century. Pierre Mariette, Cornelis Ploos van Amstel, Samuel Woodburn, or Joseph Duveen – archetypal wheeler-dealers from the seventeenth through early twentieth centuries – would likely not thrive so well in today's informed, open-market fine-arts auction system. Over the years, art scholarship, too, has become egalitarian at the museums and the academies. The scene a century ago of Wilhelm Bode, the mellifluent scholar and dictatorial director of the Berlin Museum, publicly excoriating those of lesser rank for their contrary opinions on his pronouncements of attribution and quality represents an era closed.[7, 8]

The opportunities for nonprofessionals (for example, collector-amateurs and students) to develop sound connoisseurship skills have undergone a quantum increase in recent years. The mobility of great art by way of the traveling exhibition and the accelerated enrichment of the collections at public museums have had beneficial consequences in broadening the numbers of art devotees, and in increasing the depth of their knowledge. Public access to scholarly and visual materials has proliferated with the availability of excellent photoreproductions. A new and exciting revolution leaps at us now with the global propagation of digital images and information through the electronic Internet.

From my years of admiration and observation of old-master art connoisseurs at work in institutions and in commerce, I have noted the following personal traits that seem to be essential ingredients for their knack:

1. They are richly experienced visually. Connoisseurship usually gets better with age.

2. They demonstrate excellent powers of visual memory and image recognition.

3. They possess keen spatial sense and spatial memory. (Spatial perception, like map-reading ability, is a highly variable trait among individuals.)

4. They possess color memory, which for drawings would be more useful with watercolors than with the more customary monochromatic works.

It should be said that academic success today in art history does not absolutely demand a "good eye." Some art scholars are not necessarily interested in connoisseurship. They may specialize in the social or historical context of art, eschewing technical or analytical aspects such as evaluations of quality and attribution of individual works. For example, Guillam Du Bois' drawing of the Dutch village of Noordwijkerhout (Cat. no. 6) may be more important to some historians for its architectural details of the town church, the Witte Kerk, circa late 1640s, than for its unusual blend of red chalk with gray wash or for the evidence supporting its attribution.

On the other hand, most acknowledged connoisseurs do come from the ranks of successful scholars, those who can combine their training and experience with the visual skills necessary to render reasoned judgments on quality and rightness. Given the explosion of available information and images, only a rare few today can manage the enormous visual content defining expertise across many schools, cultures, periods, and media. Therefore, the art expert often develops a reputation as a specialist in the works of a particular group of artists related in some way, such as the Rembrandt school, or the French eighteenth century, or the Pre-Raphaelite movement.

Stylistic Analysis of Drawings

Although the analysis of an artist's style provides a framework for objectivity in identifying the artist's hand, it is surely not a flawless method. Traditional connoisseurs say that an artist's style is shaped by his personality. To a great extent this is true, if personality is defined broadly as the sum of the innate and acquired mental, physical, emotional and social characteristics of an individual. Unfortunately, the actual study of artistic style falls short of the embracing scope this definition suggests. In fact, stylistic analysis of master drawings has been largely restricted to the study of volitional output – strokes, forms and shapes knowingly and caringly composed by the artist. The nonvolitional strokes – incidental, repetitive fills and backgrounds – are usually ignored. Let's take Rembrandt studies as an example.

Three scholars particularly are at the vanguard of the analytical study of Rembrandt's drawings: Peter Schatborn at the Rijksmuseum, Martin Royalton-Kisch at the British Museum, and Werner Sumowski in Stuttgart. Peter Schatborn's recent essay[9] on "Aspects of Rembrandt's Draughtsmanship" is an example of stylistic analysis at its best. He advances an evidence-based approach to recognize the master's hand by studying details in drawings, building arguments for or against attribution to Rembrandt. With visual references often to the small core of documented Rembrandt drawings, he rather thoughtfully constructs a

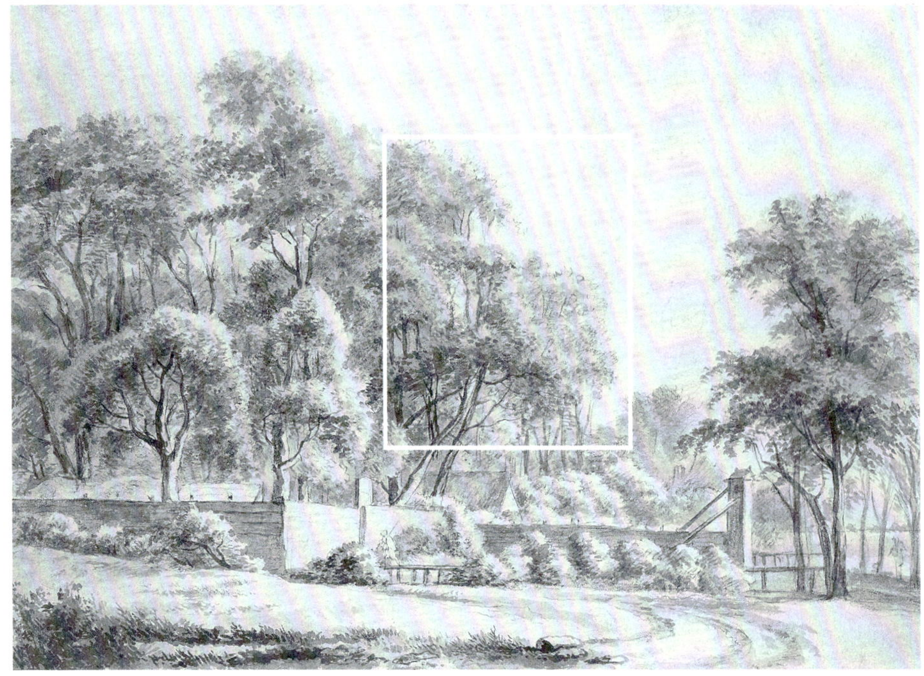

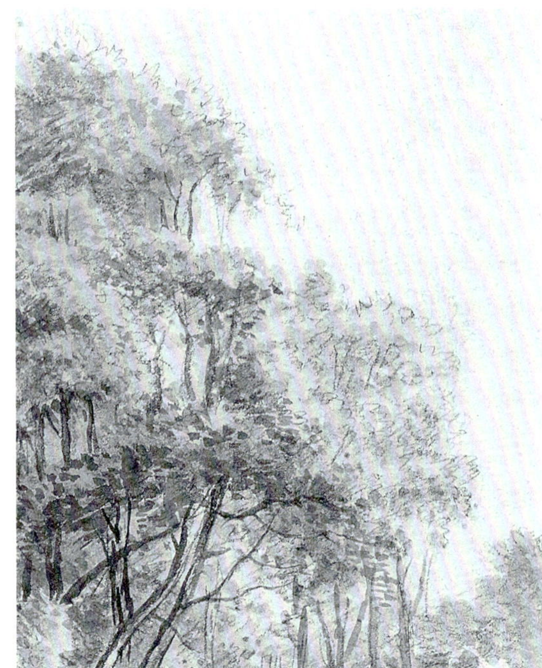

Fig. 1. Jan van Kessel, Cat. no. 17, with framed detail, enlarged at right. Zigzag tree-fill strokes in black chalk are easily observed at the right periphery of foliage.

volitional Rembrandt behind almost every significant graphic feature he interprets.

For example, Schatborn emphasizes that Rembrandt consciously conveyed the intensity and direction of a scene's light by his rapid, controlled accents and modulation of lines, clearly outshining his teacher Pieter Lastman. We also learn that Rembrandt was not reluctant to add corrections to his drawings, using bolder strokes or applying a white opaque wash. As Schatborn further notes, Rembrandt usually left his skies empty (see Cat. no. 22), unlike most of the cloud-loving Dutch landscapists of his time. Also, he followed a deliberate process of starting his landscape drawings at the horizon with very thin lines, then progressing to the foreground with much darker strokes and washes.

Despite fascinating and useful insights such as these about the intentional working methods of Rembrandt and other studied artists, little mention is made by scholars today of an artist's nonvolitional personality, of the possible analytical value of his seemingly insignificant, repetitive strokes. What can be said about the almost automatic, incidental lines in a drawing, those executed below the artist's level of awareness? What may we learn from the quick zigzags or hatching representing shadows and shading, the humdrum fills, the innocent scribbles, the curlicue leaves on a tree, or hairs on a head? Wouldn't the artist especially reveal himself in these informal, mechanical passages of a composition?

One amateur in the nineteenth century, Giovanni Morelli (1816–1891), seems to have had an incredible eye for this kind of artistic content. Morelli was a physician by training and an art lover by nature. He particularly took issue with the generous attributions given to many Renaissance pictures hanging in his native Italy. Morelli's awareness of human anatomy and his diagnostic eye led him to challenge many traditional attributions that were grounded in grandiose assumptions. He based his objective analyses on the habitual and idiosyncratic ways different artists seemed to form basic morphological details,

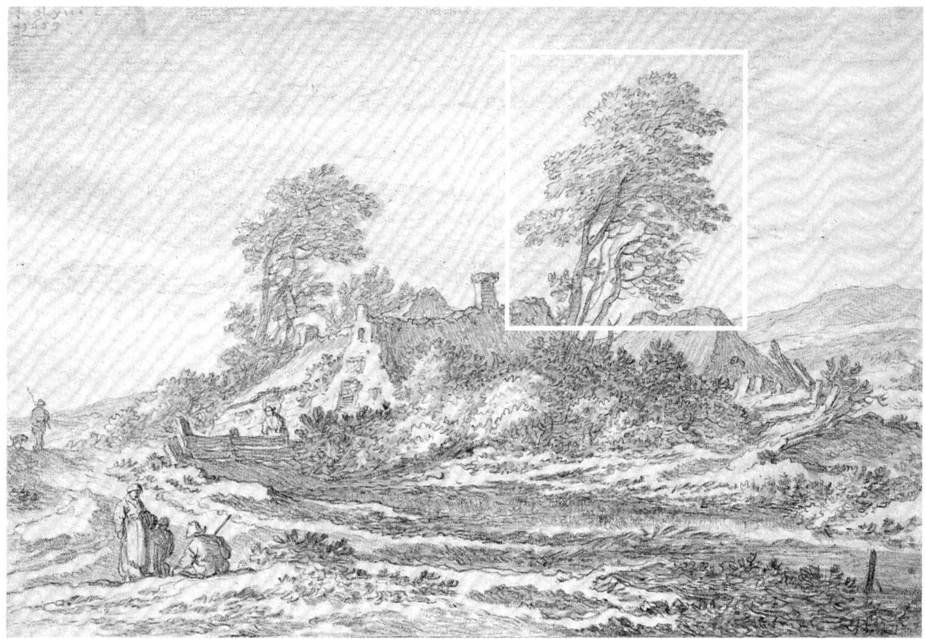

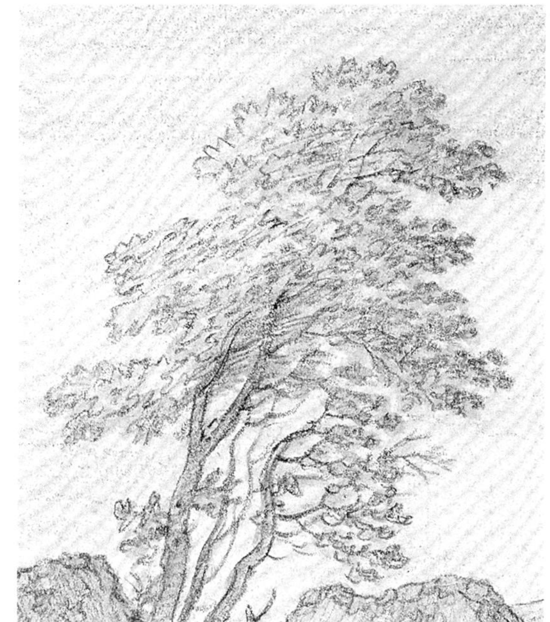

Fig. 2. Pieter Molyn, Cat. no. 20, with framed detail, enlarged at right. The artist delineates almost all of the peripheral and frontal foliage with tree-fill strokes of connected, inverted U's in black chalk.

like the ears, eyes, nose, and hands. He felt that exacting study of these small features could often reveal the artist's highly personal – and identifiable – artistic handwriting. Morelli received severe criticism for his pioneering semi-quantitative approach to help sort out masters from their imitators among European old master painters. He was forced to publish his life's work under a Russian pseudonym; only posthumous editions carried his name.[7]

Now, over a century later, Giovanni Morelli may be vindicated. The prescientific observations he promulgated as an aid to stylistic analysis of art have, I believe, some new biological underpinnings. Simple pictorial or graphic solutions, we learn, may be naturally embedded in an individual's brain and at the mercy of his upper-limb anatomy. This understanding points us to some new possibilities in advancing the state-of-the-art of drawings analysis.

Objective Analysis of Graphic Stroke Formation

The art of drawing has recently attracted close scrutiny from neuroscientists and psychologists. These researchers have shown convincingly that handwriting and drawing strokes and the "style" with which they are applied are under certain invariant biologic controls. (A selection of scientific reports in this field is referenced.[10–19]) Part of the biologic control for these manual activities derives from limb-muscle limits peculiar to the individual's hand, wrist, and arm, and part comes from programmed pathways innately "wired" into the central nervous system.

New research instrumentation has triggered a boom in the number of published studies examining factors involved in the production of human graphic tasks. Specialized computer software and digitized writing tablets are now available to record electronically every stroke, curve, and pattern in the dynamic processes of writing and drawing. At present, this apparatus can recognize and process

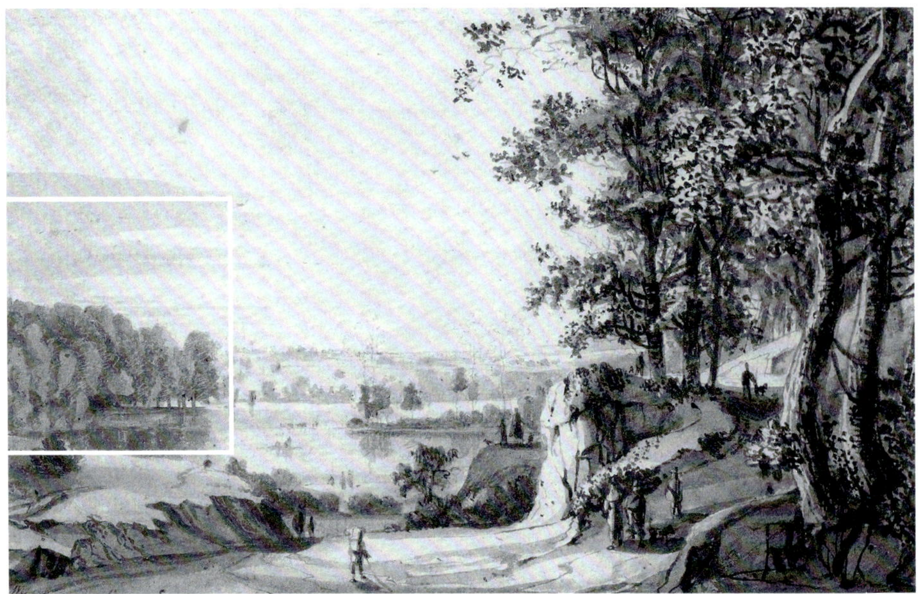
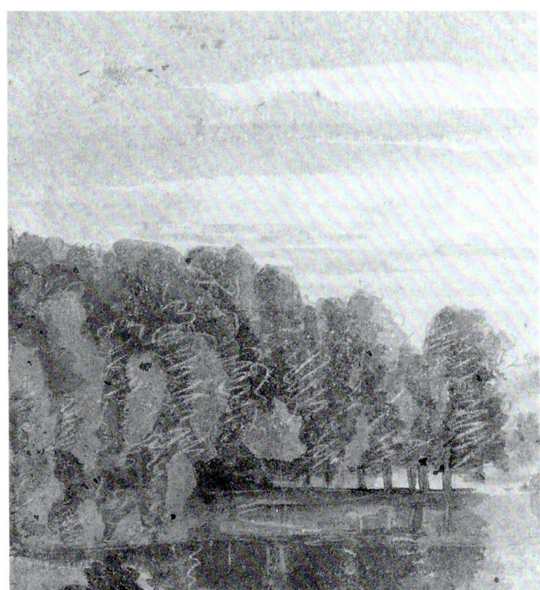

Fig. 3. Roelant Roghman, Cat. no. 23, with framed detail, enlarged at right. Tree-fill strokes are visible as thinly penned outlines under washes.

strokes less than 0.02 millimeters in width, 25-times narrower than a fine-point pencil lead.

Cursive handwriting is particularly targeted in investigations, since there is great commercial promise for a technology that may be able to claim a breakthrough such as signature recognition.[20] Writing familiar words like one's name is almost identical to practiced, repetitive drawing movements. Therefore, the results of these handwriting experiments are also applicable in the development of a scientific basis to help identify the subtly encoded graphic "signatures" of artists.

We are living in a digital age that encourages the eye to welcome novel ways of seeing images. In this context, we should suspend, for the moment, the usual focus on esthetics and style to concentrate on a drawing's less obvious character. Drawing experiments indicate that the hand of an individual follows characteristically repeatable pathways in creating cursively drawn lines. For example, a surprisingly limited number of graphic shortcuts exist for a landscape artist to fulfill the task of rapidly drawing in the foliage for trees and forests with pen or pencil. Leaves on trees – or *tree-fill*, as I call it – are most frequently represented in old master drawings by zigzag patterns resembling connected U's or V's (Figs. 1, 2).

The often inconspicuous, rapid zigzags of tree-fill can offer telltale clues about the specific anatomy and motions of the artist's drawing hand. In other words, these strokes may carry the unique imprint of the draftsman's arm-wrist-hand characteristics, elements of his identity. In kinesiology (the study of body movements), the "principle of least effort" establishes the way we physically carry out tasks, including manual work. Thus, from their student days onward, most artists execute their drawing strokes, especially the rapidly repeated forms and hatching, in the most efficient manner for maximum conservation of muscular, articular, and cerebral energies. By studying the slants of the angular loops or vertices of the connected "U" strokes and "V" strokes, a useful diagnostic

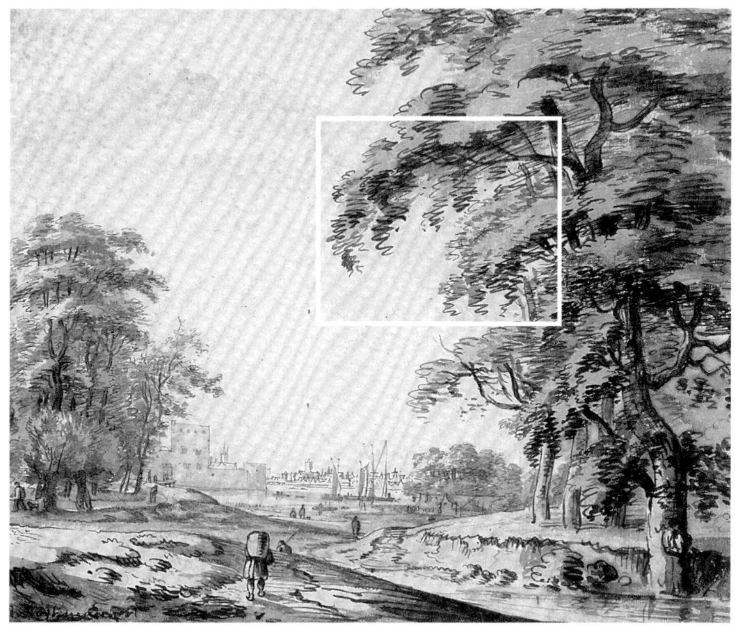

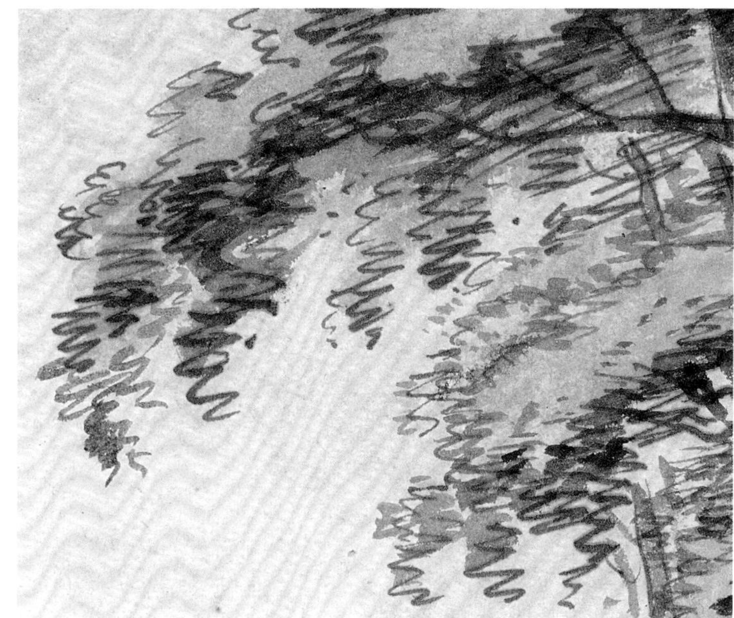

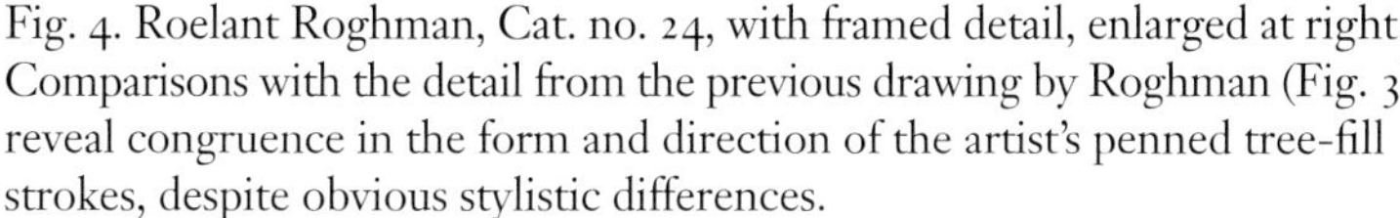

Fig. 4. Roelant Roghman, Cat. no. 24, with framed detail, enlarged at right. Comparisons with the detail from the previous drawing by Roghman (Fig. 3) reveal congruence in the form and direction of the artist's penned tree-fill strokes, despite obvious stylistic differences.

factor becomes available to help determine if a drawing is right. The most readable tree-fill strokes are found usually around the borders of foliate trees with the closed side of the U's and V's facing out. I describe the direction of these graphic forms using clock-face nomenclature. For example, tree-fill positioned at 8 o'clock indicates strokes inclined downward around 30 degrees from the horizontal with the U-shaped and V-shaped elements facing outward towards the lower left border of the tree. Usually, an artist's tree-fill is set down in two principal, and opposite, directions along closely related, if not identical, axes; this bidirectionality is made possible by elasticity in finger maneuvers in the presence of relatively inelastic arm-hand movements. Some circumstances are responsible for exceptions and atypical variations: right-left handedness differences; variables involving the artist's angular placement of the paper; whether the artist was seated or standing; and differences that may be associated with age-related physical or mental infirmities. Nonetheless, experimental studies and my own observations indicate that the favored form, slant and direction of such tree-fill strokes are largely invariant for the individual.

Examples of this biologically based graphic constancy are seen in the landscape drawings of Roelant Roghman, a talented member of Rembrandt's Amsterdam circle. Roghman demonstrates several graphic styles in his 149 known, signed drawings (see Sumowski[21] and van der Wyck[22]). Close analysis of his tree-fill, the shorthand artistic representations for leaves, boughs, and leaf clusters, provides remarkable evidence of a qualitative unity throughout his stylistically assorted range of drawings. In this exhibition, the two signed landscape drawings by Roghman show obvious stylistic differences. Yet, the form and orientation of his tree-fill strokes are identical in both (Figs. 3, 4). His "Broad river view with wooded shores" (Cat. no. 23) shows a delicate style with tree-fill executed by thinly penned outlines under brushwork. Contrast this with his majestic "High trees by a river with a town in the dis-

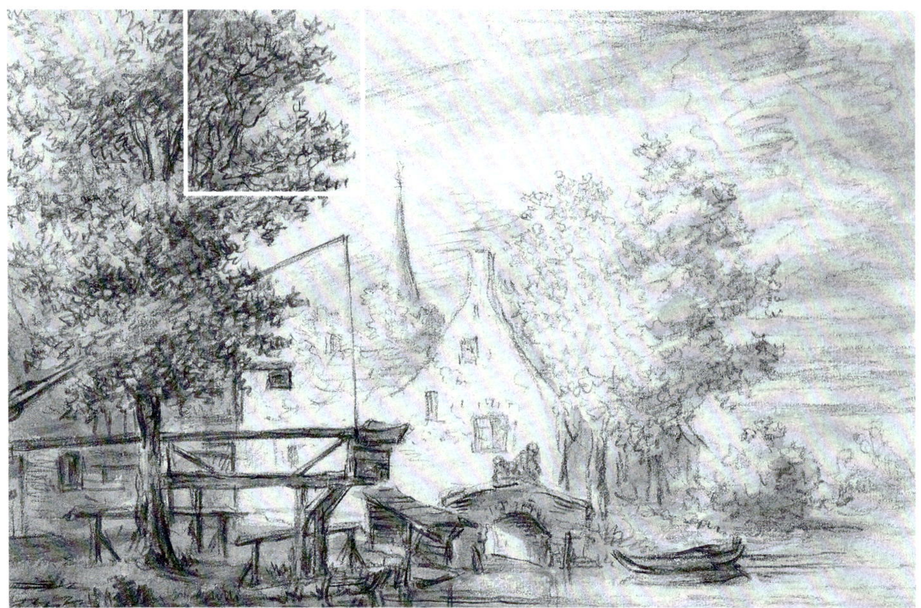

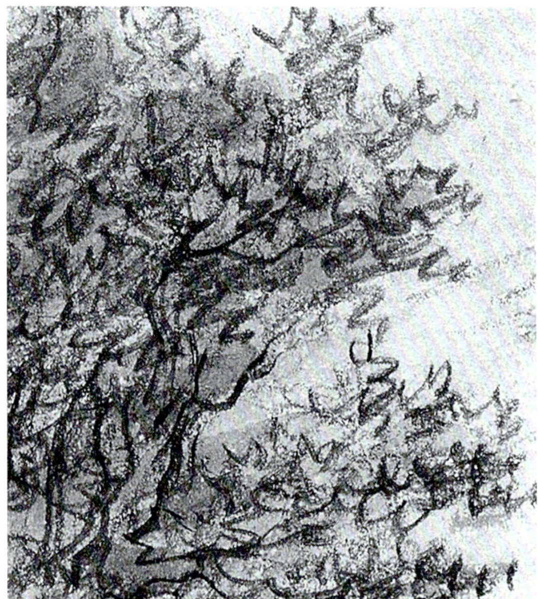

Fig. 5. Jacob van Ruisdael, Cat. no. 27, with framed detail, enlarged at right, showing Ruisdael's exceptional control of tree-fill hatching to represent the stellate lobes of oak leaves at the tree's upper periphery.

tance" (Cat no. 24), exhibiting sweeping pen strokes and wash as tree-fill. In both drawings, the orientation of the tree-fill pen strokes is the same: Roghman characteristically drew his tree-fill favoring 8 to 9 o'clock and 2 to 3 o'clock. Roghman's drawings oeuvre as catalogued and illustrated by Sumowski[21] and van der Wyck[22] generally conforms to this pattern. Two notable exceptions (Sumowski nos. 2282[XX] and 2283[XX]) are weighted with vertical (12 and 6 o'clock) tree-fill, rather than his customary horizontal strokes. This anomaly, coupled with other problems, leads me to conclude that these two unsigned drawings are not by Roghman.

Applying this criterion to left-handed artist Jan van Goyen, we find that the slope of his tree-fill belies his hand preference. It is not unusual for a left-hander to learn early how to camouflage his sinistrality by jockeying his hand and arm positions. Van Goyen's tree-fill (see Cat. nos. 11–13) is angled like that of a typical right-hander, with a slight change seen in his last decade: before 1650s, 7 to 8 o'clock, 1 to 2 o'clock; 1650s, 8 to 9 o'clock, 1 to 2 o'clock. Pieter Molyn, a right-handed artist whose unsigned drawings have sometimes been confused with van Goyen's work, seems to have a somewhat distinctive tree-fill "signature." He articulates tree-fill with vertical strokes, mostly facing 10 to 2 o'clock, documented in this exhibition with two signed and dated drawings (Cat. nos. 19 and 20, and see Fig. 2), made at ages 39 and 64, two years before his death.

The truly profound artists seem to be more versatile in overriding the graphic shortcuts of tree-fill, and in developing original and utterly amazing ways to depict foliage. Jacob van Ruisdael is one such giant. Stylistically, both Ruisdael drawings in this exhibition (Cat. nos. 26 and 27) appear to be from the early 1650s, one of his most productive periods as a young artist. His primary tree-fill device at this time was multidirectional zigzags composed of three to six connected "V" or "U" units. Seymour Slive was among the first specialists to recognize that Ruisdael favored oak trees in his landscapes. Both of the Ruisdael drawings here prominently feature oaks. Quite remarkably, Ruisdael deliberately distorts his rapid tree-fill hatching along some of the bough tops to replicate the stellate lobes of oak leaves. This brilliant, naturalistic device is particularly clear high on the wonderfully articulated oak in the left foreground of Cat. no. 27 (Fig. 5).

With these examples, I have attempted to demonstrate some of the strikingly individual constancy in execution and articulation of basic drawing tasks, even by artists of the highest skill and originality. Invariant graphic stroke traits, such as those evident in tree-fill, may indeed give connoisseurs another modus operandi. Bold, innovative artists, like Jacob van Ruisdael, may often consciously overpower some of the biologically determined stroke patterns and will surely stand out; controversial works at the border of their oeuvres may now be reassessed in light of this new criterion.

For the eager specialist, a sampling of other natural, drawing-related articulatory constraints and biases are:

1. In the formation of connected vertical strokes, the down-strokes are always stronger than the up-strokes and a down-stroke is usually the initial vertical stroke in a series.

2. In the formation of connected horizontal strokes, stroke order is from top to bottom of the series.

3. Right-handers start horizontal strokes from the left, and left-handers start them from the right.

4. Copying is characterized by strokes of shorter length than in the original, more pauses ("pen-up" moments), and angles drawn more acutely than in the original.

What works for drawings may not be so useful for paintings. Max Friedländer aptly contrasted the nature of drawings to paintings as the difference between wit and humor. The spontaneity of sketching is a prerequisite for the success of a analytical method based on the artist's innate psychomotor limits. Detecting and sorting the involuntary elements from the willful elements in the less spontaneous, more elastic painting process, therefore, may well be beyond this type of method. Unlike the solid stroke delivery of the draftsman's stylus, the tip of the painter's brush is highly elastic and thus less reliable for stroke analysis.

These and other aspects of neuropsychology and human limb kinematics should have transferable value for connoisseurs, scholars, and students of drawings. I hope this introduction may serve to open artistically inclined eyes to new analytical directions, and to fuel efforts at this interface from others. Stroke analysis is simply another tool to add to the serious student's armamentarium for an understanding of authenticity. Goethe, who drew copiously and collected drawings, noted that we hear and see only what we understand. The study of old master drawings with their stimulating challenges in connoisseurship surely must have extended his grand sensory range. I believe the field remains just as exciting and promising for us today.

– Sheldon Peck

References

1. Asher, Richard. Six honest serving men for medical writers. *Journal of the American Medical Association* 1969, vol. 208, pp. 83–87.

2. Frey, Karl. *Der literarische Nachlass Giorgio Vasaris.* vol. 2, Munich, 1930, pp. 901–902.

3. Hirst, Michael. *Michelangelo and his Drawings.* New Haven, Yale University Press, 1988, pp. 16–21.

4. Perrig, Alexander. *Michelangelo's Drawings. The Science of Attribution.* (M. Joyce, transl.) New Haven, Yale University Press, 1991, pp. 1–34.

5. Van de Wetering, Ernst. *Rembrandt. The Painter at Work.* Amsterdam, Amsterdam University Press, 1997, pp. 47–73.

6. Brown, Jonathan. *Kings and Connoisseurs. Collecting Art in Seventeenth-Century Europe.* Princeton, Princeton University Press, 1995.

7. Morelli, Giovanni. *Italian Painters. Critical Studies of Their Works.* (C. J. Ffoulkes, transl.), 2 vols., London, John Murray, 1893–1900.

8. Tietze, Hans. *Genuine and False. Copies, Imitations, Forgeries.* New York, Chanticleer Press, 1948, pp. 46–47.

9. Schatborn, Peter. Aspects of Rembrandt's draughtsmanship. In: Holm Bevers, Peter Schatborn, Barbara Welzel. *Rembrandt: The Master & his Workshop, Drawings & Etchings.* New Haven, Yale University Press, 1991, pp. 15–34.

10. Van Sommers, Peter. *Drawing and Cognition: Descriptive and Experimental Studies of Graphic Production Processes.* New York, Cambridge University Press, 1984.

11. Van Sommers, Peter. A system for drawing and drawing-related neuropsychology. *Cognitive Neuropsychology* 1989, vol. 6, pp. 117–164.

12. Thomassen, Arnold J. W. M.; Teulings, Hans-Leo. Constancy in stationary and progressive handwriting. *Acta Psychologica* 1983, vol. 54, pp. 179–196.

13. Teulings, Hans-Leo; Schomaker, Lambert R. B. Invariant properties between stroke features in handwriting. *Acta Psychologica* 1993, vol. 82, pp. 69–88.

14. Meulenbroek, Ruud G. J.; Thomassen, Arnold J. W. M. Exploitation of elasticity as a biomechanical property in the production of graphic stroke sequences. *Acta Psychologica* 1993, vol. 82, pp. 313–327.

15. Lacquaniti, F.; Ferrigno, G.; Pedotti, A.; Soechting, J. F.; Terzuolo, C. Changes in spatial scale in drawing and handwriting: Kinematic contributions by proximal and distal joints. *Journal of Neuroscience* 1987, vol. 7, pp. 819–828.

16. Maarse, Frans J.; Thomassen, Arnold J. W. M. Produced and perceived writing slant: Difference between up strokes and down strokes. *Acta Psychologica* 1983, vol. 54, pp. 131–147.

17. Wing, Alan M.; Nimmo-Smith, M. Ian; Eldridge, Margery A. The consistency of cursive letter formation as a function of position in the word. *Acta Psychologica* 1983, vol. 54, pp. 197–204.

18. Meulenbroek, Ruud G. J.; Rosenbaum, David A.; Thomassen, Arnold J. W. M.; Schomaker, Lambert R. B. Limb-segment selection in drawing behaviour. *Quarterly Journal of Experimental Psychology* 1993, vol. 46(A), pp. 273–299.

19. Desbiez, Dominique; Vinter, Annie; Meulenbroek, Ruud G. J. Biomechanical and perceptual determinants of drawing angles. *Acta Psychologica* 1996, vol. 94, pp. 253–271.

20. Plamondan, Réjean; Suen, Ching Y.; Simner, Marvin L., editors. *Computer Recognition and Human Production of Handwriting.* Singapore, World Scientific, 1989.

21. Sumowski, Werner. *Drawings of the Rembrandt School.* vol. 10, New York, Abaris, 1992, pp. 4992–5173.

22. Van der Wyck, H. W. M. *De kasteeltekeningen van Roelant Roghman.* vol. 1, Alphen aan den Rijn, Canaletto, 1989, pp. 21–242.

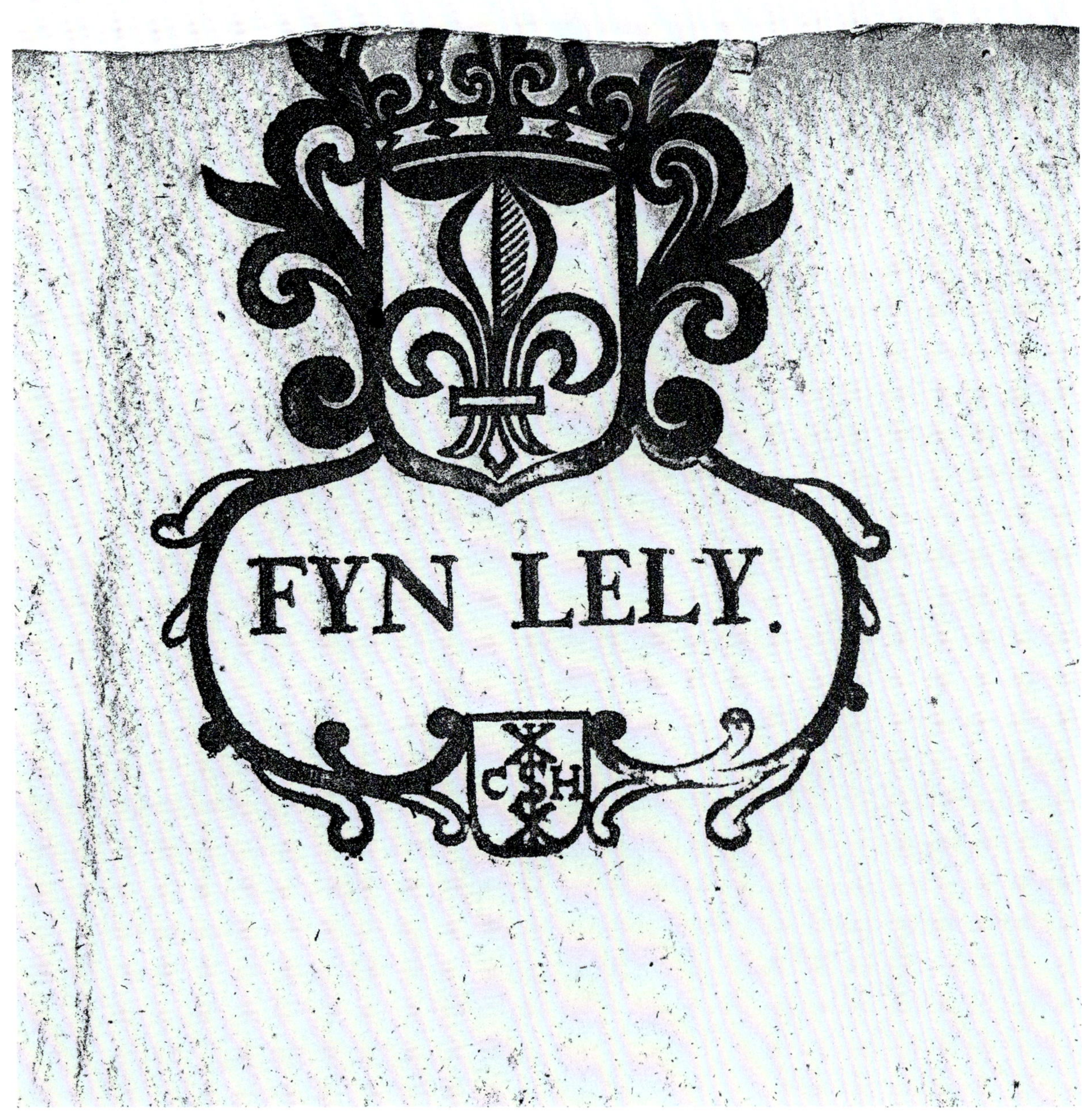

Fig. 1. "Fyn Lely" ream wrapper, 1689, mark of Cornelis Simonsz. van Huysduynen, one of the early white-papermakers in the Zaan near Amsterdam. (Collection of the author.)

Paper in the Netherlands

THE PAPER USED for old drawings and prints only recently has been given serious analytical attention as a source of documentary evidence. Most earlier scholarly studies were restricted to art historical considerations and to matters regarding composition and subject. In 1985, research on the paper used by Rembrandt was begun in earnest in Holland, because of increasing demand for more and better ways to examine issues of authenticity. Since research on paintings had advanced significantly through the scientific analysis of the wooden panel or canvas carrying the artwork, it was thought that detailed study of the paper supporting an old master print or drawing would yield equally valuable information. The following brief history of paper in the Netherlands is intended to illuminate the origins of the paper used by Dutch seventeenth-century artists, with the particular objective of improving the typing and dating of the paper. Some practical aspects of paper analysis are addressed at the conclusion.

The first papermakers in Europe came from the Arab culture in North Africa. They crossed the Mediterranean at the beginning of the thirteenth century and settled in the south of Spain and in southern Italy. The production of paper in Spain did not grow very fast, and one can hardly speak of export at that time. Italian paper, however, was taken abroad by traveling merchants, especially to northern Europe, so it appeared on the Dutch market by the thirteenth century. Thirteenth- and fourteenth-century paper in Dutch archives is, practically without exception, from Italy.

The early papermakers tried to protect their industrial secrets as closely as possible to avoid losing their monopoly. Despite these efforts, the art of papermaking slowly spread to northern Europe. In the fifteenth century, paper mills were established in northeastern France. The first paper mill in Switzerland was built in Basel in 1433. Germany followed soon, with mills along the Rhine.

Soon afterward, the Dutch got used to having a ready stock of paper but remained dependent for many years on supplies from traveling merchants, mainly coming from Lombardy in Italy. Prices for this so-called "Lombards" paper were high because of the long distance between producers and users. In time, foreign users like the Dutch experienced great relief with the development of nearby production centers, specializing in paper and other marketable commodities.

The northern French city of Troyes, with its famous market, developed into a commercial production center, supplying paper to eager Dutch importers. Paper from Troyes was called "Troys papier" in the Netherlands.[1] In addition to being cheaper, this paper was also whiter and finer than the old Lombards paper.

The city of Troyes kept its important position throughout the sixteenth century as a main supplier of paper for the Dutch. In addition, some paper was imported from the Rhine area. Paper also traveled in the direction of the Netherlands from Lorraine, the Jura (Montbéliard), Switzerland and southern Germany through commercial centers such as Basel, Strasbourg and the Frankfurter Messe. Moreover, paper from southwestern France reached the Netherlands over sea, transported through harbors, such as La Rochelle and Bordeaux.

Political problems in Europe, however, eventually strangled some of these burgeoning routes for the paper trade. The Spanish authority had to answer the rebellion in the Dutch territories, and one of the results was the so-called Fall of Antwerp in 1585, that is, the closing of Antwerp's harbor, which was of great importance to the Dutch; the Spaniards blockaded the southern inland border at this time. All land routes from France were closed. Furthermore, the shipping channels from southwest France were hindered severely. Suddenly, the Dutch faced acute paper shortages from this embargo.

In 1586, one year after the Fall of Antwerp, a few entrepreneurs tried to build the first paper mill in the Netherlands. They put a floating water mill on the river near

Zwijndrecht. The mill had to get its power from the tides in the river. It was not a success, and it became clear why paper always had been imported from abroad: the Netherlands did not have at its disposal plentiful sources of energy. It simply could not run machines. The French and Swiss paper mills were all built on fast-streaming rivers; the Netherlands lacked these powerful water resources, and the techniques of harnessing wind power were still too feeble and inefficient to drive papermaking machinery.

The only successful Dutch paper mills were water mills on little streams in the hilly area in the center of the country, known as the Veluwe. The production from these little mills, however, was far from sufficient for the national demand. An enterprising businessman, Cornelis van Lockhorst (1547–1617), from Utrecht, frequently visited the Frankfurter Fair.[2] He noticed that, despite the Spanish blockades, shipping on the Rhine continued to thrive. He understood the commercial possibilities immediately and traveled to Basel in order to buy as much paper as he could. He recognized that the paper industry there was waning. The golden days of Swiss papermaking indeed seemed over, and mill operators were longing for new orders. Van Lockhorst's activities were stimulating. In a short time, the Swiss paper industry fully recovered, and Dutch paper consumption continued to grow rapidly.

Another aspect of the Dutch need for paper was international trade. Dutch merchants tried to develop markets for paper in England, Scandinavia and Russia. There was no papermaking activity yet in those countries; in fact, many English believed that paper was exclusively a Dutch product. By the late sixteenth century, van Lockhorst had a firm grip on the Swiss paper industry. He moved to Amsterdam and founded the *Compagnie van Duytsche Papieren* (Company of German Paper) in 1595 with agents in Strasbourg and Basel. Paper from eastern France and southern Germany also found its way through these agents. Paper from Baden-Hochberg and Württemberg was picked up along the Rhine riverside during the voyage to Holland. The paper from all these areas was called "Bovenlands papier" in the Netherlands.

The Company had a few co-financiers, mainly printers and publishers, all friends of van Lockhorst. The agents in Basel (Ludwig König) and in Strasbourg (Dietrich Krasselt) formed, together with the Dutch bookkeeper Albert Tjason, an important nucleus in the Company, which flourished through the close cooperation among these four men. Their activities in Basel consisted not only of buying paper, but also of financing wages and raw materials for several mills. The Company assisted in the financing on the condition that they would be sold the entire paper production.

It would be interesting to trace in the Dutch archives the ratio among Bovenlands, French, and Dutch paper from this period. On the basis of experience, we may conjecture that more than 80 per cent was Bovenlands in origin. The Company flourished until 1609, when the warring and tired parties in the Eighty Years' War concluded the Twelve Years' Truce. During that period, international trade recovered, and, for the paper situation, the land and sea routes to France were reopened. Even Spanish and Italian paper was now freely exported to Holland. This resulted in growing competition, which was not good for the Company of German Paper. Moreover, in 1618, the Thirty Years' War began in Germany, causing problems for the Company. Tensions on the Rhine, even river closings now and then, hindered free access to the Swiss paper producers. Also, harsh business tactics among paper merchants compounded these problems. As if to symbolize the swelling commercial uncertainties of the times, Cornelis van Lockhorst died in 1617. This amiable and important man was succeeded by his son Cornelis II (1593–1629).

The situation within the Company changed totally. Cornelis II was an arrogant young man who wanted to become rich as soon as possible. He tried to get rid of his father's partners, and he maneuvered to shift the debts of the Company into the accounts of these partners. He undermined the Company and started to do business on his own account. The foreign agents subsequently did the same, and in the 1630s the Company collapsed. Cornelis II did succeed personally; he became one of the richest merchants in Amsterdam. However, he also succeeded in destroying one of the finest of the city's enterprises.

When the Twelve Years' Truce ended in 1621, both parties – the Spanish and the Dutch – could hardly wait to resume the war. The Spaniards wanted to curtail the Dutch impact on their economy, and the Dutch expected to earn more during the war than during peace. The wood for building Spanish men-of-war, for instance, was sold by Dutch lumber merchants who bought it in the Baltic and transported it to Spain on Dutch cargo ships.

Termination of the truce was disastrous for the Dutch paper supply arriving from abroad. The route over sea from southwest France to Dutch harbors was virtually shut down by the Spanish fleet with help from the Dunkirk privateers. Transport over land was completely sealed. Again, the Dutch market was condemned to the Bovenlands paper, but now from a crippled Company of German Paper. The Rembrandt Paper Research Project[3] has shown that during the ten-year period from 1621–31 "German" paper was used in substantially increased quantities in the Netherlands.

The smaller role of Swiss paper imports was due to friction between the Dutch and the Swiss. The Swiss as a matter of policy never sold their paper mills; they only sold the finished paper products. The profits naturally stayed in Switzerland, an intolerable situation in the eyes of Dutch tradesmen. The business ethos of the Dutch mercantile class had been, "If we see a profit-making industry, it has to be taken over by us." For years, the Dutch tried to break up Swiss mill ownership, but in vain.

The Swiss were well aware of their powerful position, and they abused this power by producing inferior paper at shamefully high prices. The Dutch were distressed by these developments, which ultimately led to the contraction and demise of the Swiss paper industry.

In the German city of Münster, international negotiations started in 1643 to put to an end all European wars. Five years later, in 1648, this diplomacy concluded with the Peace of Münster (for the Eighty Years' War) and the Peace of Osnabrück (for the Thirty Years' War).

One can hardly imagine the broad impact of the Peace of 1648. For the Dutch paper trade, it provided enormous relief. Quite a few Dutch papermakers were already installed in France, and now they could start sending goods to the Dutch market. It all happened immediately after 1648; the Rembrandt Paper Research Project shows that the use of Swiss paper abruptly stopped at that time in the Netherlands and was replaced by paper from French mills. Unlike the Swiss situation, French establishments, including paper mills, were always on the sales block. It was only a matter of money. This triggered a renewal of golden times for Dutch entrepreneurs, who quickly bought up all the paper stock they could find, including paper made for local use, and shipped it all to Holland. This is the reason that some unusual watermark images, rarely seen in the Netherlands before, like the phoenix and the paschal lamb (see radiographs, no. R27, Cat. no. 27, Jacob van Ruisdael), suddenly appeared on the Dutch market for a brief time (c. 1648–1652).[4]

A few Dutch dealers like Abraham Jansen and Gillis van Hoven capitalized on the traditional English belief that all good paper originated with the Dutch. They sold French-made paper to the English and brought the profits to Amsterdam. This scheme was extremely successful from mid-century to about 1690, when the English got the notion that they could start their own papermaking industry with help from French paper mills. Abraham Jansen did not like this idea and tried to wreck these plans with the help of the French Ambassador in London. He did not succeed, and as a result of his losing English business, he had to find new markets for his French-made paper. He sent his son back to Holland and now tried to capture a share of the Dutch paper market. Thus, if we find a Rembrandt etching on paper with the Abraham Jansen watermark, we know it was posthumously printed, after c. 1690.

The paper manufactured in France for the Dutch market soon was customized with Dutch watermarks. For example, in the early 1650s we already see the coat of arms of Amsterdam in French-made paper. They called it in France "Papier Stradam." It became so popular that even French independent papermakers copied this watermark for their own local papers. The old Rhine route from Strasbourg was kept in use, and land routes were also heavily trafficked. Therefore, the 1650s were the first time in Dutch history that Holland had an abundance of paper.

During the second half of the seventeenth century a new development, nevertheless, again changed the paper situation in the Netherlands. The Dutch had gained so much experience with building windmills that they now could use them for the production of white (blank) paper. These Dutch mills were stronger than the average Swiss or French water mill. A new industrial complex with small windmills had developed since 1600 in open wetlands about 15 miles northwest of Amsterdam, the Zaan area. The strength of the mills continued growing over the years, and they were used as sawmills, oil and paint mills, and paper mills. The paper mills could be recognized very easily because of their long drying sheds. In these mills only raw basic material was produced, that is, gray board and blue paper. The equipment was not yet able to produce the finer paper stuff (ground paper stock) for use in white writing, and printing, paper.

The Zaan was particularly well chosen for this mill-park because of its flatness and openness. The wind could be exploited optimally, there were good traffic connections on land and on water, and there was plenty of clean water, so essential in the paper industry. The production of paperboard and blue paper grew dramatically after 1640 (Table I).[5]

Table I. Total annual paper production in the Zaan area (after Voorn[5])

YEAR	APPROXIMATE ANNUAL PRODUCTION (KILOGRAMS)
1640	250,000
1650	450,000
1660	650,000
1670	800,000
1680	1,100,000
1690	1,450,000
1700	1,950,000

The Dutch white paper industry started in 1673. In that year a group of papermakers from Gelderland arrived in the Zaan. The French occupation army had forced them to leave their Veluwe mills, and they were looking for a new future in the neighborhood of Amsterdam. They brought a revolutionary device to the Zaan: a new machine, which could prepare the paper stuff in a shorter time and with finer quality. This "Hollanderbeater" or "Hollander" replaced the old hammer-beater, but it needed a windmill with considerable power. These mills were indeed available in the Zaan and so the production of white paper could be started. Dutch production of white paper rose significantly after 1673 (Table II).

Table II. Annual production of white paper since 1673

YEAR	APPROXIMATE ANNUAL PRODUCTION (KILOGRAMS)
1680	200,000
1690	425,000
1700	700,000

Among the first white-papermakers in the Zaan were the families Van der Ley, Honigh, Blauw, and Van Huysduynen (Fig. 1). Due to the Hollanderbeater, this new Dutch white-paper industry could compete successfully with French imports. The Dutch manufactured paper of superior quality, and, because of the shorter production time, they could offer these goods at moderate prices.

The Hollander was such a technological breakthrough that papermakers elsewhere soon embraced the idea. By 1700, it was in use throughout Europe, even by the French. In the late seventeenth century, another improvement – probably of Dutch invention – was a newly designed sieve on which the paper was made. The sieves for papermaking were woven of copper wires that had become finer and finer since the fifteenth century. The thinner the copper wires, the finer the resulting paper. Then, the Dutch paper producers suddenly reversed this trend. They began using thicker copper wires and they wove them into a wider pattern. This resulted in water that dripped through the sieve much faster. The surface of the paper, thus, became a little bit wilder in appearance, more irregular and rougher, but actually that did not make much difference to the users. More significantly, the new sieve shortened production time, and that meant greater profits for the papermakers. This new development was eventually adopted by all European papermakers, and the changeover in sieve construction occurred between 1690 and 1700.

This succession of events and developments affecting

paper availability and quality in the Netherlands during the seventeenth century is corroborated in the sequence of papers Rembrandt used for his etchings, according to the findings of the Rembrandt Paper Research Project over the past 10 years. The watermarks provide a picture book of the history of paper supply. Recent research on the paper used by Adriaen van Ostade for his etchings shows the same remarkable historical veracity.[4]

There is, however, a difference between the use of reams of paper for print editions and the incidental use of one sheet for a drawing. When paper was used to print an edition of an etching, the printer used a stack of new paper, so all the impressions would have the same watermark in the same relative location. On the other hand, an artist who wanted to make a drawing could take a single sheet of unknown origin or age. Rembrandt worked always with one or more "books" (stacks of 24 sheets) of new paper when he printed his etchings. For his drawings, he used all kinds of single pieces or scraps of paper. He even made a drawing on a printed proof sheet which had been thrown away in a book printing office. It also could happen that an artist showed a particular preference for a special kind of paper, for example, Italian. The dating of drawings on the basis of the paper, therefore, is a little less secure than in the case of prints. Generally the age of the paper corresponds well with that of the drawing, but there is always the possibility of an exception.

Many old master drawings are on pieces of paper showing only a fragment of a watermark. Other works are on paper pieces with no watermarks. Dating in such cases has to be determined on the basis of the pattern of the chain and laid lines, and from the thickness of the copper wires. These lines show rather clearly in the so-called "verge" structure of the paper. Moreover, there are regional differences in the preferred methods of placing the sieve wires, and these differences often provide clues. When the chain lines and laid lines follow a sloppy pattern with thick, uneven copper wires, this indicates in many cases that the paper is Italian (see radiographs, nos. R2, R3, R13, R29). A neat and fine pattern, on the other hand, always points to Switzerland or Germany as the country of origin.

Sometimes a watermark can be connected with a particular historic event. As described earlier, all kinds of paper were transported suddenly to the Netherlands just after the Peace of 1648. Among them are watermarks that only appeared for a short period on the Dutch market (1648–1652), thus precisely identifying a time window for the papers' immediate use.

Lastly, it is absolutely impossible that a seventeenth-century drawing would be made on eighteenth-century paper. This may seem like a simplistic remark, but experience tells us that such scholarly rationalization happens all the time. That is why it is so important that a drawing's art-historical evidence and its paper evidence agree with each other.

The artists' paper for the forty works in this exhibition of seventeenth-century Dutch landscape drawings from the Peck collection was compared with the available references. The paper evidence and drawing evidence corresponded well in all cases. In addition to the watermark descriptions contained in the catalogue, commentaries on some of the individual drawing sheets and their watermarks are given in the radiographs section of this volume. For sheets without watermarks, the pattern of the chain and laid lines was examined to authenticate the paper. Where possible, the country of origin has been mentioned.

– Theo Laurentius

References

1. H. Voorn. "Lombards en Troys, Frans en Bovenlands papier." In: *Opstellen over de Koninklijke Bibliotheek en andere studies.* Hilversum, 1986, p. 312.

2. H. Voorn. "Uit de oudste geschiedenis van de Amsterdamse Papierhandel." *Proost-Prikkels* 303, Amsterdam, 1967.

3. Th. Laurentius; H. M. M. van Hugten; E. Hinterding; J. P. Filedt Kok. "Het Amsterdamse onderzoek naar Rembrandts papier: radiografie van de watermerken in de etsen van Rembrandt." *Bulletin van het Rijksmuseum*,1992, vol. 40, pp. 353–384.

4. P. Van der Coelen; Th. Laurentius; S. W. Pelletier; T. Rassieur; L. J. Slatkes. *Everyday Life in Holland's Golden Age. The Complete Etchings of Adriaen van Ostade.* Amsterdam, 1998, pp. 61, 85.

5. H. Voorn. *De Papiermolens in de provincie Noord-Holland.* Haarlem, 1960.

Catalogue of Drawings

Notes to Readers

The catalogue entries are ordered alphabetically by artist and chronologically within an artist's work. Dimensions of the drawings are given in millimeters (and inches), height preceding width. Abbreviations L. stands for Lugt number and R indicates the radiograph number in this catalogue. Color illustrations are direct digital images reproduced no larger than actual size.

All drawings in the exhibition are on white laid rag paper. The orientation of the paper's chain lines (horizontal or vertical) is given for each work, followed by the distance between chain lines in millimeters. Watermarks are described, typed, and compared with published references. Notations for watermark comparisons are made according to a graded system from Laurentius (1993) and Ash and Fletcher (1998): similar to…; nearly identical to…; identical to….

Franklin W. Robinson wrote the entry narratives (except Cat. no. 17). The data for the entries were compiled by Sheldon Peck.

Bartholomeus Breenbergh
Deventer 1599/1600–1657 Amsterdam

1 *Travelers on a hilly road near Bomarzo*

Pen in black and gray ink, brush in gray ink, over black chalk; black ink framing lines.
91 x 148 mm (3⅝ x 5⅞ in).

WATERMARK: none. (R1)

CHAIN LINES: horizontal, 25–26 mm.

INSCRIPTIONS: numbered *28* at upper right (pen in light brown ink, 17th century?); verso, at lower left *Strada di Bracciano.* (pen in dark brown ink, in the hand of Valerius Röver).

PROVENANCE: Valerius Röver (1686–1739), Delft (L. 2984a–c), posthumous catalogue, c. 1739. Pieter de Haan (?), sale, Amsterdam, 9 March 1767, lot 692, 694, 768 or 774. Private collection, Amsterdam, 1965. Hans van Leeuwen, Amerongen (L. 2799a), his sale, Amsterdam, Christie's, 24 November 1992, lot 38, acquired at the sale.

LITERATURE: Roethlisberger 1969, under no. 64.

EXHIBITIONS: Cat. Bonn/Saarbrücken/Bochum 1968–9, no. 26 . Cat. Amsterdam 1975–6, no. 22 (illus.). Cat. Utrecht 1978, no. 26 (illus.). Cat. Bremen/Braunschweig/Stuttgart 1979–80, no. 25. Cat. Rome 1982.

The three drawings by Bartholomeus Breenbergh in this exhibition give an overview of one of the most important Dutch artists in Italy. Although he spent the last three decades of his life in the Netherlands, Breenbergh's sojourn in Rome in the 1620s defined his work for the rest of his career. In his many paintings, prints, and drawings, he helped create the vision of Italy as a kind of Arcadia, a timeless, picturesque mixture of ancient Roman ruins, medieval battlements, and contemporary buildings, peopled with happy peasants and the occasional tourist or traveler, the whole bathed in late afternoon golden sunlight. This vision was a product of the work of several Dutch artists, including Cornelis van Poelenburgh, Jan Both, and Nicolaes Berchem, and continued in the Netherlands into the eighteenth and even nineteenth century; in fact, Breenbergh's drawings in particular are close to those of Claude Lorrain and may have influenced his classic views of the Roman countryside.

This drawing is from a series of sketchbook sheets which Marcel Roethlisberger dates to the last year of Breenbergh's stay in Italy, 1629. It probably shows the road to Bracciano (the ancient Via Claudia, which later crosses the Via Cassia; Breenbergh worked for Duke Paolo Giordano II Orsini, whose summer residence was at Bracciano). Valerius Röver's inscription, "Strada di Bracciano" on the verso, refers to this hill town north of Rome (and, probably, the area around Bomarzo). The drawing has the feeling of a quick sketch made on the spot; in 1627 he also recorded the Lake of Bracciano, with the Duke of Bracciano and his party, in the Fitzwilliam Museum, Cambridge, as well as other views in the area.

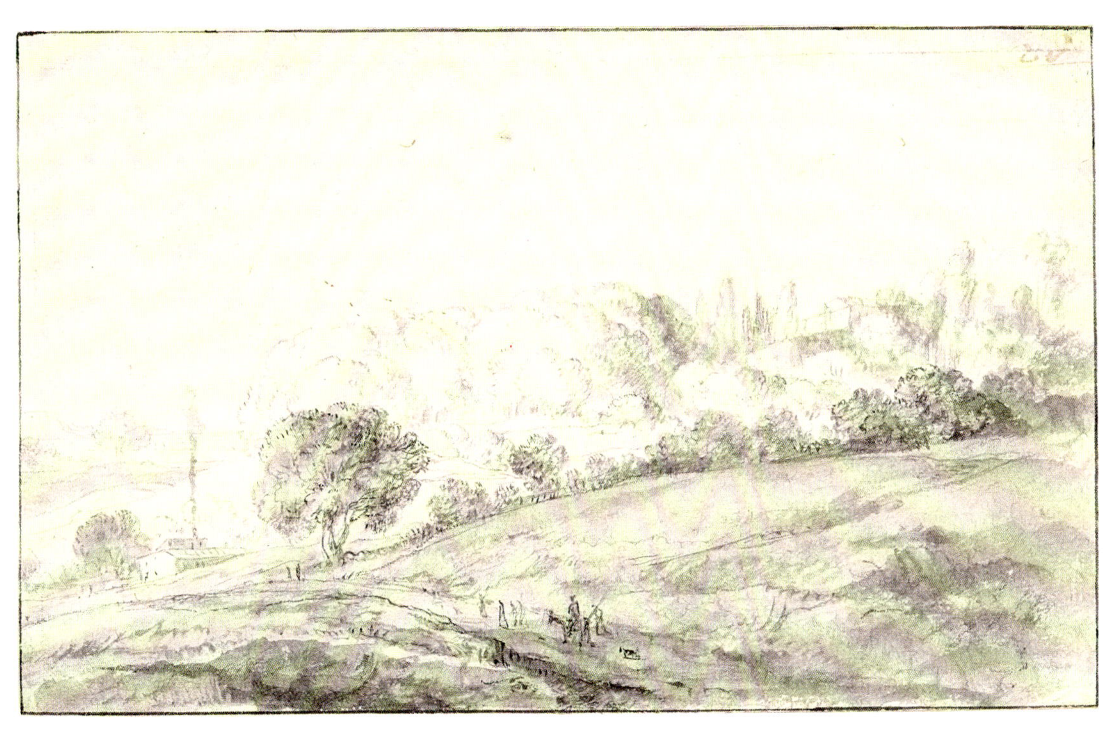

Bartholomeus Breenbergh
Deventer 1599/1600–1657 Amsterdam

2 *Cliff near Bomarzo*

Pen in brown ink, brush in brown and gray ink; laid down; traces of dark brown ink framing lines. 252 x 324 mm (9⅞ x 12½ in).

WATERMARK: crown with five points below a six-pointed star, nearly identical to Heawood no. 1116 (Rome, dated 1570); identical to watermark on two other Breenbergh drawings, *Castello Bomarzo*, monogrammed and dated 162[5], in the Rijksprentenkabinet, Amsterdam (Schapelhouman and Schatborn, 1998, cat. no. 75), and *Ruins of a castle on a hill*, c. 1625, in the National Gallery of Scotland, Edinburgh (Andrews 1985, cat. no. D853); backing paper with countermark ADS (unidentified). (R2)

CHAIN LINES: vertical, 30–32 mm.

INSCRIPTIONS: none visible through backing paper.

PROVENANCE: Sale, Amsterdam, Christie's, 26 November 1984, lot 66. Ian Woodner, New York, his sale, London, Christie's, 2 July 1991, lot 209, acquired at the sale.

LITERATURE: Roethlisberger 1991, p. 91.

EXHIBITIONS: none.

This drawing is one of four very similar views of this dramatic spot, perhaps near Bracciano or Bomarzo. Three of the drawings include not only the cliff we see here but also a road to the left, a small house on the road, and a boulder in the foreground, with two or three travelers. One of these last three is by the Netherlandish artist Paul Bril, whose Italian landscapes were an important influence on his contemporaries; this drawing is in the Louvre (Fig. 1), while the other two drawings, in the Albertina and in a private collection, Amsterdam, are given to Breenbergh.

The relationship among these four drawings is hard to determine. The drawing in Amsterdam is the loosest and most summary of the four and may well be a copy. Of the other three, the Albertina version shows the most complete view of the scene, including the diamond-shaped cliff on the far right, the road and building on the far left, and the foreground boulder and travelers. Interestingly, the vertical fold in the Albertina sheet is down the center of the paper. The Bril in the Louvre stops, on the right, just before the diamond-shaped cliff; appropriately, the vertical fold here is to the right of center, suggesting the sheet was cut down on the right. The present drawing, which stops before the road and house on the left, has its fold to the left of center, implying it was cut down on the left. (In each of the four drawings, the fold goes through the same part of the landscape.)

There are certain details that the Bril and the present drawing share, and the Albertina drawing lacks, for example, in the architecture at the top of the cliff and in the hut below; this suggests that the Bril and this sheet are directly related, and the Albertina work is dependent on one or the other of them, before they were cut down. Close as the Bril and the present drawing are, the latter has all of Breenbergh's dramatic play of light and shadow, especially evident in the brilliant device of shading the whole cliff on the right.

A sheet with just the lefthand part of the

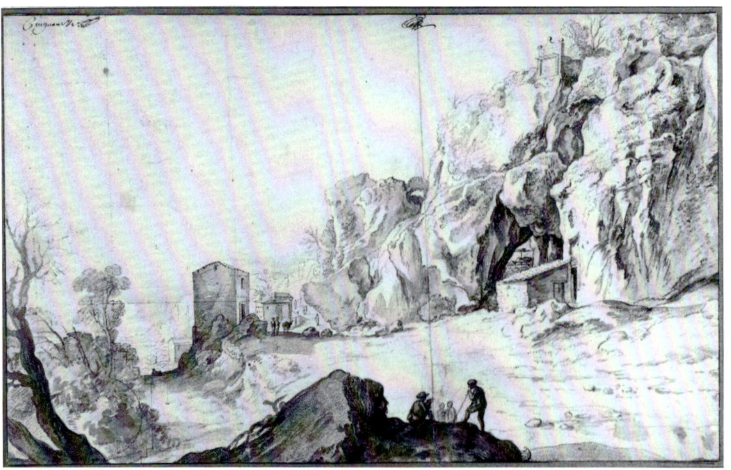

Fig. 1. Paulus Bril, *Rocky landscape with house*, pen and ink with wash. Louvre, Département des Arts Graphiques, Paris.

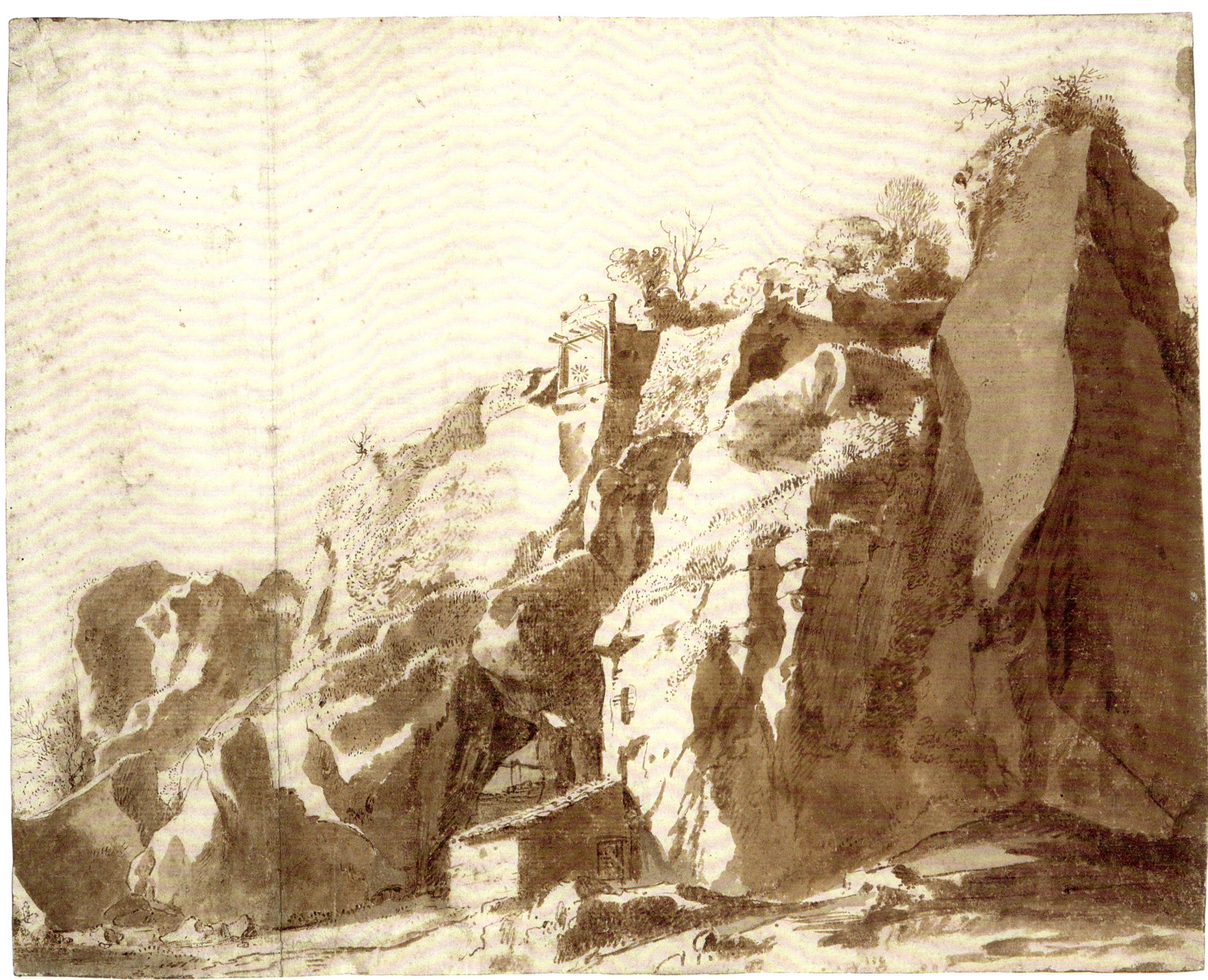

whole view (the road, building, and foreground rock) was at B. Houthakker, Amsterdam, in 1969 (cat. no. 6, illus.). Different elements of the landscape found their way into the artist's paintings.

Other connections between the drawings of Bril and Breenbergh have been discussed by Carl Depauw (1989). He shows that a Bril drawing is clearly the model for a Breenbergh work in the National Gallery of Scotland, Edinburgh (Andrews 1985, cat. no. D853, p. 13).

This site was clearly popular with seventeenth century Dutch artists, for it was the subject of drawings by Nicolaes Berchem, dated 1654 (location unknown), and Anthonie Waterloo (sale, Amsterdam, Christie's, November 14, 1988, no. 102). At the top of the cliff in the present drawing, the portico of an estate may be seen, with a large shade showing a sunburst design, rolled down to keep out the glaring midday light.

Bartholomeus Breenbergh
Deventer 1599/1600–1657 Amsterdam

3 *View under an archway or inside a vault*

Brush in brown ink over traces of black chalk; brown ink framing lines.
261 x 215 mm (10¼ x 8½ in).

WATERMARK: none. (R3)

CHAIN LINES: vertical, 30–32 mm.

INSCRIPTIONS: signed and dated *Bartholomeüs Breenborch.f/ A°* *1657*[?] at lower right (pen in brown ink), bottom of date cut off; verso, at lower center *Ecole hollandaise, Deventer-/ Bartolomé Breenbergh actif vers.1629–1660* (pencil); at upper right *V. 37/ 21651/37* (pencil).

PROVENANCE: Unidentified collector's mark RVZS[?] (verso, gray stamp). Einar Perman, Stockholm, 1953. Sale, London, Sotheby's, 27 June 1974, lot 117. Richard L. Feigen, New York, 1974. Richard L. Feigen and Co., New York, 1991. Acquired 1991.

LITERATURE: Roethlisberger 1998 (illus.).

EXHIBITIONS: Cat. Stockholm 1953, no. 160. Cat. New York 1991, no. 31 (illus.).

Most of Breenbergh's many paintings, prints, and drawings of Italian sites were executed after his stay in Rome, when he had settled in Amsterdam. Often he integrated religious scenes into a Roman setting, for example, putting Christ and the rich youth in front of the Pantheon.

He was particularly fond of views from inside caves and vaults, in the arcades of the Colosseum, the caves or villas in and around Tivoli, or the grotto of Egeria. There is no precise precedent for the present drawing, topographically or stylistically, and indeed, the image is unusually haunting and powerful, with the intense darkness in the foreground and the full sunlight beyond.

M. Roethlisberger (op. cit.) has suggested a date circa 1627, based on a drawing in Rotterdam dated that year and with almost the same form of the signature ("Breenberch"). However, because of, as he says, "some exceptions to this rule of thumb," the clarity of the artist's own inscription, and the unusual subject and style of this remarkable work, we propose 1657, the last year of Breenbergh's life.

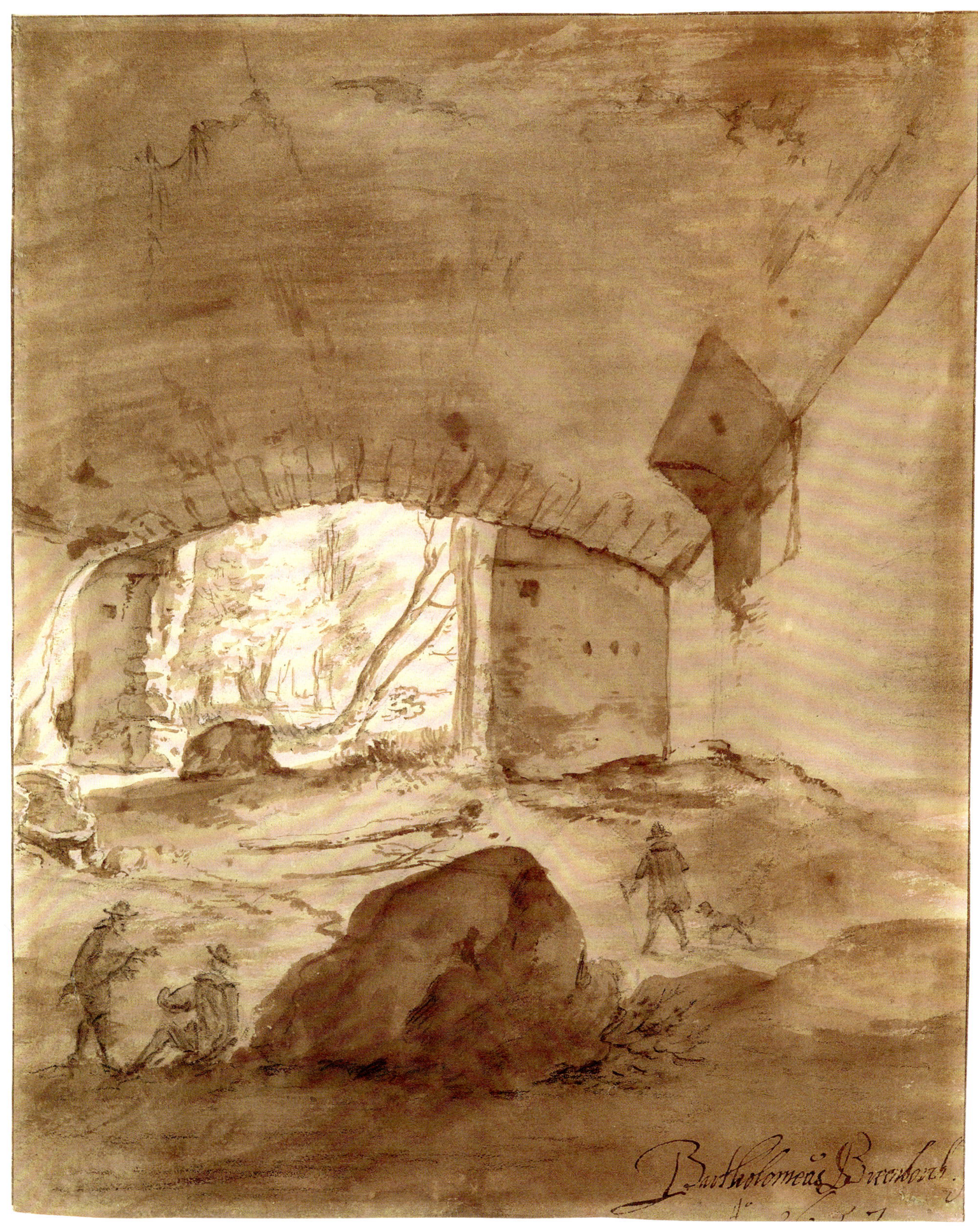
Bartholomeüs Breenborch

Michiel Carrée
The Hague 1657–1727 Alkmaar

4 *River scene with boats, a windmill and a natural arch*

Pen and brush in brown ink over traces of graphite; brown ink framing lines.
162 x 247 mm (6¼ x 9¾ in).

WATERMARK: fragment, Strasbourg lily, at upper center, similar to Heawood no. 1734 (Paris, dated 1677). (R4)

CHAIN LINES: vertical, 25–27 mm.

INSCRIPTIONS: signed *M Carree* at lower right (pen in brown ink); verso, shelf-mark *1802 WE. P.29* at lower left (pen in dark brown ink, in the hand of William Esdaile); at upper left *479* (pen in brown ink); at upper right */6* (pen in brown ink); at center *Carree 8/* (pencil).

PROVENANCE: William Esdaile (1758–1837), London (L. 2617), his sale, London, Christie and Manson, 22 June 1840, lot 1172. Estes Galleries, New York, 1958. Norbert L. H. Roesler, his sale, New York, Christie's, 31 May 1990, lot 99, acquired at the sale.

LITERATURE: none.

EXHIBITIONS: none.

The work of Michiel Carrée is one of the special pleasures of seventeenth-century Dutch drawing. His paintings are conventional variations on the formula for Italianate Dutch landscapes, with cattle and sheep wandering among fountains and classical statues – a formula established by his master Nicolaes Berchem and other artists of his generation.

It is in his drawings that Carrée comes into his own. This sheet, with its charmingly chaotic mixture of Dutch windmill, Rhine landscape, and Italianate natural arch, is typical for him. The outpouring of detail, with an equal variety of human and animal activity, is matched by Carrée's quick and energetic touch and summary descriptions of figures, clouds, and hills. Aside from his Arcadian views of cattle in Italian fields, he did many drawings, and paintings, of monkeys imitating humans, stag hunts, deer parks, and deer resting or playing.

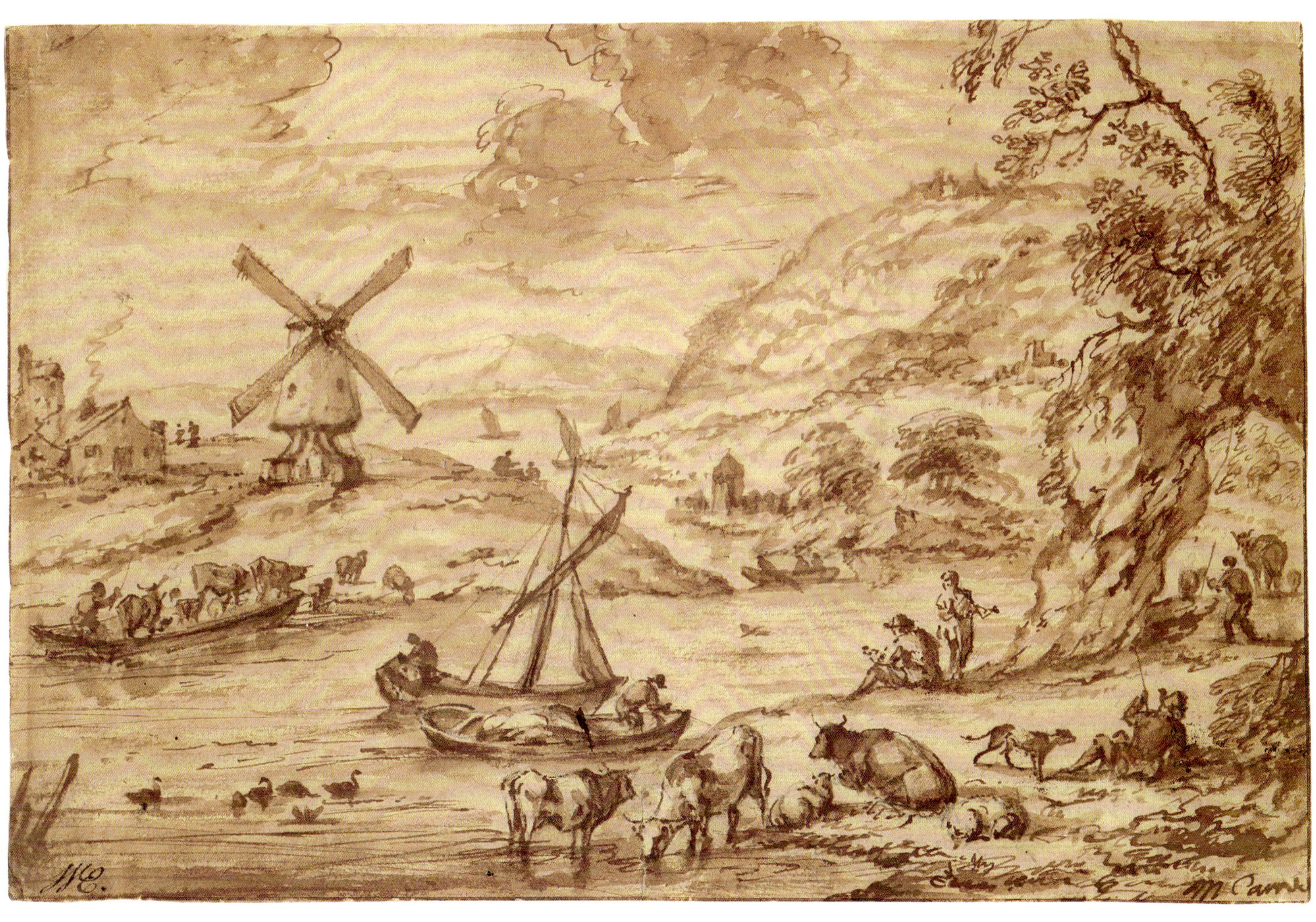

Guillam Du Bois
Haarlem 1625–1680 Haarlem

5 *Cottages along a wooded road*

Black and red chalk; dark brown ink framing lines.
134 x 189 mm (5¼ x 7½ in).

WATERMARK: none. (R5)

CHAIN LINES: vertical, 22–24 mm.

INSCRIPTIONS: none.

PROVENANCE: Jacob de Vos Sr. (1735-1833), his sale, Amsterdam, de Vries, Roos, 30–31 October 1833. J. A. G. Weigel, Leipzig, his sale, Stuttgart, H. G. Gutekunst, 8 May 1883. Belmon collection, Amsterdam, 1967. Hans van Leeuwen, Amerongen (L. 2799a), his sale, Amsterdam, Christie's, 24 November 1992, lot 56, acquired at the sale.

LITERATURE: Giltay 1977, p. 152, fig. 11.

EXHIBITIONS: Cat. Bonn/Saarbrücken/Bochum 1968–9, no. 38. Cat. Utrecht 1978, no. 18.

Guillam Du Bois is one of the most interesting landscape draftsmen active in the middle years of the seventeenth century. He was a member of the Haarlem guild by 1646, and in 1652–53 he traveled in Germany with Dirk Helmbreker, Cornelis Bega, and Vincent Laurensz. van der Vinne. This drawing in red and black chalk is typical of the artist at his best: the low, heavy cottages hugging the ground contrast with the short, staccato strokes of the trees and grass.

In many ways, Du Bois is a transitional figure; he responds to early landscapists, such as Salomon van Ruysdael, Jan van Brosterhuisen, and Pieter Molyn, but is clearly influenced by Jacob van Ruisdael, Salomon's nephew. Jacob's dense and heavy paintings and etchings of the late 1640s, with their gnarled and twisting trees and impenetrable underbrush, are close to Du Bois's less monumental, but equally intense, and intimate forest and village scenes. Jeroen Giltay (op. cit.) dates this drawing to c. 1647 on the basis of a closely related painting, dated 1646, in the Staatliche Museen, Berlin.

Remarkable similarities in the nature and orientation of the paper, framing lines and old mounting suggest that the two Du Bois drawings here are from the same period in the artist's work and that they may have had a shared provenance in the seventeenth and eighteenth centuries.

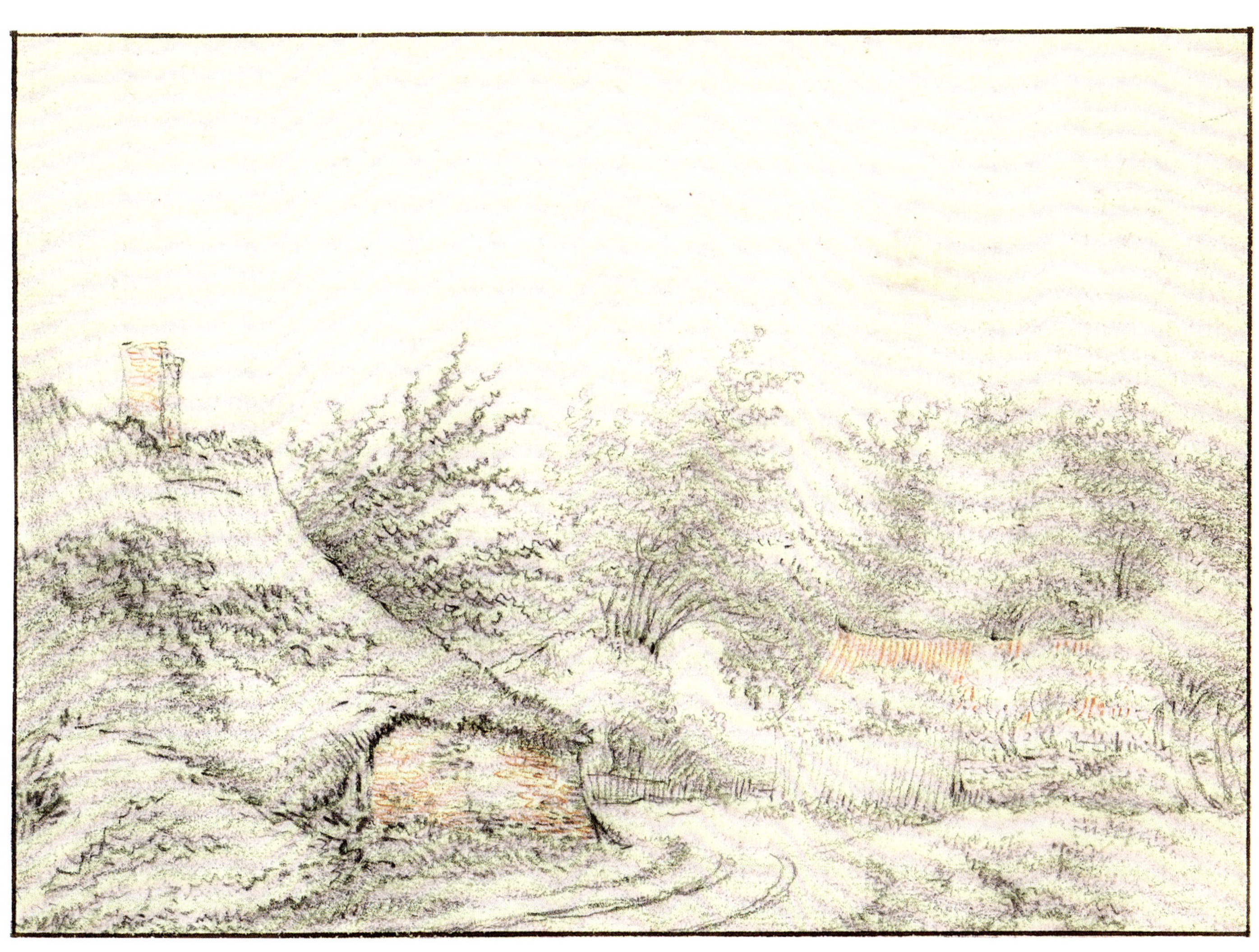

Guillam Du Bois
Haarlem 1625–1680 Haarlem

6 *View of Noordwijkerhout, with the Witte Kerk*

Brush in gray ink over traces of black chalk, red chalk; dark brown ink framing lines.
115 x 188 mm (4½ x 7⅜ in).

WATERMARK: none. (R6)

CHAIN LINES: vertical, 22–23 mm.

INSCRIPTIONS: annotated *noortwykr hout* at upper left (pen in brown ink, 17th century?); verso, at lower center *Noortwykr hout* (pencil); at lower left *za f 880.8 f14-* (pencil).

PROVENANCE: C. G. Boerner, Düsseldorf, 1962. Bernard Houthakker, Amsterdam, 1965. Sale, Amsterdam, Sotheby Mak van Waay, 3 May 1976, lot 101. Sale, Amsterdam, Christie's, 15 November 1993, lot 100, acquired at the sale.

LITERATURE: Giltay 1977, p. 159, note 50.

EXHIBITIONS: Cat. Amsterdam 1965, no. 57 (illus.).

This drawing, which Jeroen Giltay dates 1646–1650, makes an interesting comparison with the previous work, also by Du Bois. Although the buildings and trees of Noodwijkherhout still cluster together as before, the foliage is more open and impressionistic, there is more variation of light and shadow, and clouds scud across the sky.

Nevertheless, these two drawings are more closely related, at least in subject, than they first appear. Although these particular sheets (with different recent provenances) are not pendants, two similar paintings exist that, in fact, are pendants; one shows a church among trees and houses on the right, and a road in the left foreground, and the other depicts a simple cottage in the left foreground, with a road on the right leading back toward other houses and trees. Both paintings, on panel, are the same size (32.5 x 36.5 cm), and they were together in their one known sale, from the D. Komter collection (Amsterdam, Mak, March 9, 1926, no. 51). These pendants, so different in subject, are a good reminder that other such pairs by Du Bois may have been separated over the years. (Related paintings are in the Musée des Beaux-Arts, Bordeaux, and the Statens Museum for Kunst, Copenhagen.)

This church was rebuilt in the early seventeenth century after the Spanish attacked it in 1573; interestingly, the ruins of the previous church were left standing, abutting the apse of the new church. This created an unusual juxtaposition that was often the subject of topographical prints and drawings by a series of artists, including Jan van Goyen.

This drawing of a modest, rural church is a reminder of the Dutch rage for documentation; in the seventeenth-century Netherlands, there was an openness to new ideas, in science, commerce, engineering, and other fields, a fascination with the visible world, whether buildings and cities or botany and astronomy, which led to an extraordinary demand for works of art that recorded that world. Prints and drawings were the most common and most affordable form of documentation, and drawings had the further distinction of offering not just uniqueness but the freshness and spontaneity of being at the artist's elbow as he created the work.

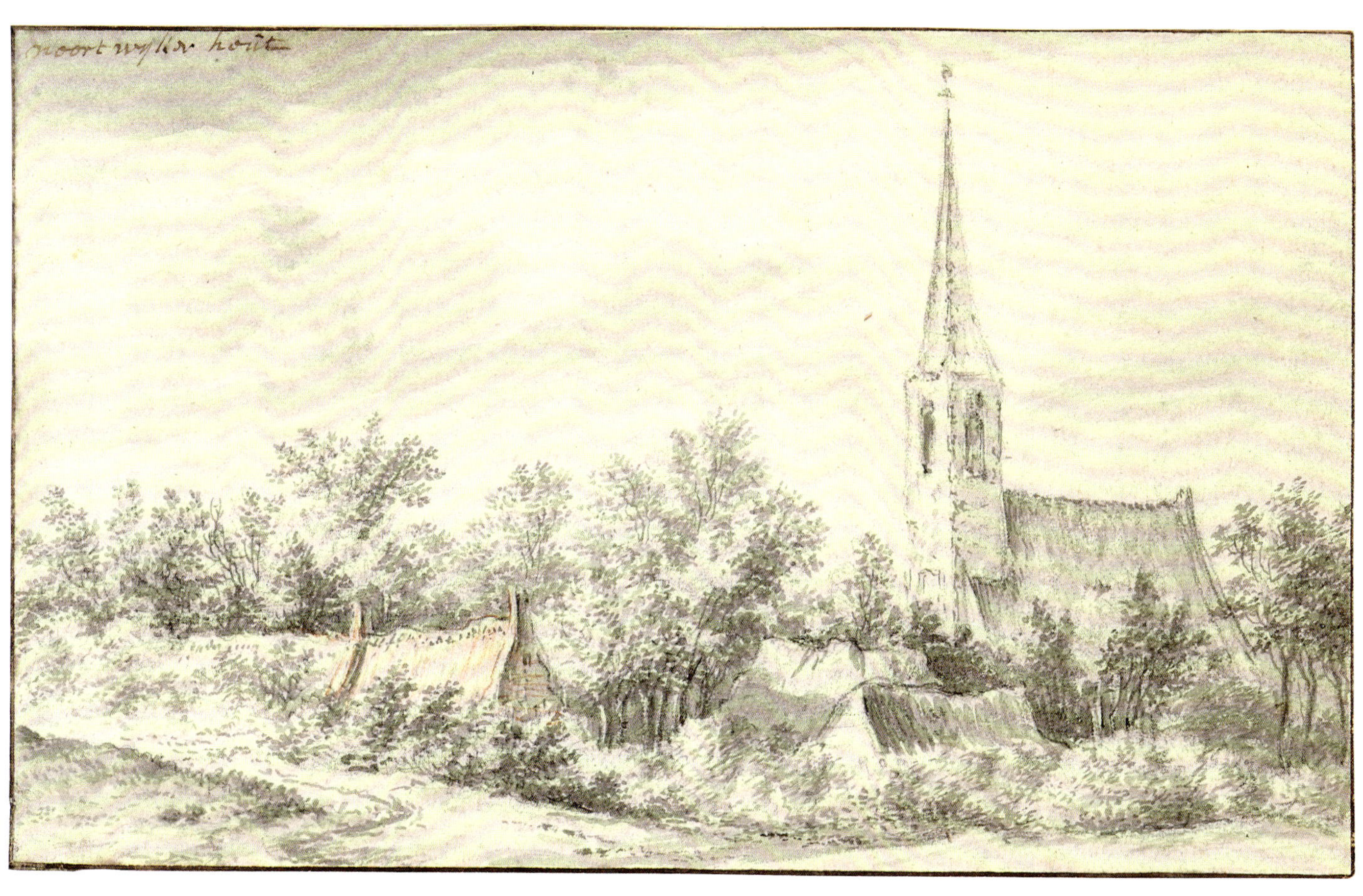
noort wyker hout

Allart van Everdingen
Alkmaar 1621–1675 Amsterdam

7 *Pulling-the-goose at a village fair*

Pen and brush in brown ink over traces of black chalk; brown ink and graphite framing lines. 103 x 93 mm (4⅛ x 3⅝ in).

WATERMARK: none. (R7)

CHAIN LINES: vertical, 25, 28, 24 mm.

INSCRIPTIONS: monogrammed *AVE* at lower right (pen in brown ink).

PROVENANCE: From an early 19th century album in an English collection. Sale, Amsterdam, Christie's, 22 November 1982, lot 168, acquired at the sale.

LITERATURE: none.

EXHIBITIONS: none.

Allart van Everdingen occupies a special place in the history of seventeenth-century Dutch landscape painting and drawing. A student of Roelant Savery in Utrecht and then Pieter Molyn in Haarlem, he traveled in the early 1640s to Norway and Sweden, where he was deeply impressed by the dramatic waterfalls, steep cliffs, massive boulders, towering fir trees, and crude huts he encountered there. Jacob van Ruisdael became acquainted with the Scandinavian landscape through van Everdingen's paintings, and it became an essential part of his conception of nature, the power of earth, wind, and weather dwarfing man and his works and catching them up in an eternal cycle of decay and rebirth.

Only a minority of van Everdingen's drawings and watercolors refers to his northern travels; rather, most, in the spirit of Jan van Goyen, are a delightful record of Dutch life in the third quarter of the seventeenth century, remarkable for their quantity (many hundreds have survived) and, in general, their small size. Clearly, there was a market among connoisseurs for these small sheets, sometimes only three or four inches wide. Many of these little drawings have borders put in by the artist himself, who also often signed or monogrammed them. There is no sign that the works were meant to be exhibited in the modern sense of the word; that is, they were not pasted or pinned to another surface, but rather kept in the collectors' *kunstboeken* for occasional enjoyment.

The present drawing is an example of his looser, more open style, to be found in dozens of his works. Pulling the goose (which hangs from a rope above the road) was a fairly common subject in Dutch art, as early as David Vinckboons, as well as in such contemporaries as Salomon van Ruysdael and Pieter Molyn, his teacher. It is fascinating, also, to see the market for an artist's work divide along the lines of subject and medium: paintings, with Scandinavian landscapes, and works on paper, with all subjects, especially the Dutch scene.

This drawing may be one of a series representing the months and seasons. According to Alice Davies [letter, 1988], another van Everdingen drawing of comparable size could be part of the same series (Fogg Museum, inv. no. 403.1922, "Peasants reaping hay," 102 x 102 mm). Davies further points out that the present drawing is "similar in size and medium to the atypical Kansas set (see Davies 1972). It is tempting to try to match them up with a selection of Kansas months and to form a second set using the two sheets at Hamburg (Davies 1972, figs. 33, 34)."

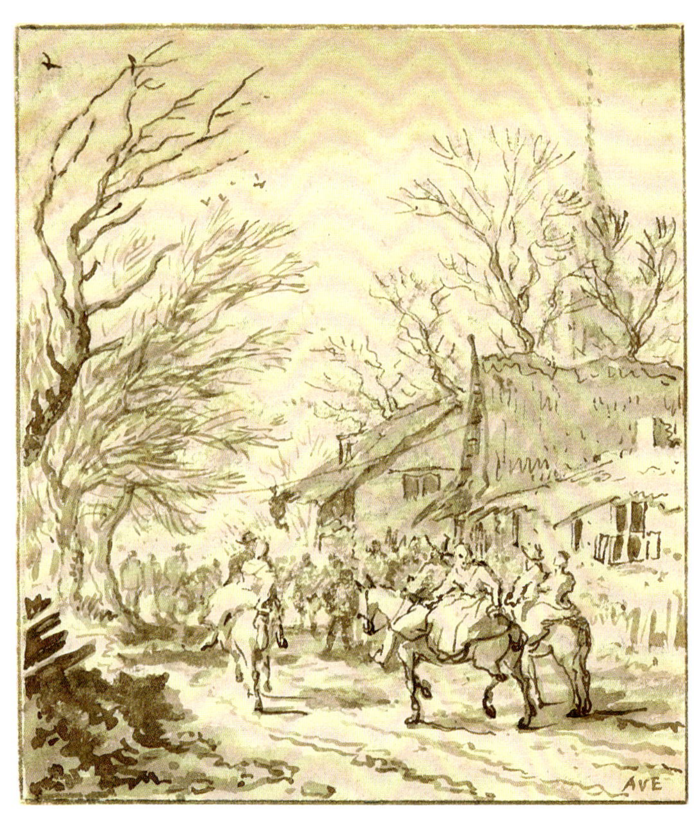
AVE

Allart van Everdingen
Alkmaar 1621–1675 Amsterdam

8 *Winter scene with skaters and hunters*

Pen and brush in brown ink over traces of black chalk; brown ink framing lines.
65 x 94 mm (2½ x 3¾ in).

WATERMARK: none. (R8)

CHAIN LINES: horizontal, 24 mm.

INSCRIPTIONS: monogrammed *AVE* at lower left (pen in brown ink); verso, lower left *A v Everdingen/ hoog 2½ d/ br 3¾ d* (pen in brown ink; in the hand of C. Ploos van Amstel); at lower right *122* (pencil); at lower left *4* (pencil).

PROVENANCE: Cornelis Ploos van Amstel (L. 3002–4), his sale, Amsterdam, 3 March 1800, lot N.30 (with another Everdingen landscape drawing). Einar Perman, Stockholm, his sale, Amsterdam, Sotheby Mak van Waay, 9 June 1975, lot 119. C. F. Karsten, New Canaan, Connecticut. Sale, New York, Sotheby's, 16 January 1985, lot 56, acquired at the sale.

LITERATURE: none.

EXHIBITIONS: none.

This tiny, fascinating drawing is remarkable not only for its size but also for its detail and finish. Alice I. Davies (1972) has discussed the various series of drawings that van Everdingen executed and this work may be from a series of the months.

A precise copy (Fig. 1), in reverse direction, is preserved in the Statens Museum for Kunst, Copenhagen (inv. no. 7307). The copy, which is almost the same size (62 x 94 mm) and in the same media as the present drawing, was discovered by Leena Peck and Sheldon Peck. It may have been made by Cornelis Ploos van Amstel, the eighteenth-century collector and printmaker who once owned the present drawing. Ploos made and commissioned numerous prints after seventeenth-century drawings, including van Everdingen's (see Laurentius, Niemeijer and Ploos van Amstel 1980, p. 271, cat. no. 36, the view of a village). The Copenhagen drawing, which is looser, less precise, and more atmospheric than the present drawing, may have been done in preparation for one of these prints.

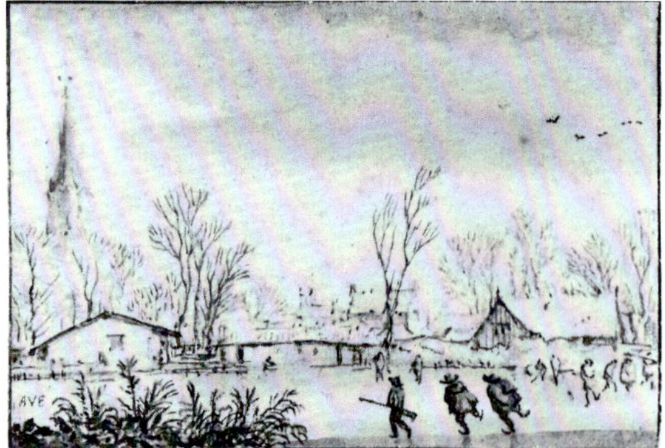

Fig. 1. Allart van Everdingen, *Skating scene*, pen and ink with wash. Statens Museum for Kunst, Copenhagen.

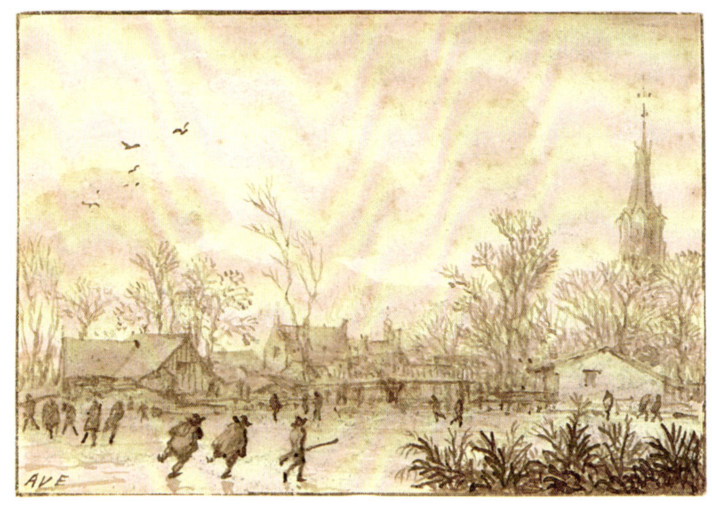
AVE

Allart van Everdingen
Alkmaar 1621–1675 Amsterdam

9 *Rocky coast with fishing boats in a stormy sea*

Pen and brush in brown ink; brown ink framing lines. 115 x 163 mm (5⅞ x 6⅜ in).

WATERMARK: fragment, crown [above horn in cartouche], at upper center, nearly identical to Heawood no. 2715 (Amsterdam, dated 1668). (R9)

CHAIN LINES: vertical, 25–26 mm.

INSCRIPTIONS: monogrammed *AVE* on a rock at lower center (pen in brown ink); verso, at lower right *A drawing by Everdingen* (pencil, 19th or 20th century)

PROVENANCE: Henri Duval, Liège, his sale, Amsterdam, F. Muller, 22–23 June 1910, lot 115. Henry Oppenheimer, London, his sale, London, Christie's, 13 July 1936, lot 243(B). Ernst Goldschmidt, Brussels, 1936. Sale, Paris, Ader Tajan, 28 October 1994, lot 13, acquired at the sale.

LITERATURE: none.

EXHIBITIONS: none.

This scene of ships on a stormy sea near the shore is a favorite one with van Everdingen; for example, the British Museum preserves a drawing by him with a large, but different boulder by the shore, with a tower behind. Perhaps the closest such scene is a larger drawing, without the tower in the background or the figures on the beach, in the Peltzer sale, Gutekunst, Stuttgart, May 13–14, 1914. Clearly, the artist often did not respond to a particular place, but rearranged the elements of his recurring, invented scenes to achieve a certain variety.

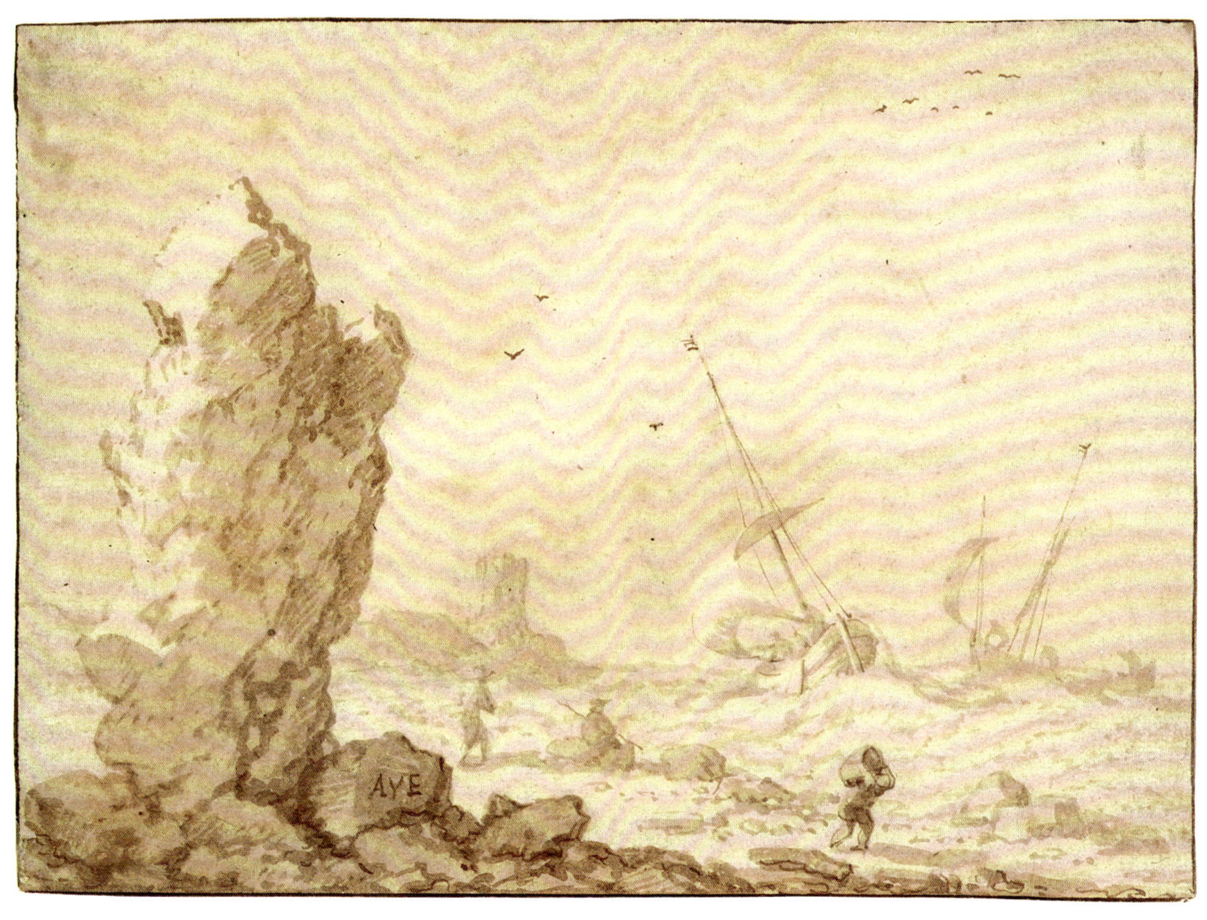
AVE

Abraham Furnerius
Rotterdam c. 1628–1654 Rotterdam

10 *Farmstead with trees by a road*

Pen and brush in brown ink; trace of gray ink framing line at lower border.
110 x 158 mm (4⅜ x 6¼ in).

WATERMARK: none. (R10)

CHAIN LINES: vertical, 24–27 mm.

INSCRIPTIONS: none.

PROVENANCE: From an 18th-century French album formerly in the British Museum, dispersed in 1943. Francis Springell, Portinscale, his sale, London, Sotheby's, 30 June 1986, lot 33. Adolphe Stein, London – Paris, 1988. Acquired 1988.

LITERATURE: Hind 1943, p. 128. Wegner 1967–8, p. 53. Sumowski 1981, vol. 4, p. 2262–3, no. 1028^{xx}.

EXHIBITIONS: Cat. London 1988, no. 23, plate 15.

In many ways, Rembrandt is the central fact of seventeenth-century Dutch art. The sheer range of his subjects, from portraits to religious scenes, animals, peasant life, landscapes, and ancient history and mythology, the quantity of his output, the social and intellectual circles he moved in and was inspired by, his international reputation, and the number and quality of the students he attracted – all these factors made him the key figure in the art of his time.

One of the finest of his students was Abraham Furnerius, who was the brother-in-law of Philips Koninck, another Rembrandt pupil and landscapist. Furnerius, who died at age 26, seems not to have made any paintings or even any drawings aside from landscapes. This sheet was taken from an album of 82 leaves, which was broken up in 1943; the British Museum acquired 65 leaves, with 252 drawings. The style is typical of Furnerius, with its long thin tree trunks with no branches at the bottom and then a mushroom-like burst of foliage spreading out; a drawing in the Museum Boymans – van Beuningen, Rotterdam (inv. no. R95), is especially close to this work.

This side view of the farm compund, with a line of trees on the left, is an interesting variation of this subject; the drawing seems to have been cut slightly at the top and bottom, making the foreground fence harder to read. This fence is reminiscent of similar devices used by Rembrandt, for example, in his so-called winter landscape in the Fogg Museum, Cambridge (inv. no. 1932.368), and the etching of a cottage with a white paling, dated 1648 (Bartsch 232), soon after Furnerius would have studied with the master.

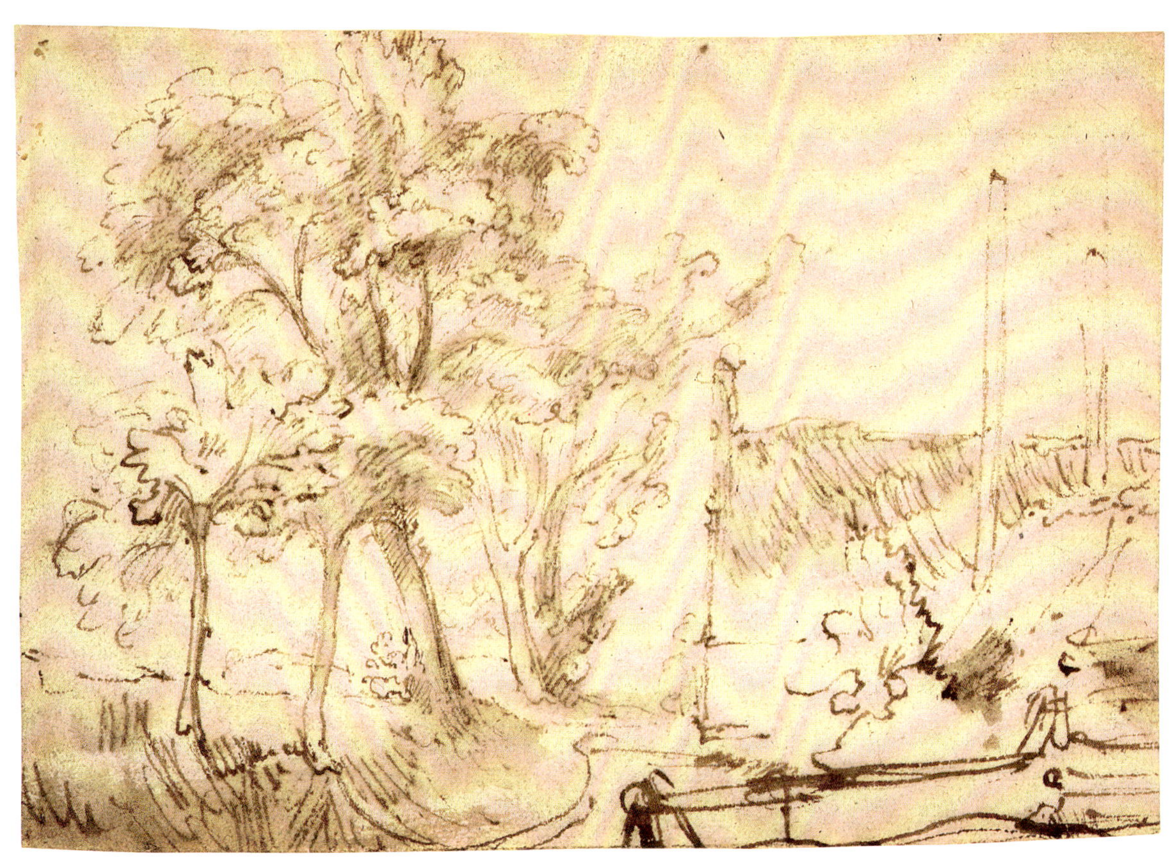

Jan van Goyen
Leiden 1596–1656 The Hague

11 *Figures, boats and cottages on the banks of an estuary*

Black chalk, brush in gray and black ink; trace of brown ink framing line at lower border. 148 x 262 mm (5¾ x 10⅜ in).

WATERMARK: none. (R11)

CHAIN LINES: horizontal, 23–25 mm.

INSCRIPTIONS: Partly erased signature and date were *I V GOIEN 1626* at lower left (pen in black ink); verso, at center *P. Molyn/ Sir Thos. Lawrence's Colln.* (pen in dark brown ink, in the hand of Samuel Woodburn); to the right *E. van de Velde* (blue ballpoint pen); at lower center *E. v. d. Velde/ 22608* (pencil); at lower right *297* (green crayon)

PROVENANCE: Sir Thomas Lawrence (1769–1830), London (L. 2445, dry stamp). Samuel Woodburn, London (L. 2584), his sale, London, Christie's, 16 June 1854, lot 909 (as Molyn). Robert P. Roupell, London (L. 2234), his sale, London, Christie's, 13 July 1887, lot 1015 (as Molyn). Mathias Komor Gallery, New York, 1962. William Suhr, Mount Kisco, New York, 1965. Sale, New York, Sotheby's, 18 January 1984, lot 209, acquired at the sale.

LITERATURE: Beck I 1972, p. 252, no. 839 (illus.). Beck III 1987, p. 116, no. 839.

EXHIBITIONS: none.

The four drawings here by Jan van Goyen, from whose hand several thousand paintings and drawings survive, give an excellent feeling for the development of this artist from 1626 to 1653, three years before his death. In the first drawing, the composition is arranged in strips parallel to the picture plane. The figures on the bank of the canal in the foreground are clearly defined, their outlines strengthened by the artist; the houses in the middle ground are looser, more atmospheric in treatment; and the background is marked by the outline of a tower on the far right. The artist moves back into space zone by zone, step by step. The verso inscription by Samuel Woodburn, "P. Molyn, Sir Thos. Lawrence's Colln.," suggests that the inscription may have been erased while the drawing was in Woodburn's hands (1830–1853) to support his Molyn attribution.

The second van Goyen shows a man rolling a barrel onto a skiff already laden with three other people and a dog; to the right is a dovecote, a common sight in the Netherlands, with wheels, barrels, and wheelbarrows stored beneath it. This drawing, from the 1640s, shows the artist in full control of the figures as they go about their business, the relaxed movement back and forth from foreground to background and back again, the range of light and shadow, the touches of gray wash, and, most particularly, the liquid, supple use of the black chalk, with its vibrating line and scattered accents. The end result is a drawing that fully expresses the busy life along a Dutch canal.

About a decade later, in 1653, van Goyen made another drawing of virtually the same scene. Now, the various details of buildings and figures are more summarily treated, there

Continued on p.60

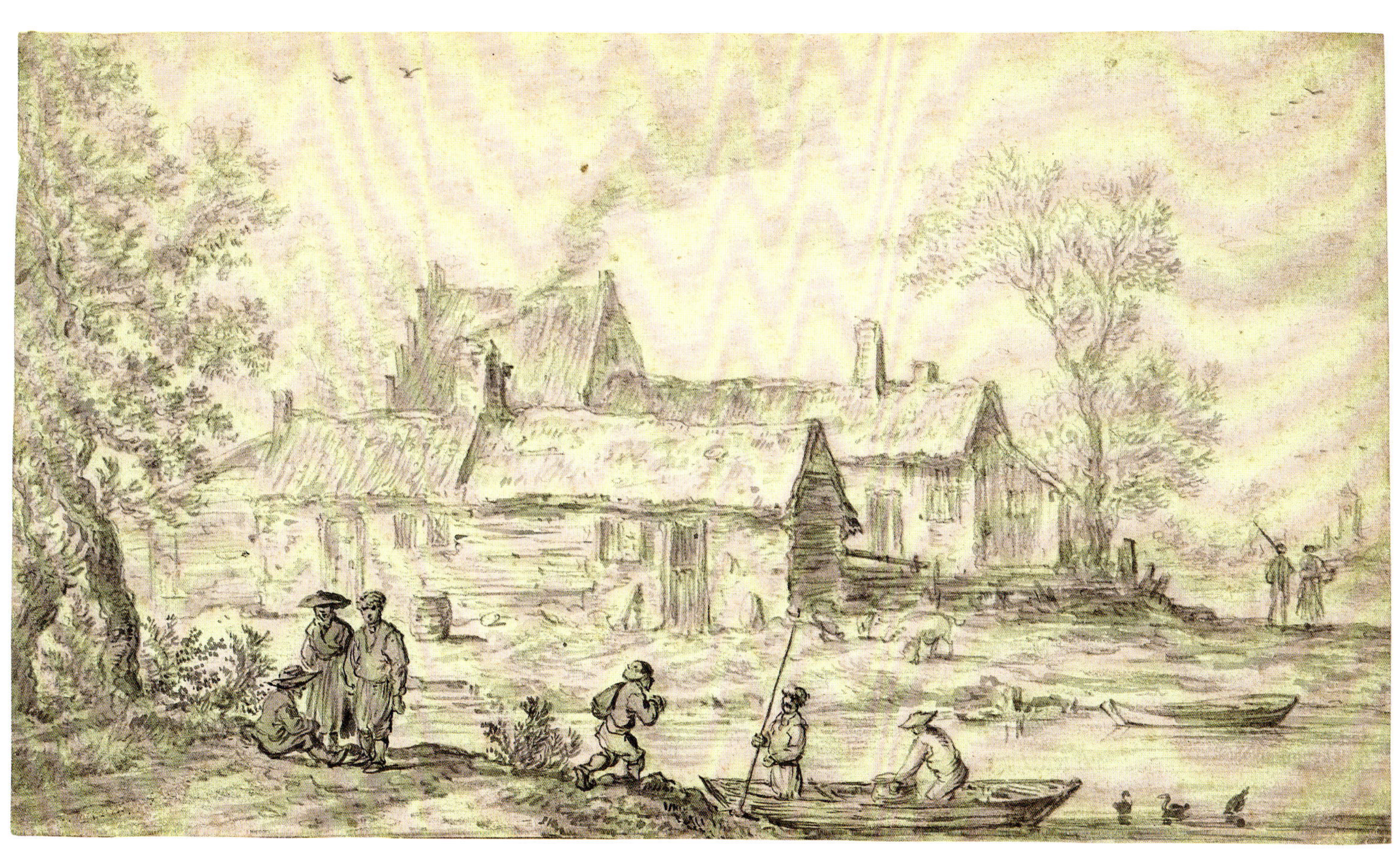

Jan van Goyen
Leiden 1596–1656 The Hague

12 *Figures in a boat near a dovecote at the shore*

Black chalk with touches of gray wash; black chalk framing lines, strengthened in some areas with black ink.
109 x 191 mm (4¼ x 7½ in).

WATERMARK: none. (R12)

CHAIN LINES: horizontal, 23–25 mm.

INSCRIPTIONS: numbered *302* at lower right corner (pen in brown ink, Flury-Hérard collector's mark number).

PROVENANCE: Flury-Hérard, Paris (L. 1015), his sale, Paris, Delbergue, 13 May 1861, lot 145. Mrs. A. L. Snapper, sale, London, Sotheby's, 10 May 1961, lot 79. Bernard Houthakker, Amsterdam, 1961. Sale, The Hague, 7 June 1966, lot 292. Sale, Amsterdam, Sotheby Mak van Waay, 18 November 1980, lot 112. Sale, New York, Sotheby's, 16 January 1985, lot 69, acquired at the sale.

LITERATURE: Beck III 1987, p. 109, no. 694A (illus.).

EXHIBITIONS: Cat. Amsterdam, 1961, no. 28 (illus.).

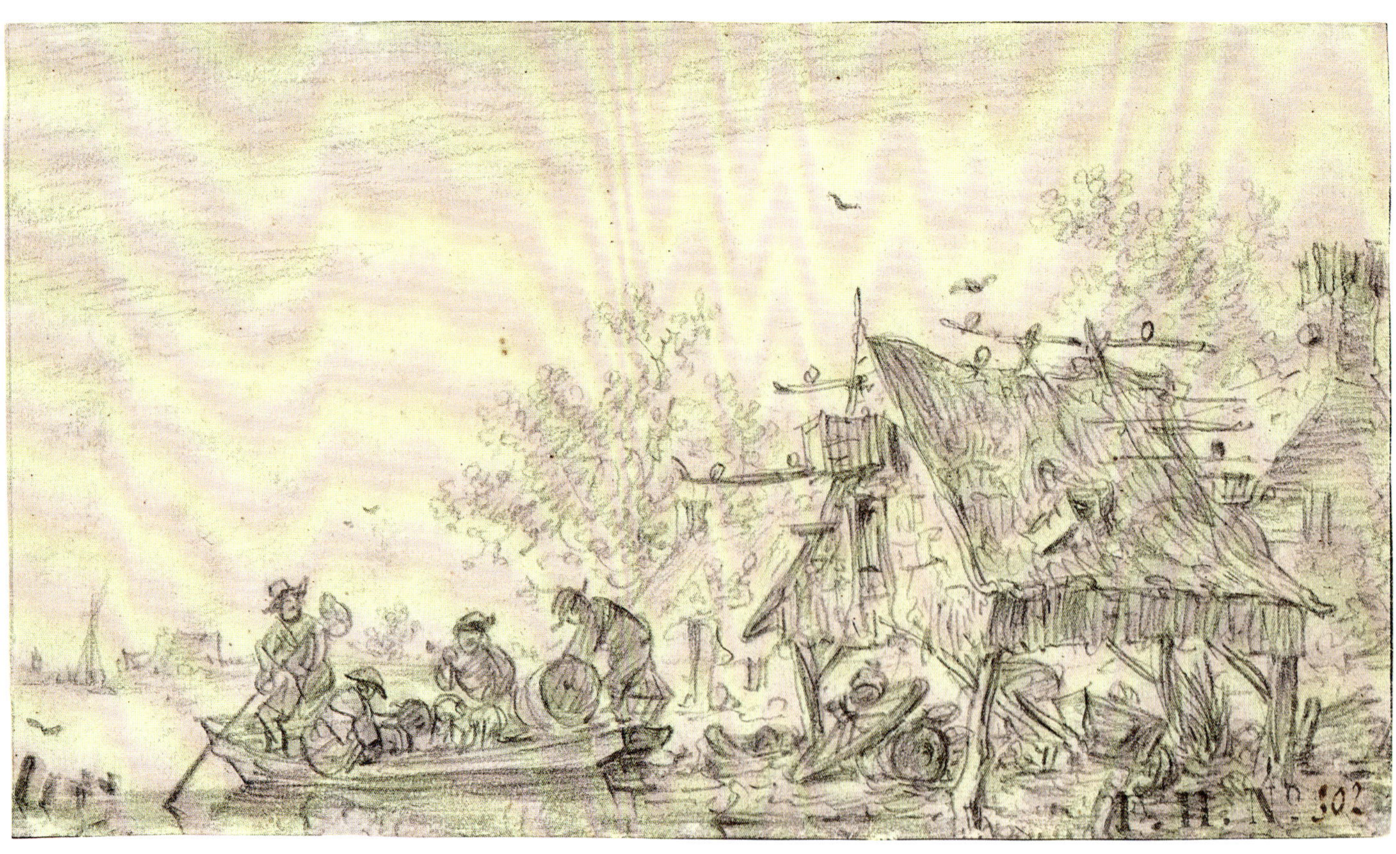

Jan van Goyen
Leiden 1596–1656 The Hague

13 *River scene with boats near a jetty by a tavern*

Black chalk, brush in gray ink; brown ink framing lines.
120 x 202 mm (4¾ x 7⅞ in).

WATERMARK: crown over three circles, similar to Beck I 1972, p. 344, fig. 69 (dated 1651–3) and Beck III 1987, p. 131, fig. 70b (dated 1651). (R13)

CHAIN LINES: horizontal, 16, 19, 29 and 33 mm.

INSCRIPTIONS: monogrammed and dated *VG 1653* at lower right (black chalk).

PROVENANCE: The Hermitage, St. Petersburg, its sale, Leipzig, C.G. Boerner, 29 April 1931, lot 92. Sale, London, Christie's, 27 June 1967, lot 101. Alfred Brod Gallery, London, 1968. L. J. Jiskoot, New York. Sale, Amsterdam, Christie's, 16 November 1981, lot 48, acquired at the sale.

LITERATURE: Beck I 1972, pp. 166–7, no. 498 (illus.). Beck III 1987, p. 89, no. 498.

EXHIBITIONS: none.

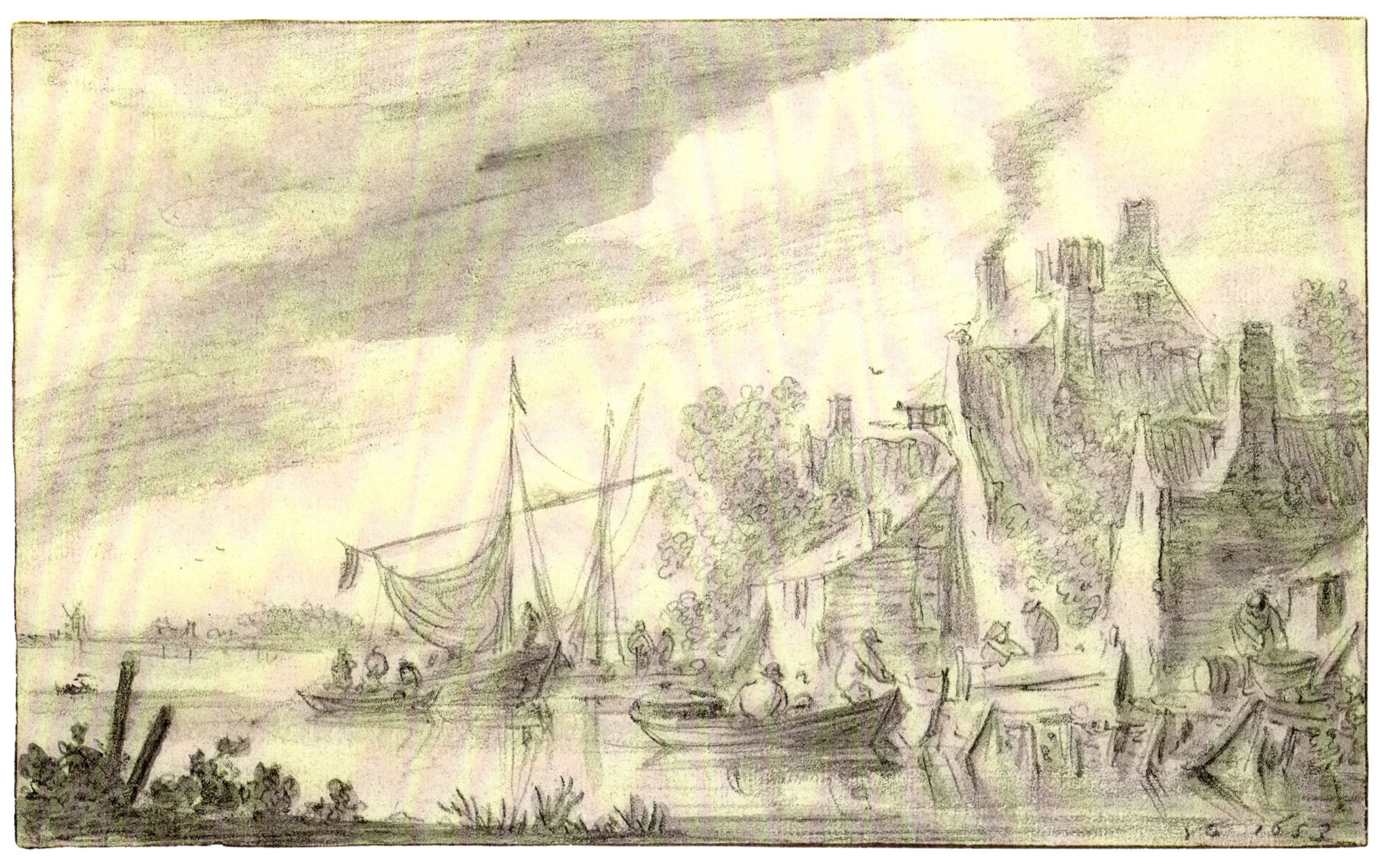

Jan van Goyen
Leiden 1596–1656 The Hague

14 *Encampment by the fortress at Gennep on the River Maas*

Black chalk with touches of light brown wash; black chalk framing lines.
173 x 280 mm (6¾ x 11 in).

WATERMARK: horn in cartouche with letters PM below, nearly identical to Beck I 1972, p. 329, fig. 19 (dated 1651); Schapelhouman and Schatborn 1998, p. 245, no. W127 (dated 1653). (R14)

CHAIN LINES: horizontal, 24–25 mm.

INSCRIPTIONS: none.

PROVENANCE: A. C. Bowring, his sale, London, Sotheby's, 23 February 1955, lot 44. Mathias Komor, New York (L. 1882a). Marion Hammer Gallery, Lugano. Sale, Amsterdam, Christie's, 15 November 1983, lot 58. Johnny van Haeften, London. Robert Noortman, London and Maastricht. Sale, Amsterdam, Christie's, 25 November 1992, lot 577, acquired at the sale.

LITERATURE: Beck I 1972, p. 249, no. 825A. Beck III 1987, pp. 116–7, no. 825A (illus.).

EXHIBITIONS: none.

Continued from p. 56
is less detail, the shift back and forth between shadow and light is even more assured, and the line itself is less sinuous and dynamic.

The last drawing of the four is also from the early or mid-1650s; Sheldon Peck has identified the site as the "Genneperhuis" fortress on the Maas, and connected it with a painting of this location by Salomon van Ruysdael (Fig. 1), in the art market, London. Here, the artist has become even more relaxed and masterful in his handling of space and light and shadow. The figures are treated in a kind of shorthand, with clusters of strokes of the black chalk. Once again, the foreground is in shadow; clumps of figures, boats, and tents move our eye from left to right as we go deeper into space, until we arrive at last at the round fort, the climax of the composition, with yet more life – people and houses – on its top. The balance between the knoll in shadow, in the left foreground, and the fort, in full sunlight, in the background right, shows the distance van Goyen – and Dutch landscape in general – have traveled in the quarter century or more since the first of these four drawings.

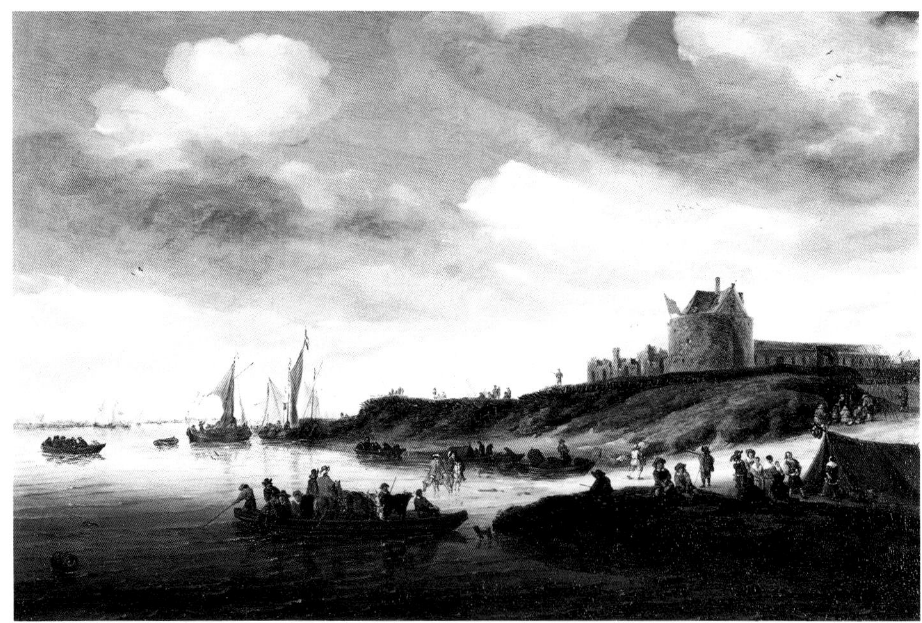

Fig. 1. Salomon van Ruysdael, *View of Gennep on the River Maas*, 1665, oil on canvas. John Mitchell and Son, London.

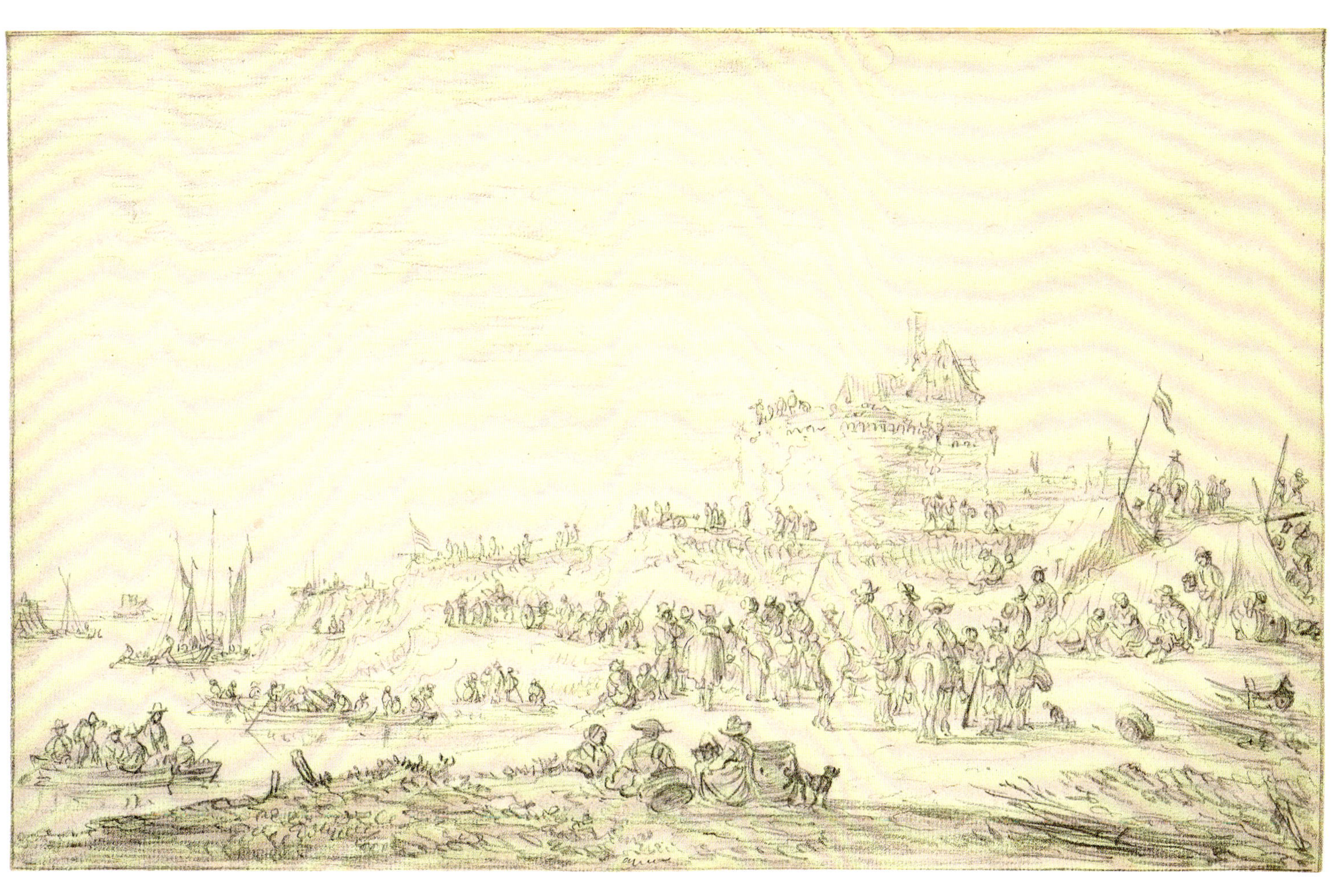

Joris van der Haagen
Dordrecht or Arnhem c. 1615–1669 The Hague

15 *Woods at The Hague with a huntsman and his dog*

Pen in gray and brown ink, brush in gray ink; gray and brown ink framing lines.
199 x 313 mm (7⅞ x 12¼ in).

WATERMARK: none. (R15)

CHAIN LINES: horizontal, 24–25 mm.

INSCRIPTIONS: signed and inscribed *dit is int haachse bos nomb...JVHagen* at lower left (pen in brown ink)

PROVENANCE: Unidentified collector's inscription *J.F. – L^{V}L. No.42* on the mount (pen in brown ink, 18th or 19th century). Antiquariaat H. D. Pfann, Amsterdam, 1956. Hans van Leeuwen, Amerongen (L. 2799a), his sale, Amsterdam, Christie's, 24 November 1992, lot 96, acquired at the sale.

LITERATURE: Brandt 1986, no. 14.

EXHIBITIONS: Cat. Arnhem, 1958, no. 46. Cat. Utrecht, 1959–60, no. 25. Cat. Laren, 1963, no. 51. Cat. Nijmegen, 1965, no. 26. Cat. Leeuwarden, 1966, no. 12. Cat. Bonn/Saarbrücken/Bochum, 1968-9, no. 55. Cat. Rheydt, 1971, no. 32. Cat. Amsterdam, 1975-6, no. 51. Cat. Bremen/Braunschweig/Stuttgart, 1979-80, no. 52. Cat. Fribourg/Passau/Trier/Aachen/Nuremberg, 1982–4, no. 40.

Joris van der Haagen, who spent most of his career in The Hague, was unusually sensitive to the simple beauties of an ordinary forest scene. Although he did many topographically accurate and identifiable scenes in Arnhem and other cities, his favorite subject was the Haagse Bos, a broad and stately stand of trees still near the center of The Hague. About thirty paintings and drawings of this forest survive, dated between 1652 and 1669; the artist seems to have added the inscriptions and dates years after the execution of most of them.

The central tree dominating the scene in this drawing has been executed in brown ink, contrasting with the rest of the forest in black ink and grey wash. The towering beauty of these trees, in van der Haagen's eternal summer, is increased by the small scale of the hunter, who is dwarfed by even the reeds in the foreground.

These woods attracted other artists of the time, such as Jacob van der Ulft (Teyler Museum); van der Haagen's love of forests is close to that of Adriaen van de Velde.

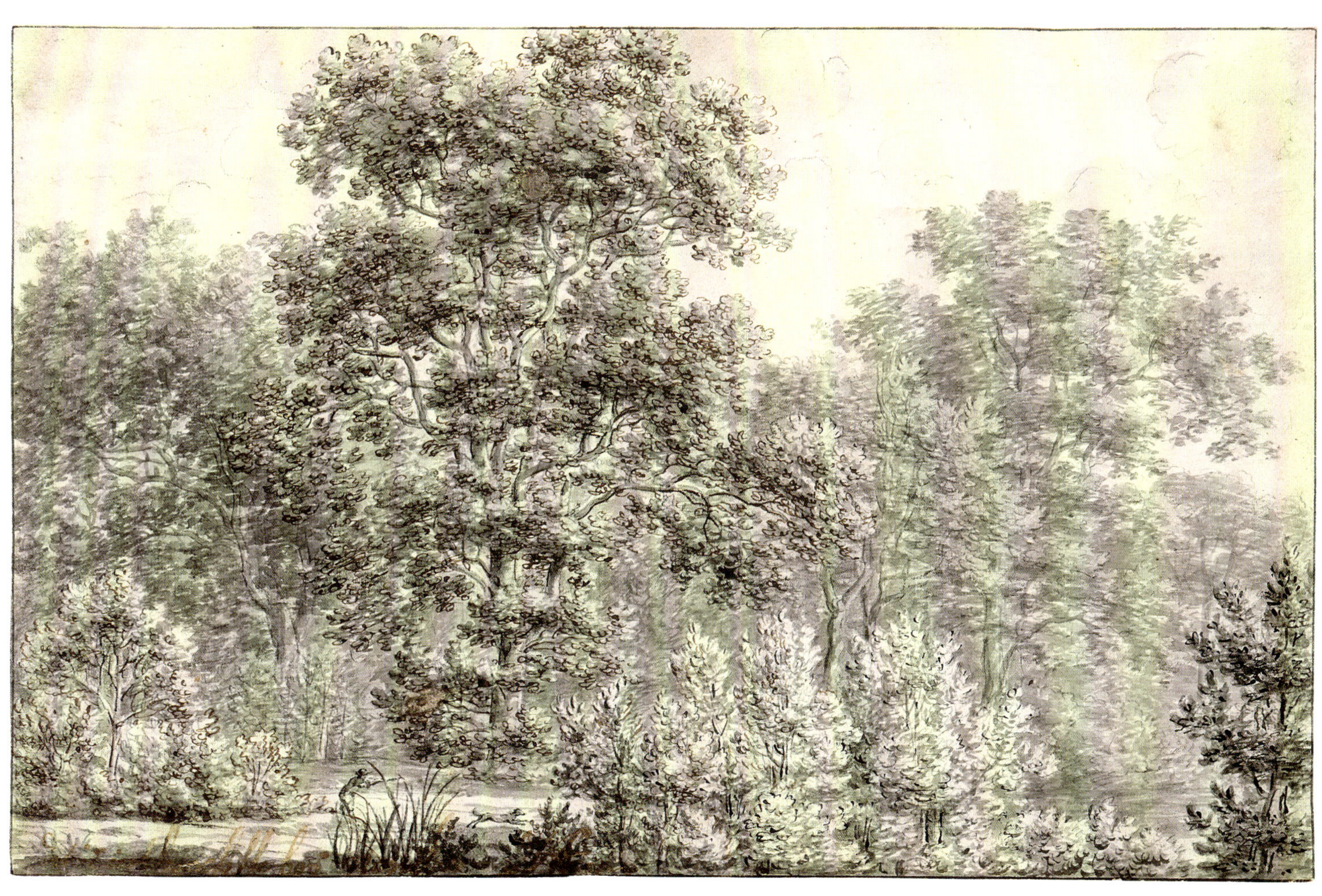

Hendrik Hondius the Elder
Duffel 1573–1650 The Hague

16 *Ruins of Castle Spangen*

Pen and brush in brown ink over black chalk; laid down; traces of black chalk framing lines. 224 x 340 mm (8¾ x 13⅜ in).

WATERMARK: cluster of grapes, similar to Heawood no. 2106 (England, dated 1622); Schapelhouman and Schatborn 1998, p. 245, no. W121 (Holland, 17th century); backing paper with Strasbourg lily, 18th or 19th century. (R16)

CHAIN LINES: horizontal, 17–19 mm.

INSCRIPTIONS: none.

PROVENANCE: Collector's mark *H DUP B* lower right, in an oval, in blue ink (not in Lugt). Sale, Amsterdam, Christie's, 18 November 1985, lot 57, acquired at the sale.

LITERATURE: none.

EXHIBITIONS: none.

Ruins were especially attractive to Dutch artists and their patrons; aside from their picturesque qualities, those ruins which were in the Netherlands were especially meaningful to a people whose independence, after an 80-year war, was newly won. Topographically precise views of famous places also satisfied the love of documentation that characterized the Dutch.

Hondius was an extremely prolific printmaker and publisher of prints; his range of interests seems inexhaustible, from a remarkable series of portraits of (mostly contemporary) artists to ancient Roman ruins, anti-Roman Catholic propaganda, a beached whale, animal skeletons, maps, and perspective constructions. Two of his most moving prints show epileptics being restrained.

The haunting and noble ruin in the present drawing, Castle Spangen (now demolished), near Rotterdam, is close in style to a Hondius view of Castle Tervueren, near Brussels, dated 1605, in the Morgan Library, New York (acc. no. 1978.40). In 1572 Spangen was burned by the Spanish (as was the church at Noordwijkerhout depicted in Cat. no. 6 by Du Bois); particularly characteristic was its central stair tower, once in the courtyard but by now clearly visible.

Castle Spangen was often the subject of topographical prints, a special love of the Dutch. These prints, from the seventeenth and eighteenth centuries, often show the castle in good condition, c.1550, as well as in ruins, after 1573; for example, Abraham Rademaker, in his famous series of Dutch cities and sites, devotes no less than five pages to different views of Spangen (Rademaker 1725, plates CXXXIX–CXLIII), the last, from behind the castle, especially close to the Hondius drawing. The castle was also portrayed in the seventeenth century by Roelant Roghman, in a famous series of about 245 such topographical drawings, and by Willem Buytewech, in a masterful study in the Fondation Custodia, Paris (inv. no. 2356).

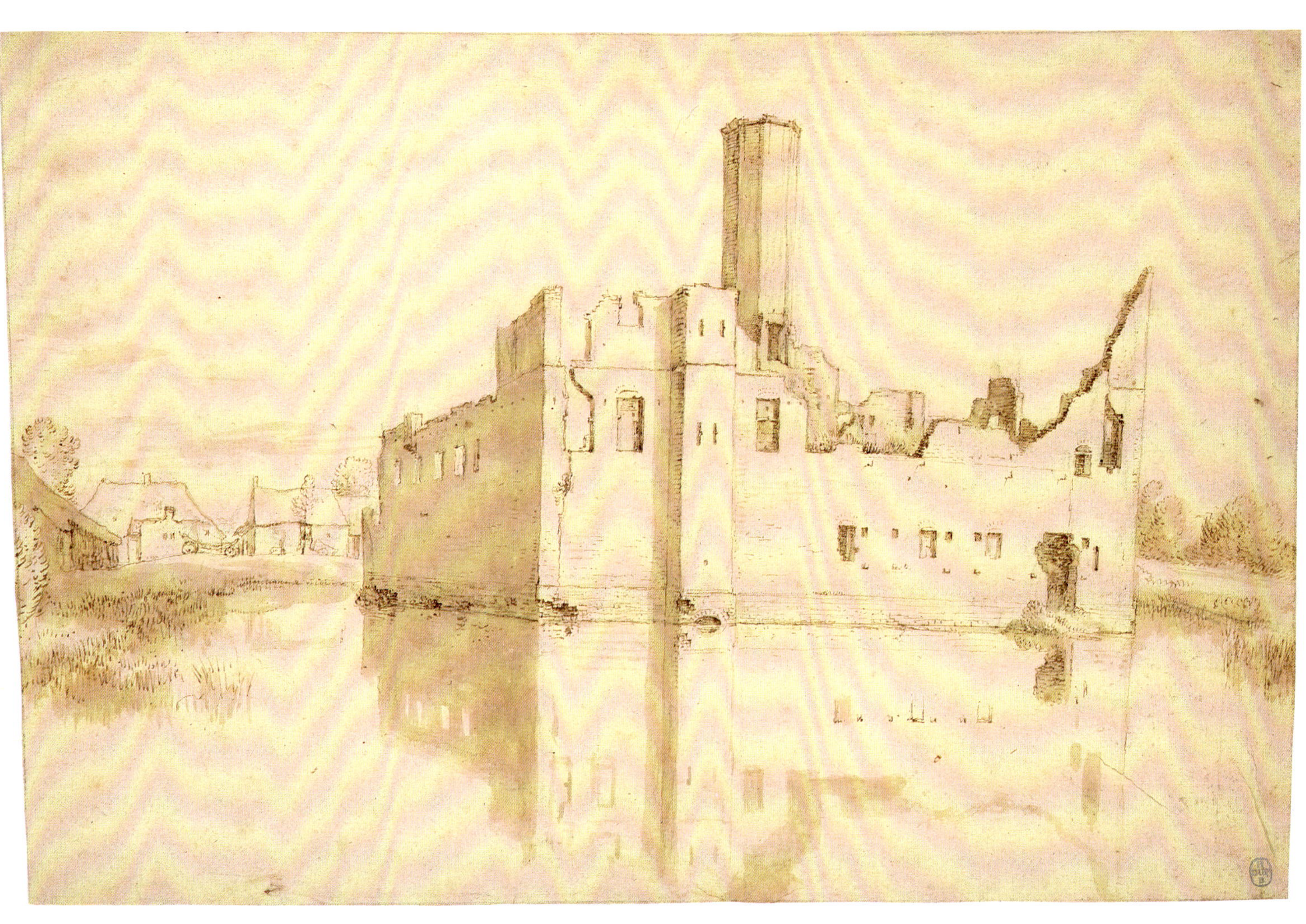

Jan van Kessel
Amsterdam 1641–1680 Amsterdam

17 *Wooded farmstead behind a wall*

Brush in gray and black ink over black chalk; gray ink framing lines.
294 x 420 mm (11⅝ x 16⅝ in).

WATERMARK: none. (R17)

CHAIN LINES: horizontal, 27–29 mm.

INSCRIPTIONS: verso, at upper left *Ah 2/63* (pencil); at lower left *AX421* (pencil).

PROVENANCE: De Jong, Wassenaar. Sale, Amsterdam, Christie's, 12 November 1990, lot 99, acquired at the sale.

LITERATURE: Davies 1992, p. 263, no. d69 (illus.). Plomp 1997, p. 454, under cat. no. 545.

EXHIBITIONS: none.

A skillful landscape specialist in and around his native Amsterdam, Jan van Kessel is credited with 120 paintings and 69 drawings (Davies 1992). In many of his drawings, his fluid use of gray wash and black chalk are comparable with the techniques practiced by his presumed master Jacob van Ruisdael from the 1660s. This landscape shows strong likenesses with characteristics of other drawings in Jan van Kessel's oeuvre, such as Davies nos. d16, d29, d35, d57, d61, d62 and d66. Davies dates the drawing to about 1665.

Van Kessel describes the foliage in this summer scene with precise dapples of brushwork over squiggly indications in black chalk, one of his customary techniques. The sunlight for the drawing is coming from the right and slightly behind the spatial plane, a direction characteristic in van Kessel's drawings, but rarer among his contemporaries' work. He tends to represent chimneys awkwardly askew of roof peaks, as seen in this drawing.

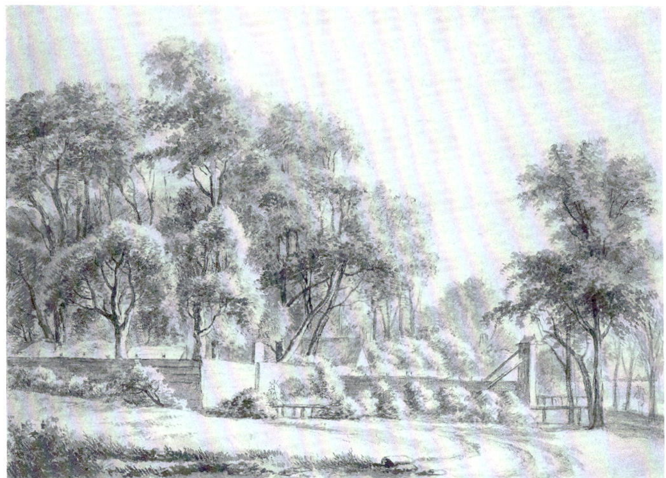

Fig. 1. Anthonie Waterloo, *Wooded landscape with houses behind a wooden fence*, black chalk with gray wash. Teyler Museum, Haarlem, The Netherlands.

Michiel Plomp (1997) in his catalogue of the Dutch drawings in the Teyler Museum published another version (Fig. 1) of this drawing, also in black chalk and gray wash and of a similar size. He attributed the Teyler's version to Anthonie Waterloo (1609–1690). Stylistically, the attribution to Waterloo seems right. The Waterloo drawing exhibits extensive use of black chalk to delineate the tree trunks, branches and the enclosure. In contrast, the van Kessel shows only some faint outlines of black chalk with the bulk of his drawing done with brush in gray ink. The question remains: Which version/artist presents the original composition and which is the copy?

In comparisons of the two works, the Waterloo fails to represent faithfully some important details found in the van Kessel version. In both versions, a gated footbridge over a stream is seen beginning at the edge of the enclosure fence near the shoreline at the right side of the sheet. A man carrying a pole is on the bridge, walking towards an opening in the enclosure. In the van Kessel drawing, this bridge runs diagonal to the enclosure wall, which itself is depicted in *back* of the bridge's gate. In the Waterloo version, the enclosure wall appears to insert in *front* of the diagonal gate, an architectural impossibility. Moreover, a tree at the outside corner of the compound is drawn by van Kessel with the trunk partially hidden behind a bough of leaves. This tree is seen branching and continuing above the bough. In the Waterloo version, the artist used black chalk to create a strangely foreshortened trunk with an unnaturally thick and rounded top – even unlike a pollarded tree – a possible result of careless "reading" of van Kessel's luminous brushwork. These kinds of "translation" discrepancies often reveal a work as a copy of a more cohesive original version.

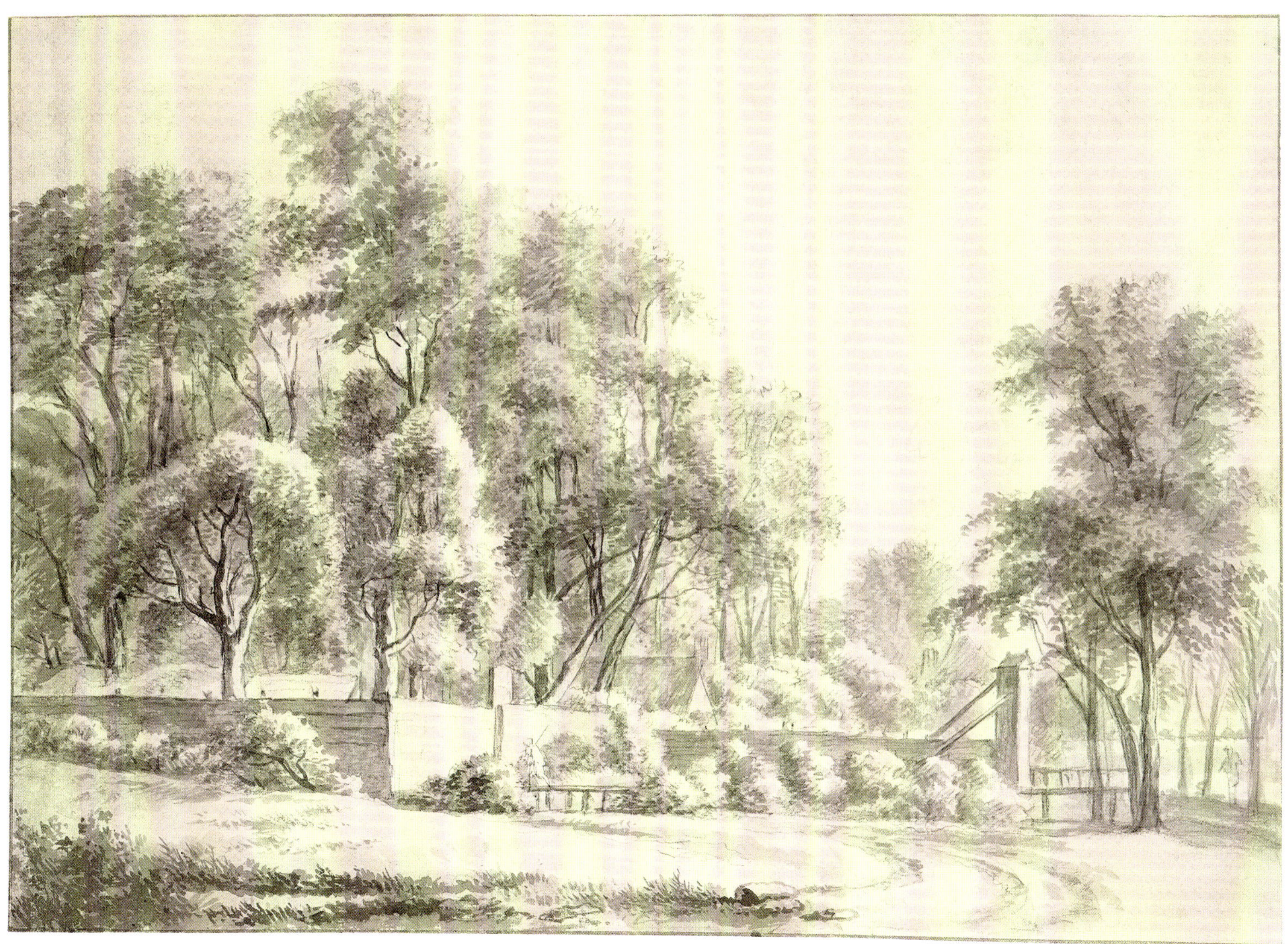

For a copy of the drawing to have been made, one of the two artists must have had both at one time. It would have been far more likely for Waterloo to have had the van Kessel, than the converse situation. Waterloo was heavily into commercial art dealings in his later years. For example, he bought the etching plates of Johannes Ruischer after the artist's death around 1675, reworked some and published them under his own address (Trautscholdt 1973). With Jan van Kessel dying at 39 years in 1680, ten years before Anthonie Waterloo's death, it is probable that Waterloo bought some of van Kessel's estate, including this handsome large drawing, for commercial advantage.

Furthermore, the van Kessel sheet has no watermark and is on thick paper, virtually impossible to trace through. Plomp reports the presence of a five-bell fool's-cap watermark in the paper for the Waterloo drawing. Paper displaying a watermark generally possesses a notable degree of translucency, making it more manageable as an overlay sheet for copying methods.

Thus, all evidence points to this tranquil farmstead scene as an original composition drawn by Jan van Kessel around 1665. The version by Anthonie Waterloo at the Teyler Museum appears to be a repetition done in the 1680s, the final decade of Waterloo's life.

S.P.

Jan Lievens
Leiden 1607–1674 Amsterdam

18 *Ruins of the castle of Brederode*

Pen in brown ink; brown ink framing lines.
292 x 383 mm (11½ x 15 in).

WATERMARK: fool's cap with seven bells and countermark PP, similar to Ash and Fletcher 1998, variant C.a., pp. 111, 116 (dated 1645); Broos and Schapelhouman 1993, cat. no. 107, p. 284 (no date); Heawood nos. 1989 (Dutch, dated 1637) and 1990 (Dutch, c. 1655). (R18)

CHAIN LINES: vertical, 24 mm.

INSCRIPTIONS: verso, at center right *slot te breederoo 3 guilden* (pen in brown ink, 17th century); at lower right 140 (pencil).

PROVENANCE: H. M. Montauban van Swijndregt (1841–1929), Rotterdam, his sale, Amsterdam, R.W.P. de Vries, 5 April 1906, lot 115. Sale, Amsterdam, R.W.P. de Vries, 4 March 1930, lot 182. H. C. Valkema Blouw (1883–1953), his sale, Amsterdam, F. Muller, 2–4 March 1954, lot 266. Bernard Houthakker, Amsterdam (L.1272), his sale, Amsterdam, Sotheby Mak van Waay, 17–18 November 1975, lot 42. Th. Laurentius, Voorschoten, 1975. F. W. A. Knight, his sale, Amsterdam, Sotheby Mak van Waay, 29 October 1979, lot 29, acquired at the sale.

LITERATURE: Schneider 1973, pp. 218, 366, no. Z.185. Kloek 1990, p. 85, fig. 134.

EXHIBITIONS: Cat. Amsterdam 1954, no. 34, (illus.). Cat. Amsterdam 1956, no. 67. Cat. Amsterdam 1964, no. 52, fig. 20.

The castle of Brederode, north of Haarlem, inspired feelings of Dutch pride, as well as being unusually evocative in its ruins and overgrown vegetation. This drawing may have been made in the 1650s or 1660s, at about the time Jacob van Ruisdael also was painting this site.

This view presents a decidedly unusual view of the castle: up close and from below, at an oblique angle that avoids the more famous views from the side. This decision was surely conscious; this surprising approach may have made the work more interesting and easier to sell. Lievens has constructed the composition brilliantly, beginning in the foreground right, with low, heavy ruins, overgrown with vegetation, in the tightest, heaviest strokes in the blackest ink. Then, the familiar ruins rise up in the middle ground, catching the sunlight, and finally, our eye drops down to the lovely copse of trees, half in shadow, quickly noted in long, energetic strokes, and reflected in a pool of water.

Jan Lievens is famous for his close association with Rembrandt in the late 1620s (they were also both students of Pieter Lastman); he later traveled to England, then Antwerp, finally settling in Amsterdam. Powerful though his paintings can be, it is in his drawings, perhaps, that he found his most original and masterful expression; his landscapes in particular take on a Flemish, Rubensian cast that fuse with their Dutch specificity of site to produce sheets of great freshness and immediacy.

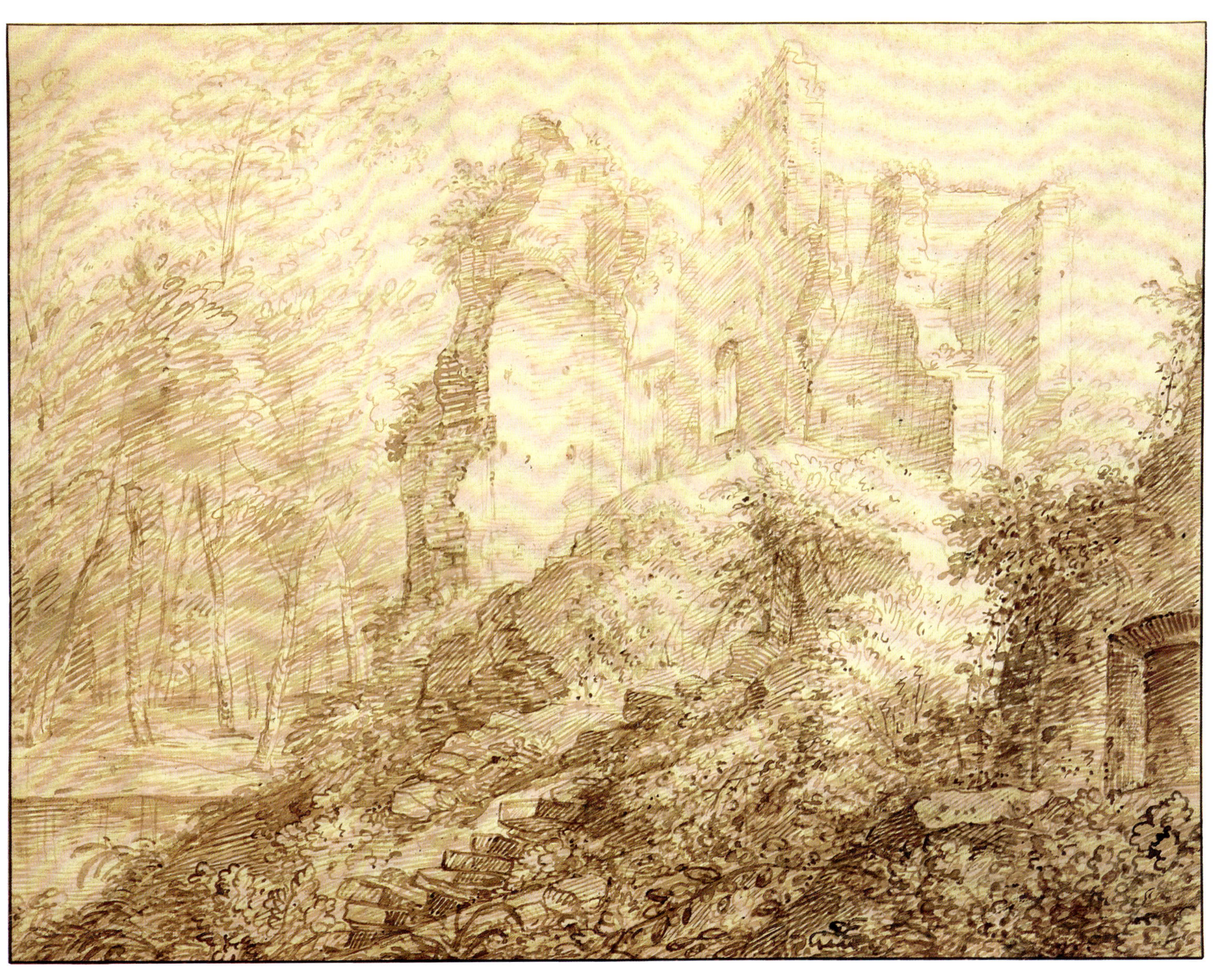

Pieter Molyn
London 1595–1661 Haarlem

19 *Wooded riverbank with a family washing and fishing*

Black chalk, touches of brush in brown ink; brown ink framing lines.
153 x 240 mm (6 x 9½ in).

WATERMARK: horn in crowned cartouche with indistinct letters below, similar to Gaudriault no. 385 (dated 1623). (R19, R19a)

CHAIN LINES: horizontal, 25 mm.

INSCRIPTIONS: signed and dated *PMolyn 1634* at lower left (black chalk).

PROVENANCE: L. X. Lannoy, his sale, Amsterdam, R.W.P. de Vries, 1 December 1893, lot 229. Sale, Amsterdam, Frederik Muller, 15 June 1908, lot 411. Sale, Amsterdam, Christie's, 9 November 1998, lot 72, acquired at the sale.

LITERATURE: Beck 1998, p. 56, no. 44 (illus.).

EXHIBITIONS: Cat. Dresden 1909, no. 244.

Molyn, who was born in London of Flemish parents but who spent his career in Haarlem, played a major role in the "making" of what we think of as the typical Dutch landscape in the 1620s and 1630s. Esaias van de Velde, Jan van Goyen, Salomon van Ruysdael, Pieter Santvoort, and Molyn, among others, created a world of villages, farms, canals, and lakes where men and women are at home, happily going about their business, at work or at play.

The present work from 1634 is an unusually important document, as it were, of Molyn's early style; according to Beck, it is the only signed and dated drawing of this period, so it establishes the artist's style of the 1630s. What is fascinating about the sheet is its relationship to other artists of the time. On the one hand, it is clearly indebted to van de Velde and especially van Goyen in subject matter and in composition, moving from foreground left to middle ground right to background left. Nevertheless, it is very different in execution and feeling from van Goyen; Molyn is more restless, more muscular, more instinctively monumental. There is here the same energy and intensity that we see in the following drawing, by Molyn a quarter of a century later, but with no hint of the indifference or even hostility of nature that is so moving in his drawings of the 1650s. Details like the juxtaposition of the stake in the foreground and the tower behind, the explosion of foliage in the center, and the intricate working of people and cottages into the profusion of trees reveal an artist already in control of his medium.

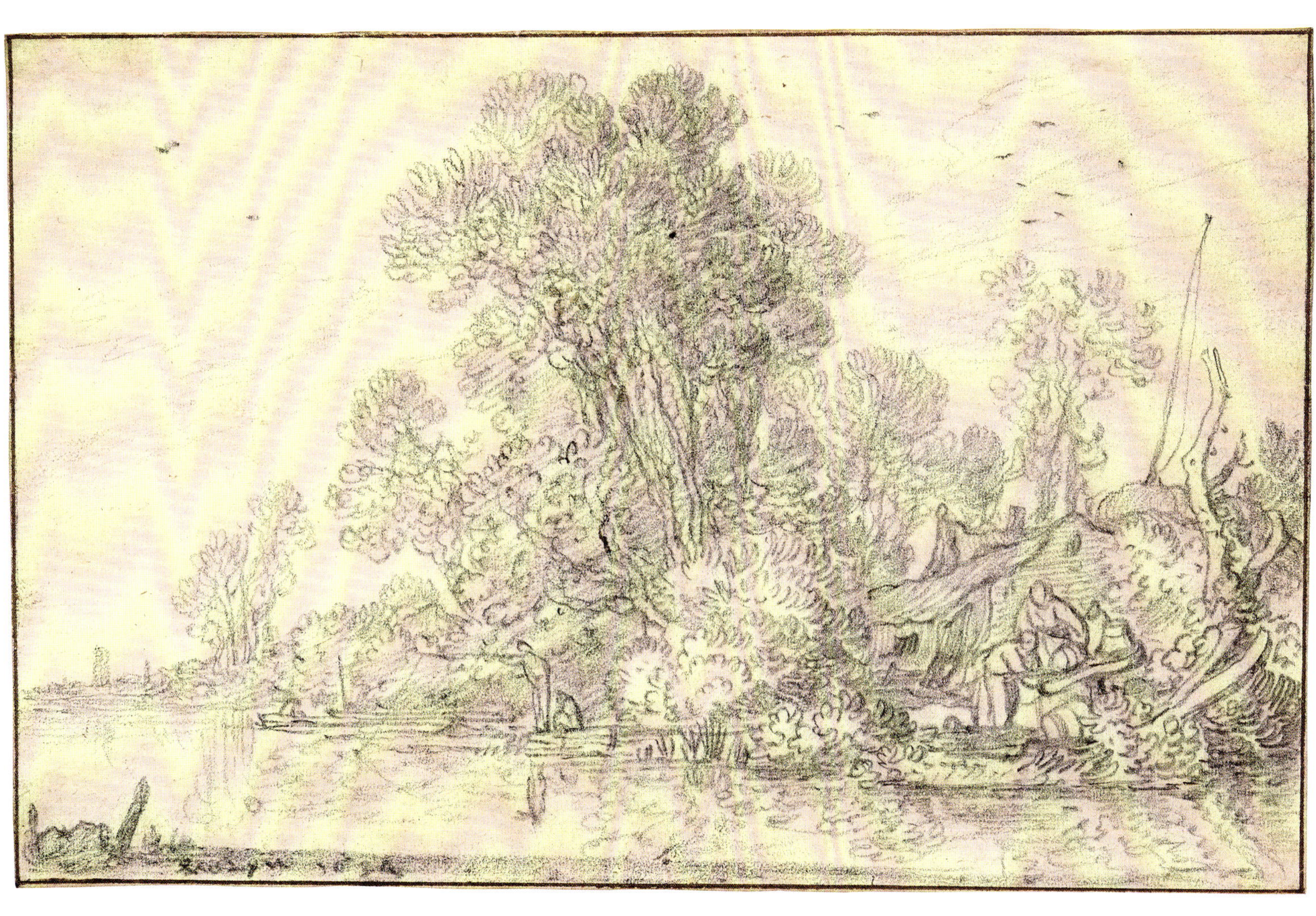

Pieter Molyn
London 1595–1661 Haarlem

20 *Cottages and figures in the dunes*

Black chalk, brush in gray-brown ink; black chalk framing lines with addition of brown ink to lower border.
191 x 276 mm (7½ x 10⅞ in).

WATERMARK: fool's cap with five bells, similar to Heawood no. 1922 (dated 1651). (R20)

CHAIN LINES: horizontal, 23–25 mm.

INSCRIPTIONS: signed and dated *PMolyn/ 1659* (PM in monogram) at upper left (black chalk); verso, at lower right *304* and *Molyn* (pencil).

PROVENANCE: Paul Mantz, his sale, Paris, Chevallier, 10 May 1895, lot 145. E. Warneck, her sale, Paris, Chevallier, 10 May 1905, lot 202b. Sale, Amsterdam, Sotheby Mak van Waay, 18 November 1980, lot 100. C. G. Boerner, Düsseldorf, 1981. Ars Libri, Ltd., Boston, 1985. Acquired 1985.

LITERATURE: Beck 1998, pp. 160–161, no. 333 (illus.).

EXHIBITIONS: Cat. Düsseldorf 1981, no. 21.

In the late 1640s and 1650s, the conception of nature as friend to human beings and their activities – so apparent in the previous drawing, by Molyn in 1634 – changed radically; this occurred largely under the influence of Allart van Everdingen, who was Molyn's pupil, and Jacob van Ruisdael. For these artists, man is overwhelmed by nature, dwarfed by towering cliffs and fir trees, crashing waterfalls, and stormy skies; people become lone travelers in forests littered with blasted tree trunks and boulders challenging the elements.

Molyn made hundreds of landscape drawings that survive; they were surely intended to be sold, since, as here, they often have borders by the artist and are clearly signed and dated. What is fascinating about Molyn's drawings of the late 1650s is not only that they are so much better in quality than his paintings at that point but also that they are a kind of intermediary between these two great streams of Dutch landscape, the van Goyen generation and the Ruisdael generation.

In this masterful drawing of 1659, for example, the composition swirls around the central farmhouse and leads our eye into the dunes in the far right; the farmhouse huddles close to the ground, and the trees bend with the weight of the wind. Although Molyn's landscape drawings are sometimes more obviously bleak and forbidding, with Nordic cliffs and fir trees, the contrast between the oasis of human habitation and the emptiness of the surrounding countryside, with a few isolated figures, is more touching and understated here. Similar scenes by Molyn are in the Morgan Library, Fitzwilliam Museum, Besançon, and the Teyler Museum, Haarlem. Virtually the same farmhouse is depicted in a drawing dated 1655 (Prestel, Frankfurt, November 12–13, 1918, no. 185).

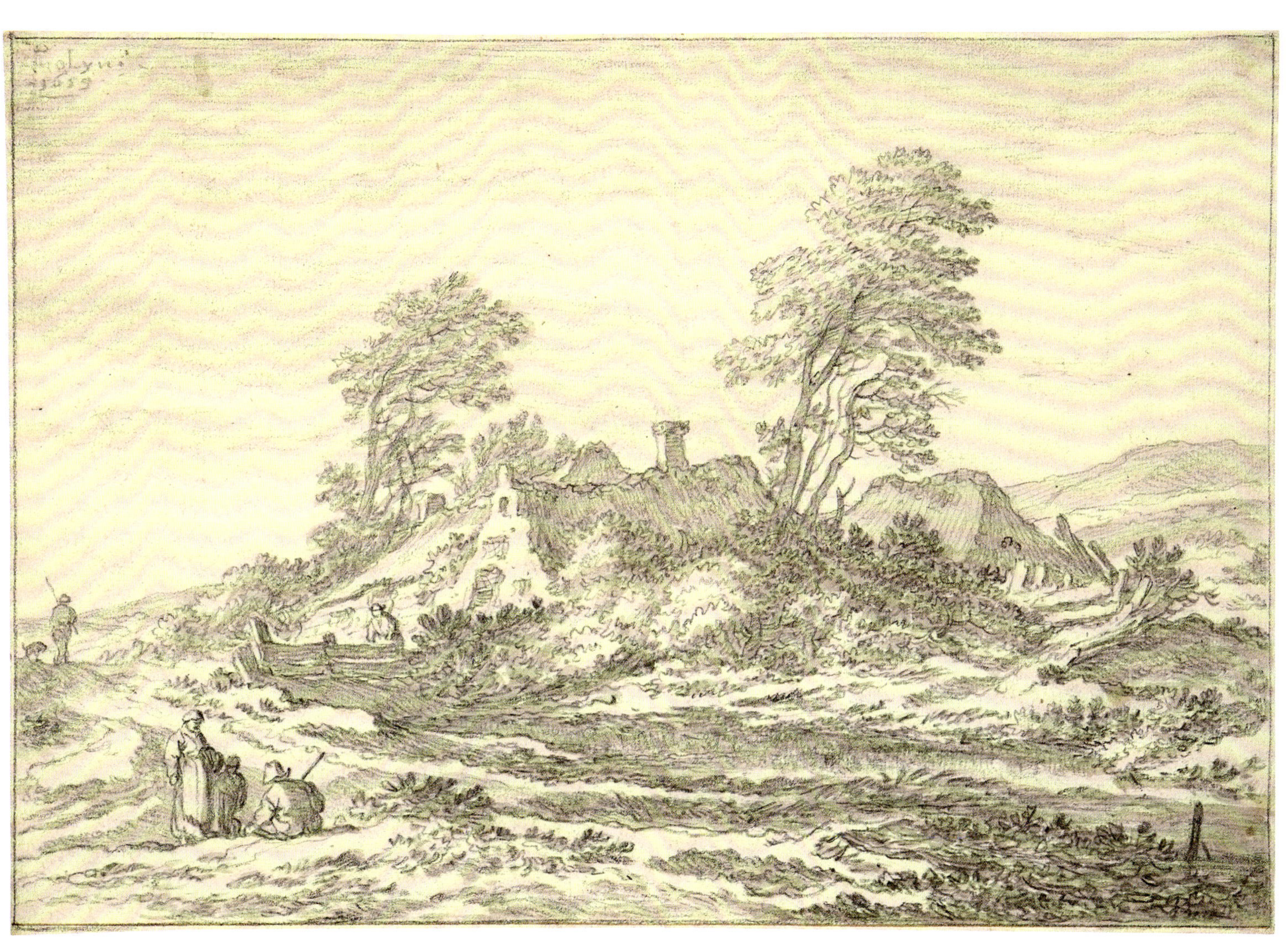

Herman Naiwincx
Schoonhoven c. 1624 – after 1651 Hamburg

21 *Knoll above a pond*

Brush in gray and black ink over black chalk; brown ink framing lines.
116 x 191 mm (4½ x 7½ in).

WATERMARK: fragment, top half of Arms of Orange-Nassau, at upper center, similar to Heawood no. 606 (dated after 1601). (R21)

CHAIN LINES: vertical, 24–26 mm.

INSCRIPTIONS: none.

PROVENANCE: Antiquariaat J. den Hartogh, Zeist, 1963. Hans van Leeuwen, Amerongen (L. 2799a), his sale, Amsterdam, Christie's, 24 November 1992, lot 145, acquired at the sale.

LITERATURE: none.

EXHIBITIONS: none.

Herman Naiwincx is yet another example of a Dutch artist of great quality who is not well-known. This is partly because he died in his twenties and his output is small; it may also be due to the possibility that he was involved in his family's large tapestry-weaving factory at Schoonhoven. Also, his work is quiet and understated; his paintings are small, as are the two sets of eight landscape etchings that make up the bulk of his graphic work, and they concentrate on cliffs and rivers, a copse of trees, that catch the late afternoon sunlight. Although he seems not to have travelled to Italy, Naiwincx captures the limpid and serene atmosphere of the Italian countryside that so attracted Jan Both, Nicolaes Berchem, Jan Asselijn, and their contemporaries.

The present drawing is characterized by a gentle fall of light on still water, picking out a fragment of a wooden fence, with a massive stone bulwark built up beneath it. This combination of strength and delicacy may be seen also in drawings by the artist in the Kunsthalle, Hamburg, the British Museum, the Fondation Custodia, Paris, and the Rijksprentenkabinet, Amsterdam.

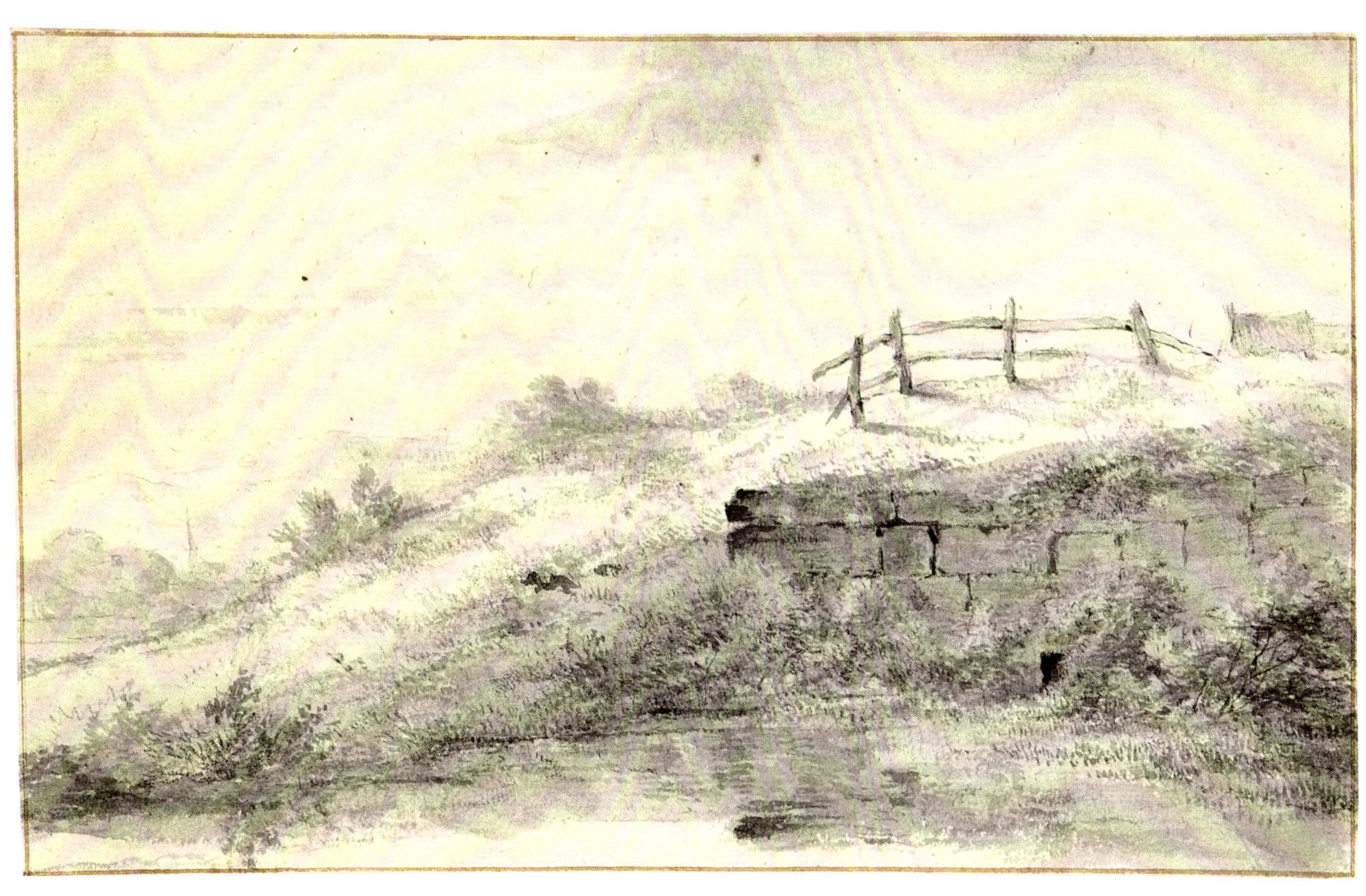

Rembrandt van Rijn
Leiden 1606–1669 Amsterdam

22 *Canal and boats with a distant view of Amsterdam*

Reed pen and brush in dark brown (iron-gall) ink; dark brown ink framing lines.
103 x 203 mm (4 1/16 x 8 in).

WATERMARK: fool's cap with seven bells, similar to Ash and Fletcher 1998, variant D.b., pp. 112, 118 (c. 1654); Heawood no. 1990 (dated 1655); Kettering 1988, nos. Gs20, p. 790; Gs22, p. 791; H214, p. 793 (all documented to 1655). (R22, R22a)

CHAIN LINES: vertical, 25–27 mm.

INSCRIPTIONS: verso (Fig. 2), test strokes of reed pen (dark brown iron-gall ink that has bled partially through, autograph?).

PROVENANCE: Municipal Library, Mainz. Städtische Gemäldegalerie, Mainz, accessioned 1892, deaccessioned 1938. H. Gilhofer, Lucerne, Switzerland. Edwin Alfred Seasongood, New York. Robert M. Light, Santa Barbara. British Rail Pension Fund, London, 1977. Sale, New York, Sotheby's, 29 Jan 1997, lot 49, acquired at the sale.

LITERATURE: *Stift und Feder* 1930, no. 4 (January 1931), Supplement, pl. 93 (as Rembrandt). Benesch 1935, p. 57 (as Rembrandt). Benesch 1954–7, vol. 6, no. 1349, p. 373, fig. 1583 (as Rembrandt). Benesch 1973, vol. 6, no. 1349, p. 361, fig. 1662 (as Rembrandt). Royalton-Kisch 1991, pp. 16–8, fig. 13 (as Rembrandt).

EXHIBITIONS: Cat. Frankfurt 1926, no. 368a. Cat. Austin 1981–2 (catalogue unnumbered).

From 1641, Rembrandt, in effect, discovers the Dutch landscape around him and creates a series of prints, paintings, and drawings that capture the famous sites and skylines of Amsterdam and other cities and also the backyards, the modest farms, fields, and canals in the countryside. In the 1650s, in particular, Rembrandt tries to get away from pure line in his graphic work, using more wash and black chalk in his drawings and, in his prints, experimenting with pure drypoint.

Especially impressive in this exceptional drawing is the definition of space. The boats, laid end to end, one on land and one in the water, define the foreground in pen and dark brown ink; there are touches of "dry pen" strokes on the side of the boat on the left and on the *zwaard*, the balance panel on the other boat, an effective way of defining a plane. The background is defined by an extraordinary horizon line of forms in pure wash, in brown, parallel to the boats, while the canal, perpendicular to both, goes straight back, then winds to the left, connecting the two. The mast set against the canal, horizon, and sky becomes a particularly dramatic accent. The dramatic contrast in focus between the foreground and the background is a good illustration of what has been called Rembrandt's "naturally selective vision" (see Cat. New York/Fort Worth 1995, no. 38).

This type of composition, emphasizing the flatness of the Dutch countryside and receding straight back from the foreground (instead of from one side or the other), is typical of Rembrandt in the 1650s, for example, in his prints, *The Goldweigher's Field*, dated 1651 (Bartsch 234), and the *Canal with a large Boat and Bridge*, dated 1650 (Bartsch 236). The wash, which is handled with such delicacy

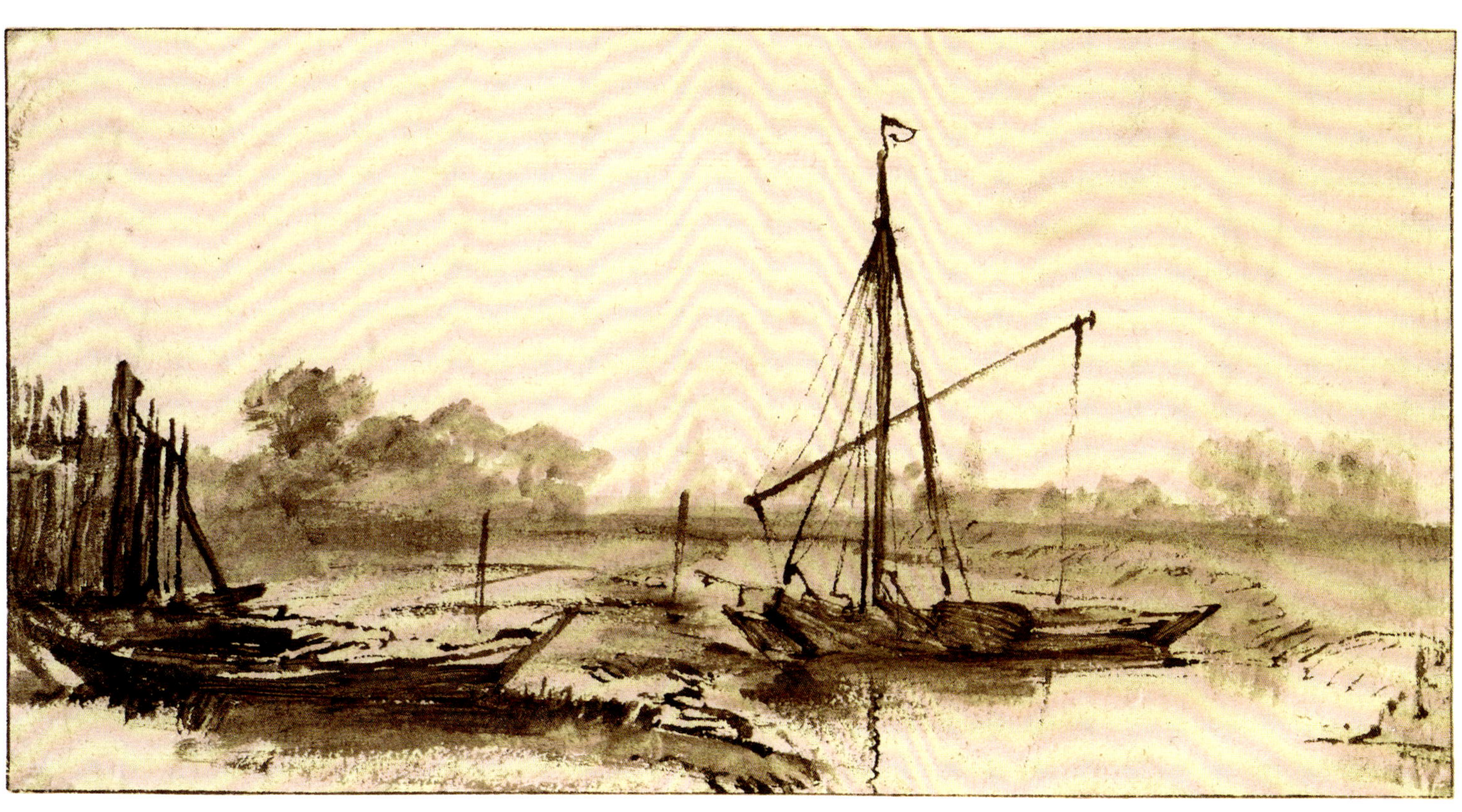

along the edges of the canal and so dramatically in the background, is also typical of Rembrandt in this decade, in landscape drawings in the Louvre (Fig. 1) and elsewhere, as is this view "behind the scenes," as it were, away from the hustle and bustle of a working farm, empty of people. In this sense, the drawing seems closer in technique and atmosphere to Claude Lorrain than to any of Rembrandt's Dutch contemporaries.

Jan Peeters and Boudewijn Bakker of the Amsterdam Municipal Archives have studied the distant townscape seen in this Rembrandt drawing. They identify it as a vignette or capriccio of Amsterdam, a view from the yard of an outlying dairy farm towards the narrow canal as it flows to the town. The linear and angular washes at the horizon appear to render brilliantly a series of farm buildings in the right middleground and dikes paralleling the distant course of the waterway on both sides and ultimately converging.

Robert Putman has pointed out that these flat-bowed canal boats were used for transporting cattle and hay or peat, and often had a mast, as here.

On the verso (Fig. 2) are calligraphic practice loops, in reed pen, possibly by the artist, cut off by the edges of the paper; this shows that the sheet was originally larger, and reminds us that in the late 1650s Rembrandt did two etched portraits of Lieven van Coppenol, the writing-master.

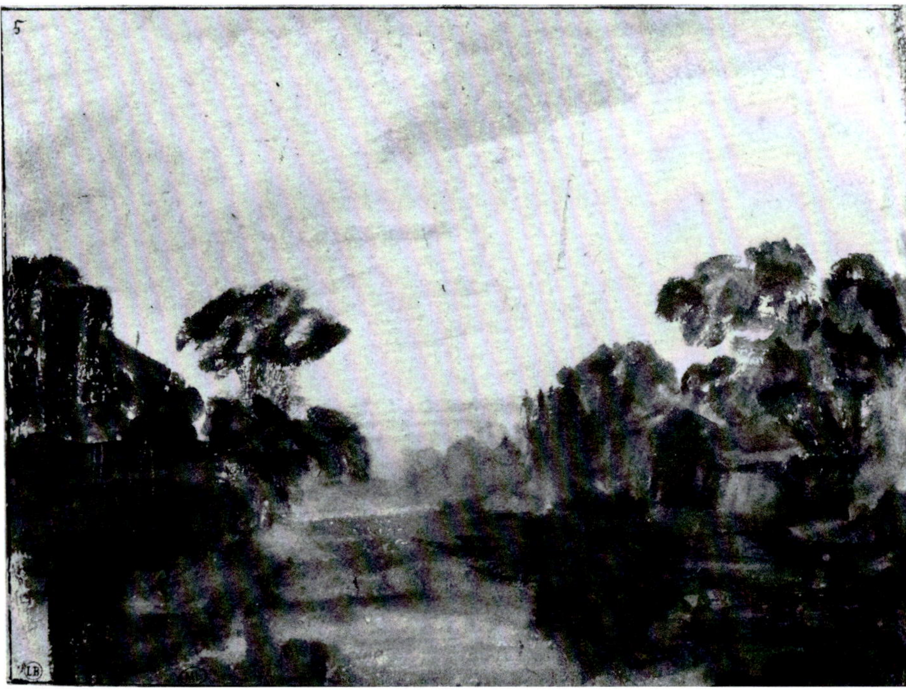

Fig. 1. Rembrandt, *River or canal with wooded banks*, brush and brown wash. Louvre, Département des Arts Graphiques, Paris.

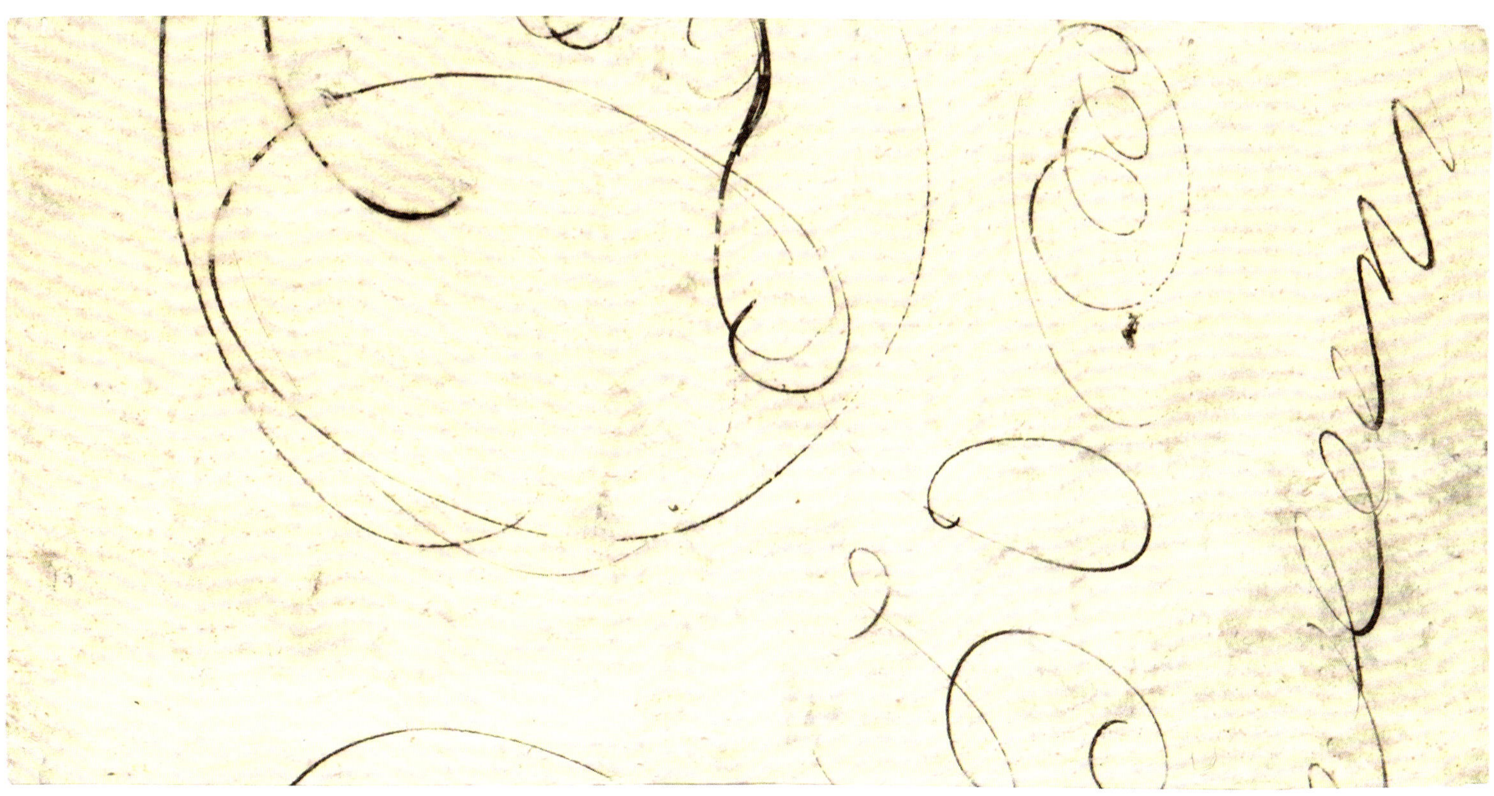

Fig. 2. Verso, test strokes of reed pen in dark brown iron-gall ink.

Roelant Roghman
Amsterdam 1627–1692 Amsterdam

23 *Broad river view with wooded shores*

Brush in brown and gray ink, pen in brown ink; laid down; dark brown ink framing lines. 218 x 347 mm (8½ x 13 in).

WATERMARK: Strasbourg lily, similar to Heawood no. 1730 (Amsterdam, dated 1646). (R23)

CHAIN LINES: horizontal, 25–27 mm.

INSCRIPTIONS: signed *R. Roghman. f.* at lower left (brush in brown ink).

PROVENANCE: William Esdaile (1758–1837), London (L. 2617), his sale, London, Christie and Manson, 22 June 1840, lot 704 or 705. Sale, Amsterdam, Sotheby Mak van Waay, 3 April 1978, lot 116, acquired at the sale.

LITERATURE: Sumowski 1992, vol. 10, pp. 5038–9, no. 2233.

EXHIBITIONS: none.

Roelant Roghman is one of the most prolific and important Dutch landscape draftsmen of the seventeenth century. Perhaps the most celebrated part of his output is an extraordinary series of topographically accurate drawings of castles and knights' residences in the Netherlands, about 245 sheets executed when he was just 20 or 21 years old.

However, Roghman's landscape drawings apart from this series have an energy, variety, and mixture of precision and imagination that are hardly rivaled in his time; the present drawing is an excellent example of how his loaded brush controls the progression of light and shadow back into space, as the pen lines in brown ink define the figures and trees. The landscape as a whole seems to melt in the late afternoon sunlight before our eyes.

This work is close to a sheet in the Teyler Museum, which Plomp (1997, p. 347, cat. no. 397) has identified as from a series drawn in the countryside around Brussels, perhaps about 1651. The scene is also reminiscent of drawings in the National Gallery of Canada, Ottawa; formerly at Colnaghi, London; and the Jonquet sale, Sotheby's, London, June 1926, no. 91, as well as a painting (Christie's, London, June 6, 1974, no. 5). In addition to the trees and hilly road on the right and lake in the middle ground, Roghman has put in a tree, isolated on the far shore, in both pen and wash; in the present drawing, this tree is executed only in pen and brown ink, and is barely visible.

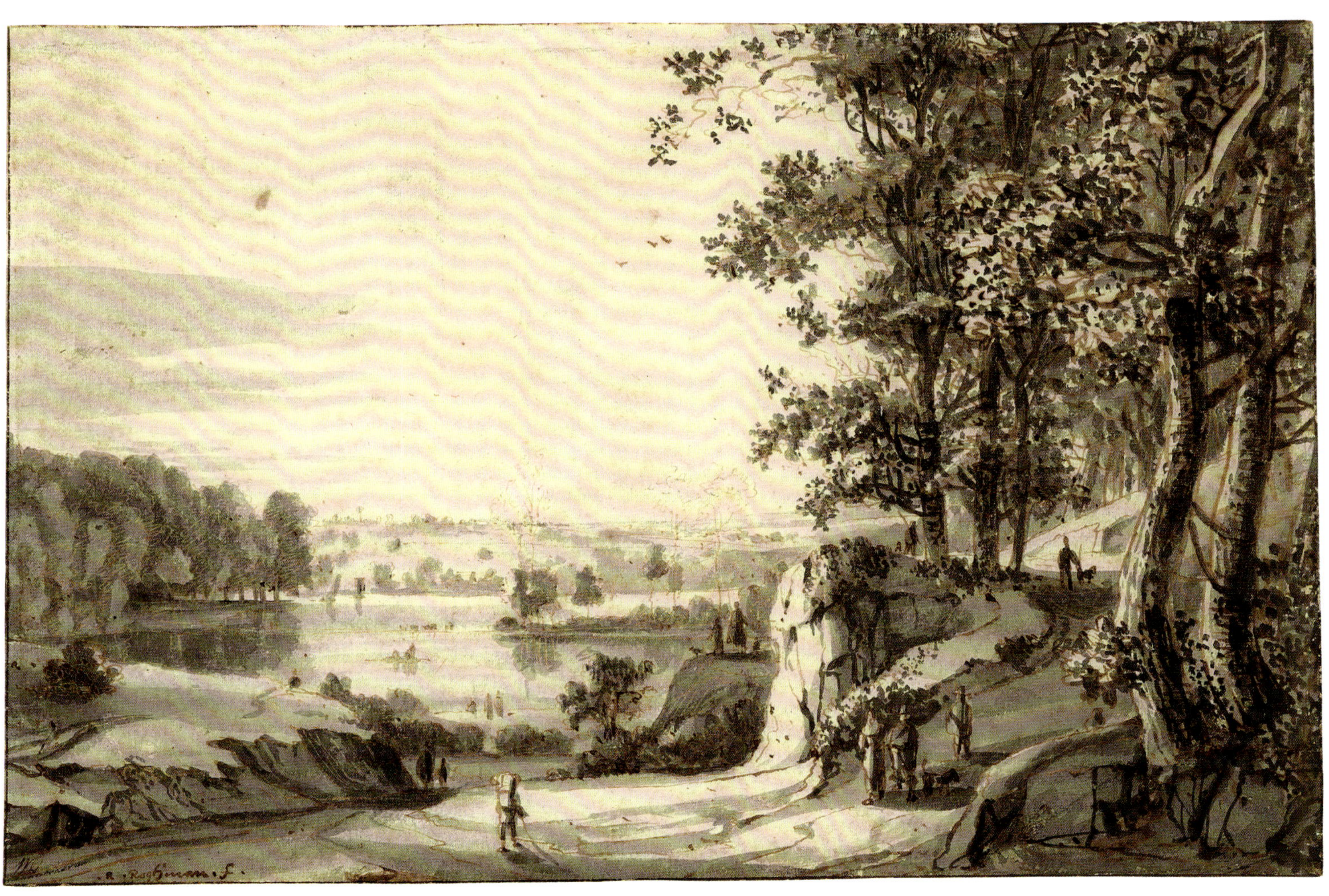
R. Roghman. f.

Roelant Roghman
Amsterdam 1627–1692 Amsterdam

24 *High trees by a river with a town in the distance*

Pen and brush in brown and gray ink on light brown paper; dark brown ink framing lines.
247 x 299 mm (9¾ x 11¾ in).

WATERMARK: Strasbourg lily with a six-petaled flower below, nearly identical to Heawood no. 1746 (Amsterdam, dated 1647). (R24)

CHAIN LINES: horizontal, 24 mm.

INSCRIPTIONS: signed *R. Roghman.* at lower left (pen in brown ink); verso, at lower left *C.I.*(?) *185* and *5-5* (pen in brown ink), and a little to the right *π32* and *30* (light pencil).

PROVENANCE: R. Collins, England. R. Peltzer (1825–1910), Cologne (L. 2231), his sale, Stuttgart, H. G. Gutekunst, 13–14 May 1914, lot 332. Toni Straus-Negbaur (L. 2459a), her sale, Berlin, Cassirer, 25–26 November 1930, lot 88. Nicolaas Beets (1878-1963), his sale, Amsterdam, 9–11 April 1940, lot 147. Bernard Houthakker (L. 1272), his sale, Amsterdam, Sotheby Mak van Waay, 18 November 1975, lot 101. Galerie Julia Kraus, Paris. Sale, Amsterdam, Christie's, 26 November 1984, lot 67, acquired at the sale.

LITERATURE: Sumowski 1992, vol. 10, pp. 5076–7, no. 2248.

EXHIBITIONS: Cat. Amsterdam 1956, no. 81. Cat. Amsterdam 1964, p. 33, no. 85 (illus.). Cat. Paris 1977, no. 38.

This drawing is even looser and more summary in its treatment of the landscape, and especially the trees, than in the previous drawing by Roghman. Before, the foliage was defined by clusters of spots in gray wash, while here, a series of arched scribbles defines its outside edges. In both drawings, the center foreground is occupied by a single traveler, seen from behind, with a pack on his back and his right foot forward. A drawing with trees arranged in this system of "shelves" is in the Witt Collection, London, dated 1652 (Sumowski, 1992, no. 2235).

Roghman's paintings, also exclusively landscapes, are characterized by a loaded brush, thick impasto, and individually visible brush strokes that recall similar effects in his drawings.

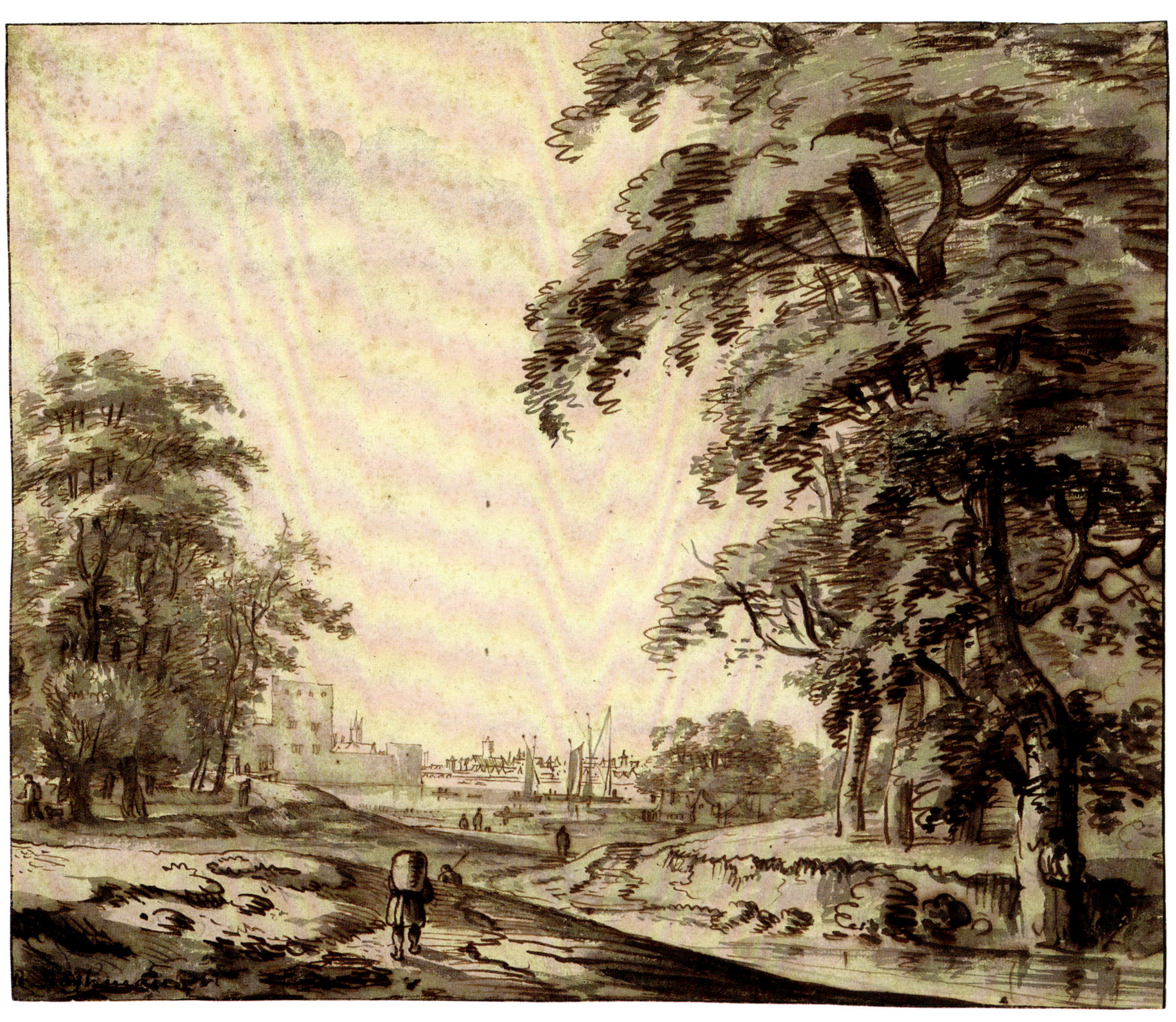

Willem Romeyn
Haarlem c. 1624 – after 1695 Haarlem

25 *Boy with two laden donkeys in the hills*

Black chalk, brush in gray ink; brown (iron-gall) ink framing lines.
195 x 322 mm (7⅝ x 12⅝ in).

WATERMARK: countermark MCMD, similar to Heawood no. 2781 (dated 1675); Gaudriault 1995, no. 4210 (dated 1661–1700). (R25)

CHAIN LINES: horizontal, 25 mm.

INSCRIPTIONS: signed and dated *WROMEYN/ 1694* at upper left corner (black chalk); verso, at center *B.4.* (pencil); at lower left *XVI* (pen in light brown ink) and to the right *Romeyn.W.van.1624-* (pencil).

PROVENANCE: Sale, Amsterdam, Christie's, 26 November 1984, lot 103, acquired at the sale.

LITERATURE: none.

EXHIBITIONS: none.

This beautiful sheet is by Willem Romeyn, another artist in this exhibition, like Michiel Carrée, whose paintings are fairly routine repetitions of the Italianate Dutch tradition created by Nicolaes Berchem and his generation but whose drawings are strikingly individual and original. Executed in 1694, long after he had returned to Haarlem from Rome in 1651, this work combines the classical and the colloquial to create a world where nothing dramatic or spontaneous occurs. These quiet peasants and their donkeys acquire a dignity and timelessness, bathed in the late afternoon light, with its long, transparent shadows. Up until the late eighteenth century, paper was made by hand with wire screens; the tooth of the paper, that is, the design of the hills and valleys left by that screen, is prominent in this drawing and easily visible, and it changes the whole feeling of the work, somehow making it more delicate and even fragile.

Many of Romeyn's finest drawings are dated in the 1690s, near the end of his life. Related drawings are in the Courtauld Institute, London, the Städel Institut, Frankfurt, and formerly the Perman Collection, Stockholm, all three dated 1694. Similar paintings, but with these elements rearranged and with new figures added, are in the Pinakothek, Munich, and the Musée des Beaux-Arts, Orléans.

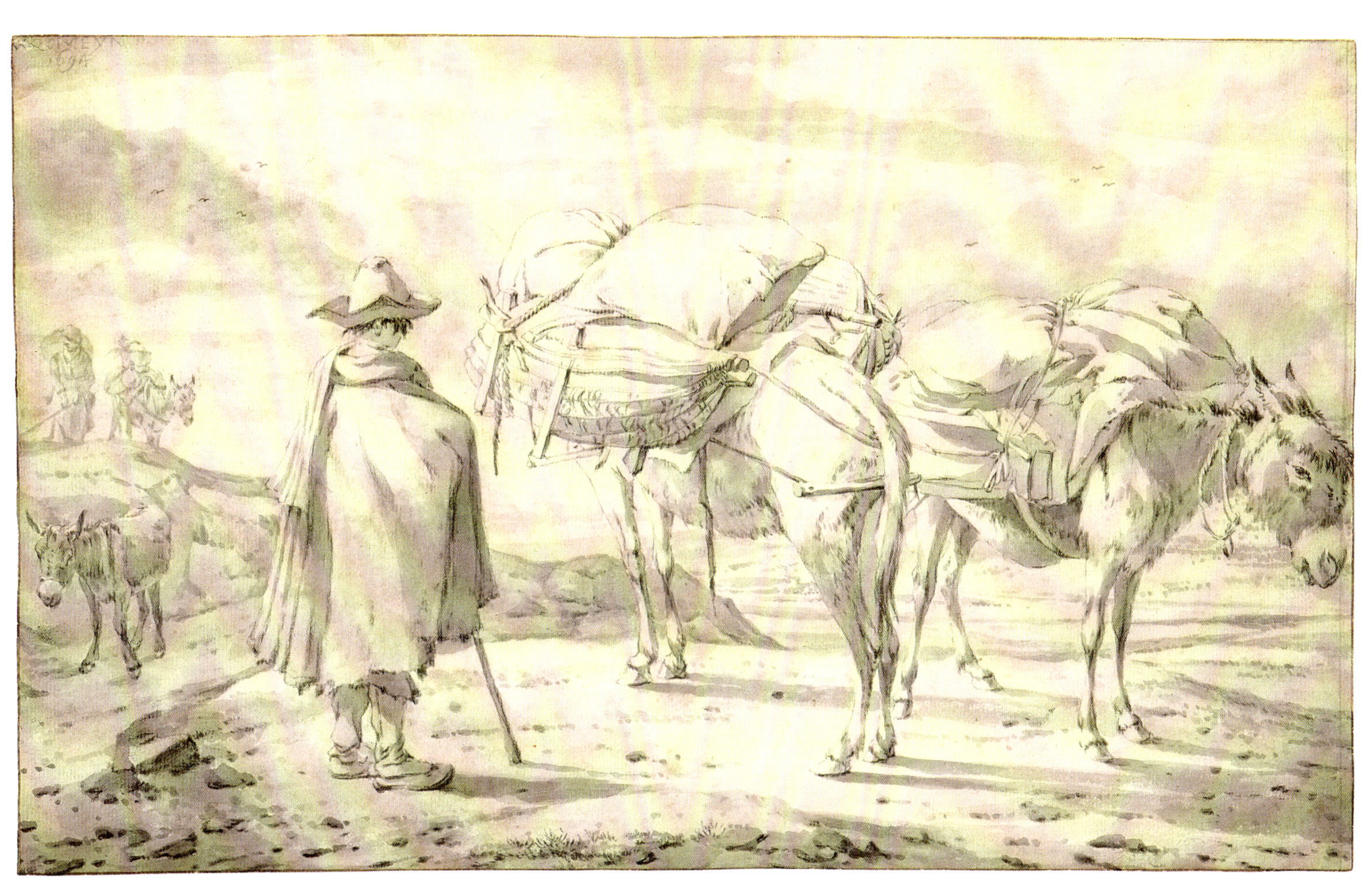

Jacob van Ruisdael
Haarlem 1628/29–1682 Amsterdam

26 *Oak trees on a rise near a stream*

Black chalk, brush in gray ink; brown ink framing lines. 146 x 200 mm (5¾ x 7⅞ in).

WATERMARK: fragment, figure 4 and three rings [suspended from a five-bell fool's cap], at lower center, similar to Ash and Fletcher 1998, variant F.a., pp. 98, 103 (dated 1654). (R26)

CHAIN LINES: vertical, 24–26 mm.

INSCRIPTIONS: none.

PROVENANCE: Sale, Amsterdam, Christie's, 15 November 1993, lot 99, acquired at the sale.

LITERATURE: Slive 1995, pp. 455–6, fig. 49. Giltaij 1995, pp. 87–8, 314, fig. 5. Bisanz-Prakken (Cat. New York/Fort Worth, 1995), p.106, note 4.

EXHIBITIONS: none.

Along with Rembrandt and Jan van Goyen, Jacob van Ruisdael is one of the great landscape draftsmen of the seventeenth-century Netherlands. It is he who created the vision of nature as a place inhospitable, or at least indifferent, to humankind, caught in an endless cycle of decay and rebirth.

On occasion, Ruisdael's drawings express the drama and power of that vision; however, many of them are surprising in their subdued treatment of modest, everyday scenes. Instead of great contrasts of scale or light and shadow, we are given an even tone, especially appropriate to their medium, black chalk with touches of gray wash. Works such as the present sheet were surely not meant to be sold, and were only occasionally used as preparatory studies for paintings. Rather, they seem to be personal notes, recording an interesting bend in the road or clump of trees, a way of stopping and looking more carefully.

This drawing is one of a large group datable to c. 1648–1655, some possibly made on the artist's journey to Bentheim, in Germany. The group as a whole, and this work in particular, are characterized by a profound response to the expressive possibilities of the medium of black chalk and gray wash, especially in the subtle control of tones and the flickering of the foliage in the sunlight and the breeze.

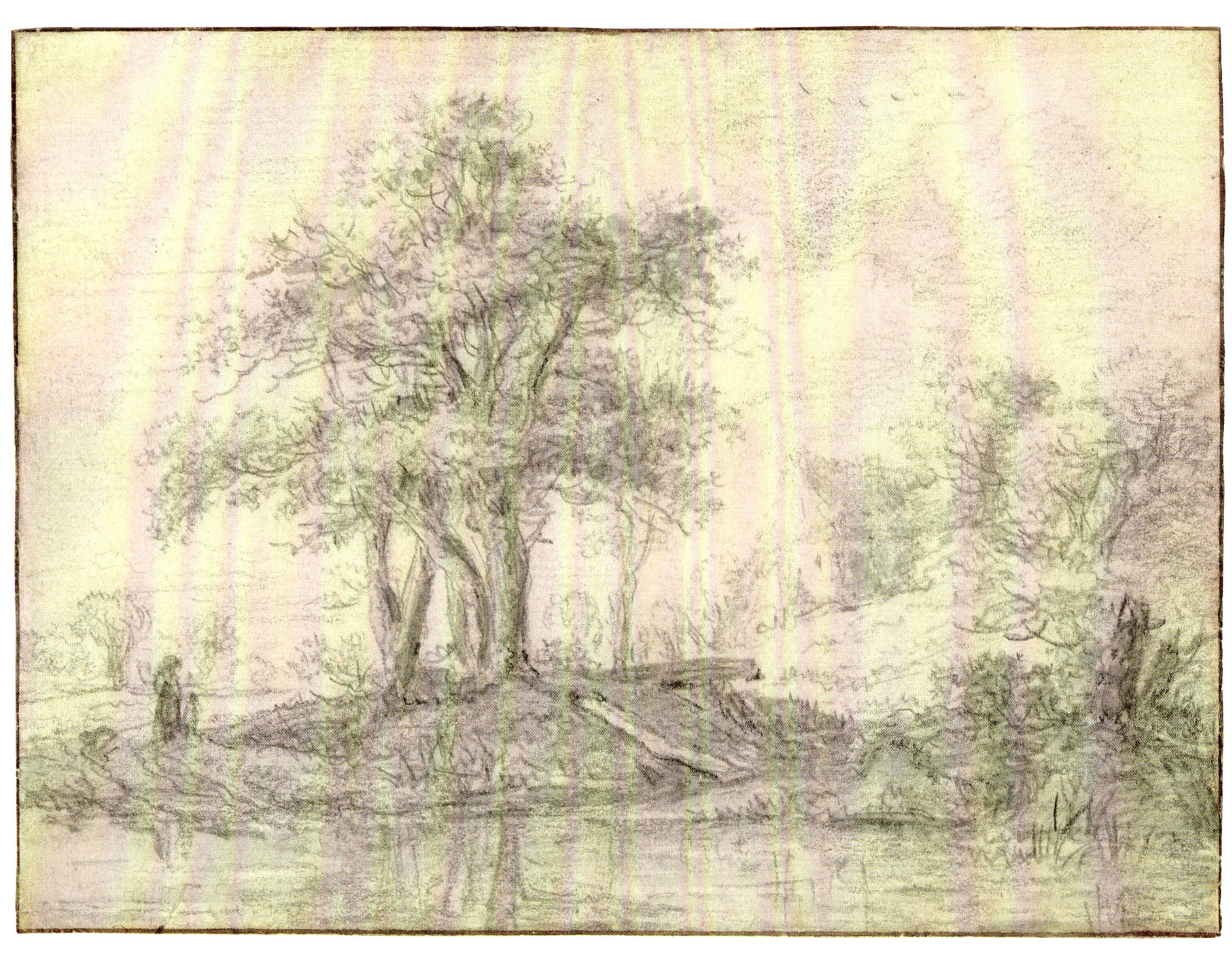

Jacob van Ruisdael
Haarlem 1628/29–1682 Amsterdam

27 *Riverbank with a wooden aqueduct and view of a village*

Black chalk, brush in gray ink; brown ink framing lines. 157 x 233 mm (6¼ x 9¼ in).

WATERMARK: paschal lamb in shield with crown, similar to Heawood nos. 2842–4 (Holland, dated 1648–51); nearly identical to Broos and Schapelhouman 1993, p. 271, cat. no. 183 (no date). (R27)

CHAIN LINES: horizontal, 25 mm.

INSCRIPTIONS: verso, in center *Jacob van Ruysdael./ Ecole hollandaise. 1628–1682* (pencil); at upper left, encircled 2 (pencil); at center left *1119* (pen in brown ink); at lower left *20* (pencil).

PROVENANCE: Count "L. G." (L. 1729), France. Paul Mathey (1844–1929), Paris. Alexis Vollon (1865–1945), Paris. Loys H. Delteil (1869–1927), Paris, 1911 (letter dated 1 July 1911, giving earlier provenance). Sale, Amsterdam, Sotheby's, 11 November 1997, lot 128, acquired at the sale.

LITERATURE: none.

EXHIBITIONS: none.

This fascinating work provides an excellent comparison with other landscape drawings in this exhibition executed in the 1640s and 1650s. This sheet, with its soft, broad strokes of black chalk and easy transitions from shadow to sunlight and back again, is very different from the sinuous, liquid shorthand of the late Jan van Goyen, or the more concentrated, even nervous intensity and detail of Pieter Molyn, the two great representatives of the preceding generation of landscape draftsmen. Even the village scenes of Guillam Du Bois, who was probably influenced by Ruisdael, are characterized by staccato strokes and a muscular density that are different from Ruisdael's more open touch. At the same time, the present sheet is broader and more spontaneous in effect than Herman Naiwincx's careful, delicate, almost fragile evocation of a lovely rustic corner or Adriaen Verboom's picturesque, gnarled trunks surrounded by sprays of leaves, each one defined by dabs of gray wash.

The present drawing, from the late 1640s or early 1650s, is typical of Ruisdael's synthesis of trees, water, buildings, clouds, light, and shadow, so evident, also, in the preceding work. Theo Laurentius has pointed out that the construction in the left foreground is a hoist, balanced in the fork of the tree trunk, to lift fresh water into an elevated aqueduct to the building on the left, a brewery, tavern or inn. Such a device is recorded by other artists, for example, Esaias van de Velde in several of his etchings and drawings. The mechanics of construction always fascinated Ruisdael, from watermills to views of Amsterdam from building platforms.

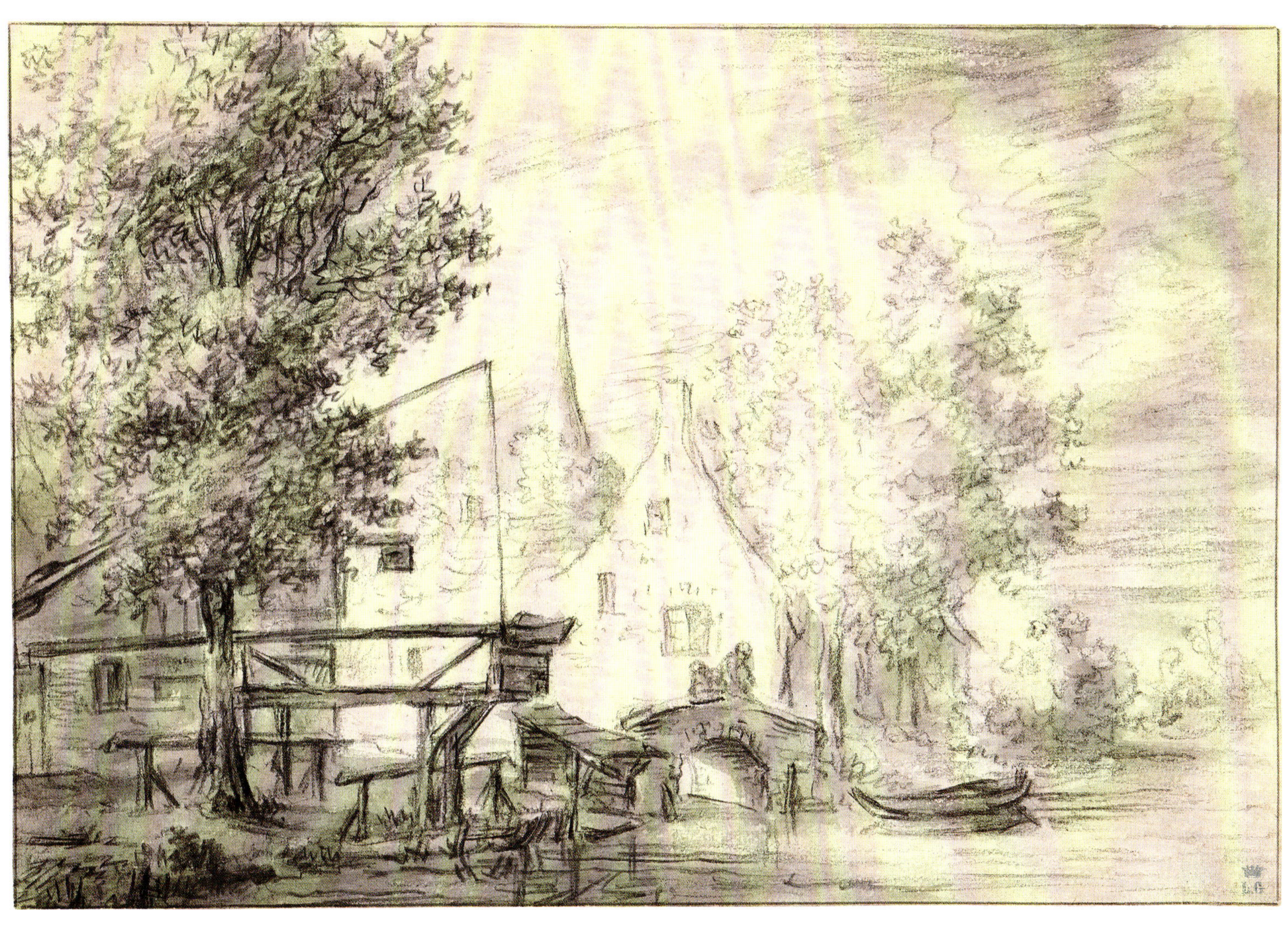

Cornelis Saftleven
Gorkum 1607–1681 Rotterdam

28 *Pigeons on a chimney with a nest of storks on a nearby church roof*

Black and red chalk, brush in gray; brown and black ink framing lines. 43 x 195 mm (5⅝ x 7⅝ in).

WATERMARK: fragment, crown [topping Arms of the Seven Provinces with lion], at lower center, nearly identical to Churchill no. 109 (dated 1656). (R28)

CHAIN LINES: vertical, 17, 22–24 mm.

INSCRIPTIONS: none.

PROVENANCE: Sale, Notarishuis, Arnhem, 1970. Hans van Leeuwen, Amerongen (L. 2799a), his sale, Amsterdam, Christie's, 24 November 1992, lot 174, acquired at the sale.

LITERATURE: Schulz 1978, no. 392.

EXHIBITIONS: none.

One of the most striking aspects of seventeenth-century Dutch draftsmanship is the fact that sometimes hundreds, and even thousands, of drawings by a single artist have survived. Cornelis Saftleven is an example of this new phenomenon; his hundreds of paintings and drawings reflect an insatiable curiosity about virtually every aspect of the world around him, from wheelbarrows to carriages, all kinds of animals, witches, people of all ages, and even political events.

Birds were one of his many interests, and here we are given not only four pigeons on the chimney to the left, above a clay bird's-pot, but also storks nesting on the church roof and a rooster weathervane on its steeple. A replica of this composition exists, cut in two parts; the left part is now in the Prentenkabinet, Leiden, and the right is in the Fondation Custodia, Paris, both monogrammed and dated by the artist 1646. (A copy of the whole drawing, formerly in the Hofstede de Groot collection and with Bernard Houthakker in 1965, sold at Swann Galleries, New York, 4 February 1999, lot 95.)

Cornelis was the son of an artist and the older brother of Herman, two of whose drawings are in this exhibition; there is also a Sara Saftleven, who apparently made watercolors of flowers. With the exception of a possible sojourn in Antwerp in his twenties, Cornelis spent most of his life in Rotterdam, and it is difficult to discover his artistic sources. He has something in common with the fresh, almost childlike delight of Anthonie van Borssum, the quirky, sharper-edged humor of Pieter Quast, and the endless curiosity of Jacques de Gheyn II, and he certainly knew the eccentric, brilliant etchings of Jacques Callot and the religious and genre paintings of David Teniers, which he could have seen in Antwerp.

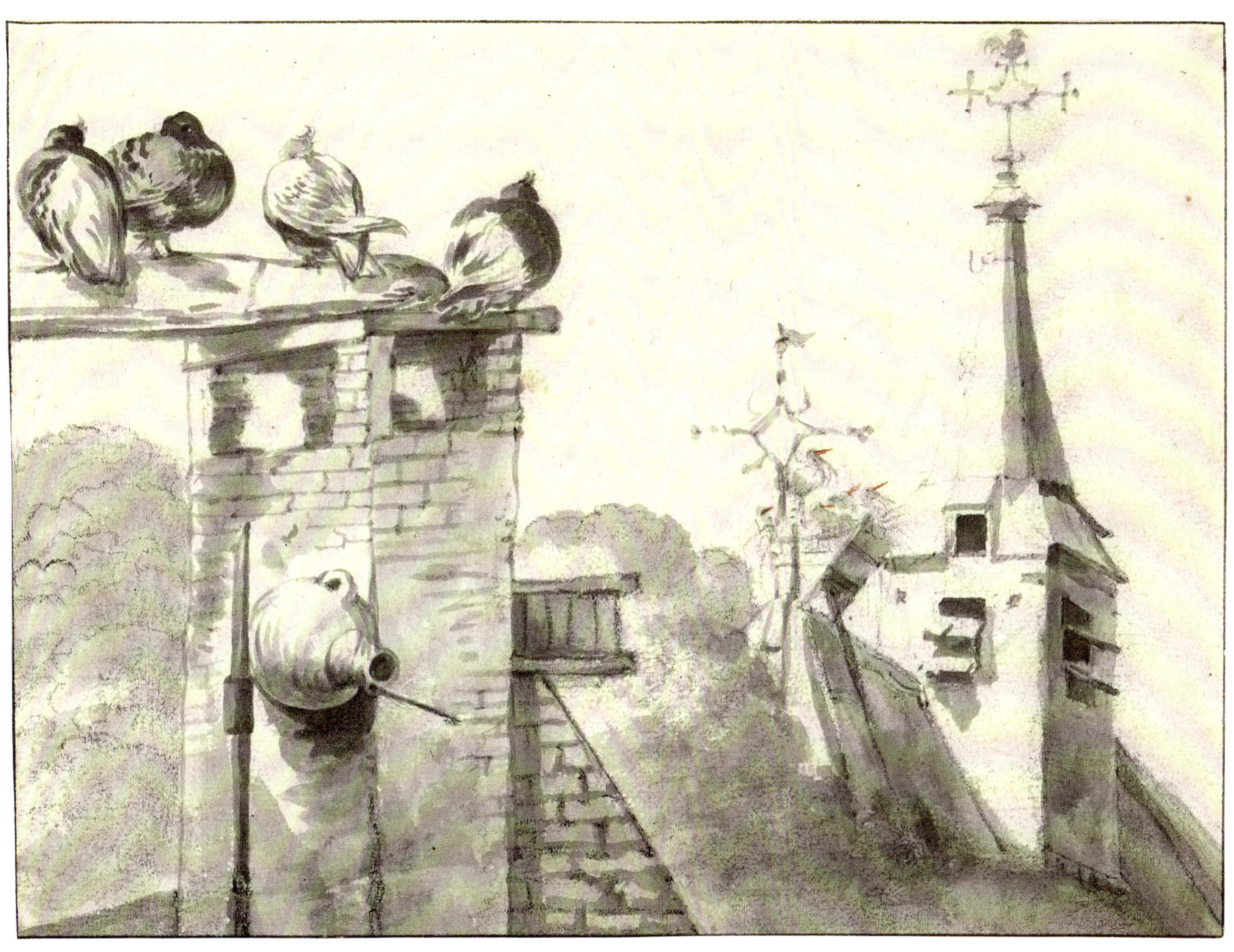

Herman Saftleven
Rotterdam 1609–1685 Utrecht

29 *Cluster of tall trees in an enclosed field by the dunes*

Black chalk; traces of brown ink framing lines.
259 x 376 mm (10⅛ x 14¾ in).

WATERMARK: bird within a circle (diameter 50 mm.), identical to Heawood no. 175 (dated 1625). (R29)

CHAIN LINES: vertical, 26–29 mm.

INSCRIPTIONS: signed *HSaft.leven (HS* in monogram) at lower left (black chalk); verso at lower left *No. 54/ Saftleven=ag3= 1/746Stug.* (pencil); at center right */815* (pencil)

PROVENANCE: Daan Cevat Gallery, London, 1963. Frans C. Butôt, St. Gilgen, Austria, his sale, Amsterdam, Sotheby's, 16 November 1993, lot 55, acquired at the sale.

LITERATURE: Bol, Keyes and Butôt 1981, p. 142, no. 54. Fechter 1989, p. 1768. Schulz (in press), no. 338.

EXHIBITIONS: none.

Herman Saftleven was the younger brother of Cornelis and collaborated with him on a number of paintings; Cornelis did a portrait of himself and Herman, making music, now in the Akademiegalerie, Vienna. Herman was, in fact, more prolific than Cornelis and concentrated almost exclusively on landscapes.

This drawing is particularly important, for it shows the earliest stage of the artist's development, c. 1627–30, that is, when he is hardly twenty years old. He is here deeply influenced by Willem Buytewech, especially his etchings of 1621, with their long supple tree trunks and clutches of tightly defined leaves. The style of the drawing in general seems derived not only from Buytewech but also from the energetic calligraphy of Esaias van de Velde and the early Pieter Molyn and Jan van Goyen, as well as, perhaps, François Rijckhals and Jan van Brosterhuisen.

Of the dozen drawings by Herman from this period, one is dated, 1630, and this dates the whole group (Amsterdam, Sotheby's, November 14, 1988, no. 34; London, Phillips, December 11, 1991, no. 140). Several of Herman's etchings probably can be dated to this period, including Hollstein nos. 20–24, and 38.

Like his brother, Herman was both energetic and original. Years after making drawings of the effects of the Delft powder explosion in 1654, he made three series of drawings documenting the devastation caused by a hurricane in Utrecht in 1674. He also turned his attention to very small drawings, often less than four inches wide, much in the manner of Allart van Everdingen.

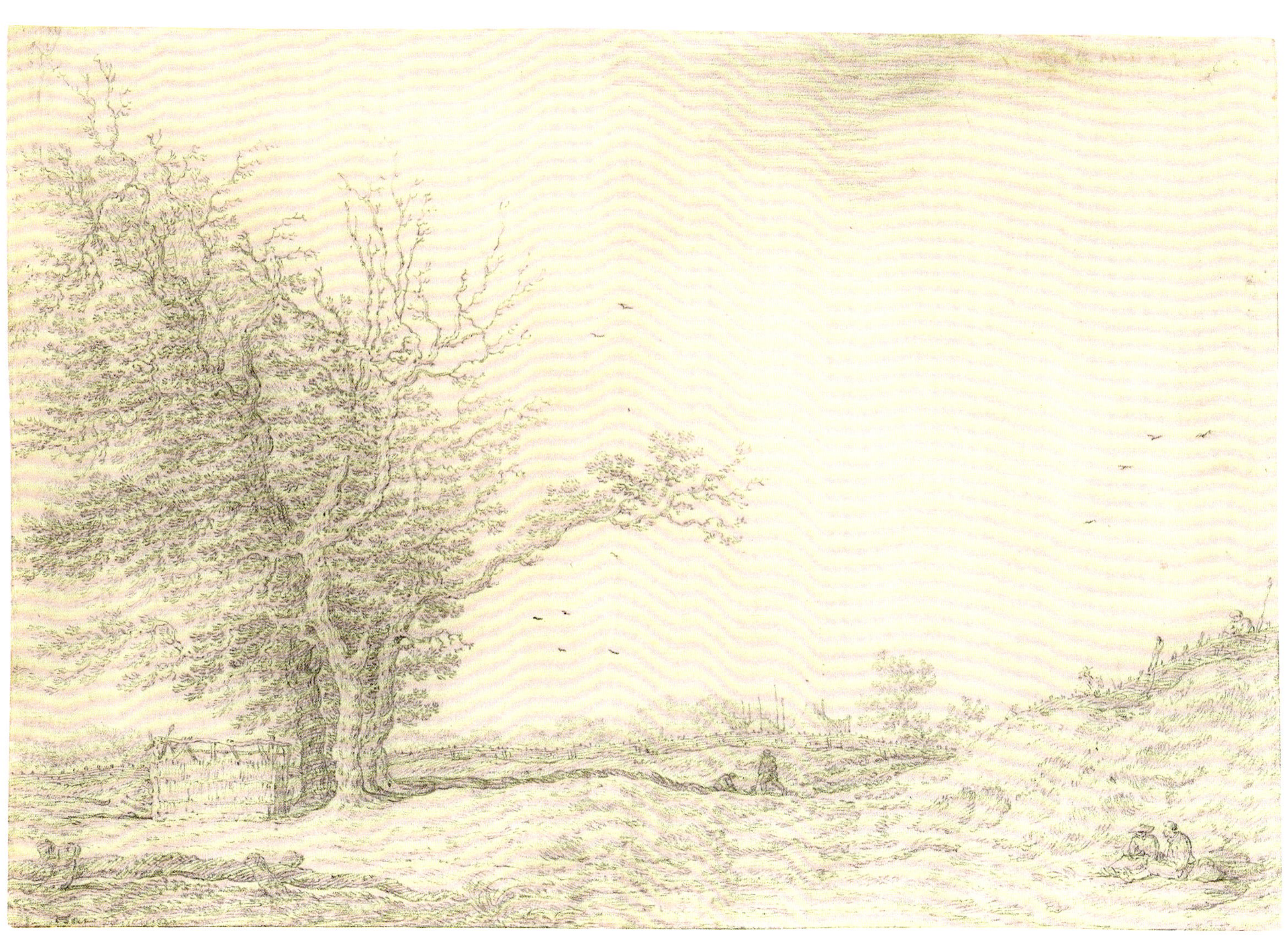

Herman Saftleven
Rotterdam 1609–1685 Utrecht

30 *Woods near Doorn with a herdsman and sheep*

Black chalk, brush in brown and gray ink; brown ink framing lines. 400 x 297 mm (15¾ x 11¾ in).

WATERMARK: fool's cap with five bells, similar to Schapelhouman and Schatborn 1998, p. 243, no. W101 (dated 1651); Beck I 1972, cat. no. 296, p. 331, fig. 23 (dated 1652); Heawood no. 1922 (Dutch, dated 1651). (R30)

CHAIN LINES: horizontal, 24–26 mm.

INSCRIPTIONS: annotated *bij Doren* at upper center (black chalk, autograph); verso, at lower center *Coll. A.../ de Hag* (pencil, 19th century?)

PROVENANCE: Antiquariaat H. Marcus, Amsterdam – Düsseldorf, 1955. Hans van Leeuwen, Amerongen (L. 2799a), his sale, Amsterdam, Christie's, 24 November 1992, lot 175, acquired at the sale.

LITERATURE: Schulz 1982, no. 632.

EXHIBITIONS: Cat. Arnhem, 1958, no. 91. Cat. Utrecht, 1959–60, no. 53. Cat. Laren, 1963, no. 98. Cat. Nijmegen, 1965, no. 21. Cat. Leeuwarden, 1966, no. 15. Cat. Bonn/ Saarbrücken/Bochum, 1968–9, no. 118. Cat. Rheydt, 1971, no. 67. Cat. Bremen/Braunschweig/ Stuttgart, 1979–80, no. 115. Cat. Fribourg/Passau/Trier/Aachen/ Nuremberg, 1982–4, no. 85.

The two drawings by Herman Saftleven in this exhibition illustrate the distance he travels stylistically in about fifteen to twenty years. The earlier work, from about 1630, is still close to the early drawings of Jan van Goyen and the etchings of Willem Buytewech, even with echoes of late Mannerist draftsmanship. By the 1640s, his style has become broader, more atmospheric, more spontaneous. He now looks forward to the work of Simon de Vlieger, Anthonie Waterloo, and Jacob van Ruisdael.

As Schulz (1982, p. 299) points out, the present drawing, which shows the artist at the height of his powers, is close to another in the Graphische Sammlung, Munich (inv. no. 1800), and his etching of 1644 (Hollstein 31).

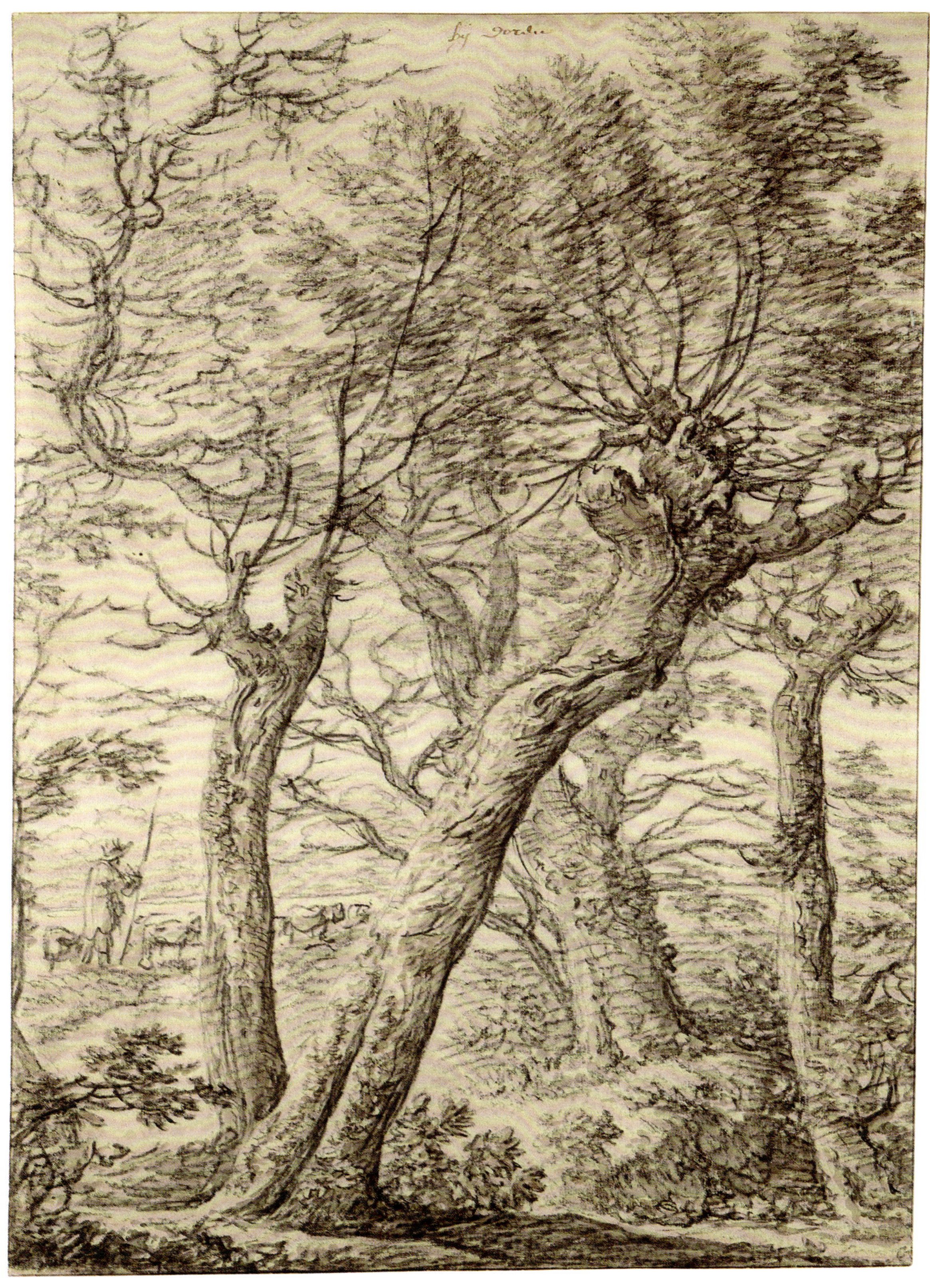

Jacob van der Ulft
Gorkum 1621–1689 Noordwijk

31 *Two trees on a hill*

Pen and brush in brown ink; traces of brown ink framing lines. 311 x 207 mm (12¼ x 8⅛ in).

WATERMARK: Arms of Amsterdam, nearly identical to Heawood no. 342 (Holland, dated 1674). (R31)

CHAIN LINES: vertical, 22–24 mm.

INSCRIPTIONS: none.

PROVENANCE: Baron van Hardenbroek, Langbroek, 18th century. Antiquariaat De Kruyff, Zeist, 1980–1. Hans van Leeuwen, Amerongen (L. 2799a), his sale, Amsterdam, Christie's, 24 November 1992, lot 195, acquired at the sale.

LITERATURE: none.

EXHIBITIONS: none.

Jacob van der Ulft was a fascinating figure in seventeenth-century Dutch draftsmanship; an amateur who never became the member of a guild, he was much involved in the municipal affairs of his native city of Gorkum. He was deeply influenced by another amateur, Jan de Bisschop, a lawyer so devoted to the ancient world that he often Latinized his name to Johannes Episcopius.

This fresh and lively image of two "embracing" trees, struck with sunlight and set against a wash of golden brown "Bisschop ink," is typical of the late style of Jacob van der Ulft. The artist often made wash drawings of one or two trees, sometimes in roundels; examples are in the St. Louis Art Museum, the Fogg Art Museum, Cambridge, and the British Museum, the last two signed and dated in the 1680s.

The present drawing was once part of an album of 63 drawings by van der Ulft in the collection of Baron van Hardenbroek.

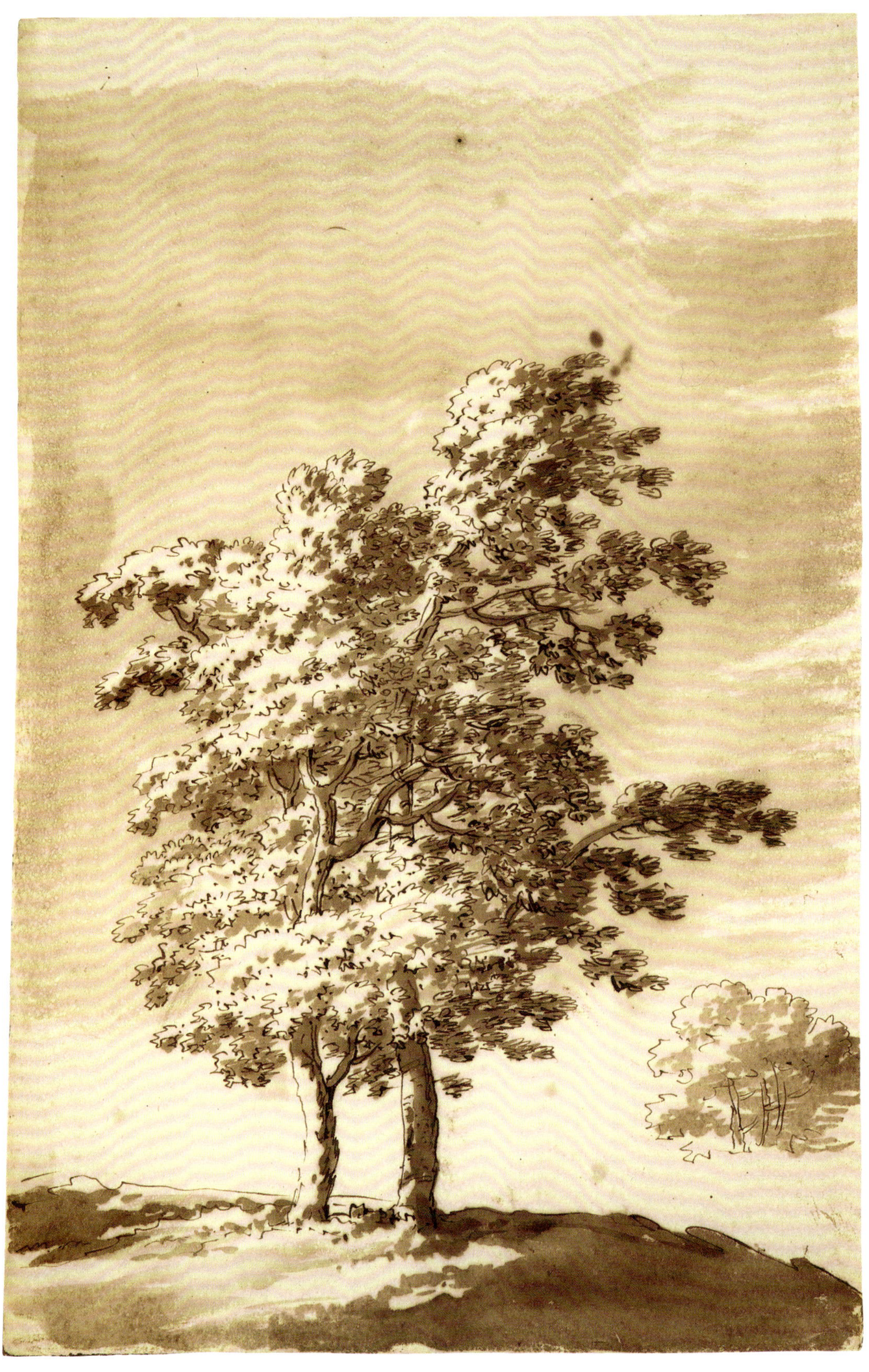

97

Jacob van der Ulft
Gorkum 1621–1689 Noordwijk

32 *Walled Italian village*

Brush in brown ink over black chalk; brown ink framing lines. 203 x 329 mm (8 x 13 in).

WATERMARK: countermark LM, similar to Heawood no. 2738 (no date). (R32)

CHAIN LINES: horizontal, 25 mm.

INSCRIPTIONS: none.

PROVENANCE: Baron van Hardenbroek, Langbroek, 18th century. Antiquariaat De Kruyff, Zeist, 1980–1. Hans van Leeuwen, Amerongen (L. 2799a), his sale, Amsterdam, Christie's, 24 November 1992, lot 197, acquired at the sale.

LITERATURE: none.

EXHIBITIONS: none.

Jacob van der Ulft, who seems never to have visited Italy himself, may have replicated many of his Italian scenes from similar drawings, in a similarly glowing golden brown ink, by Jan de Bisschop (just as he copied Pieter Saenredam's portrait of the old Amsterdam town hall).

This drawing, set down in serene and lush "Bisschop ink," is typical of van der Ulft's love of ruins and of Italy, preoccupations that characterized so many of his Dutch contemporaries. Fairly similar scenes are in the National Gallery of Scotland, Edinburgh, and the De Grez Collection, Brussels, and, in particular, in a sale, Berlin (Max Perl), November 8–9, 1926, no. 714.

Like the preceding drawing, this richly washed sketch was part of a Jacob van der Ulft album in the collection of Baron van Hardenbroek. The present sheet is preserved on a blue laid album page, which has a watermark dating to 1769, Amsterdam (countermark D & C BLAUW, Heawood no. 3267).

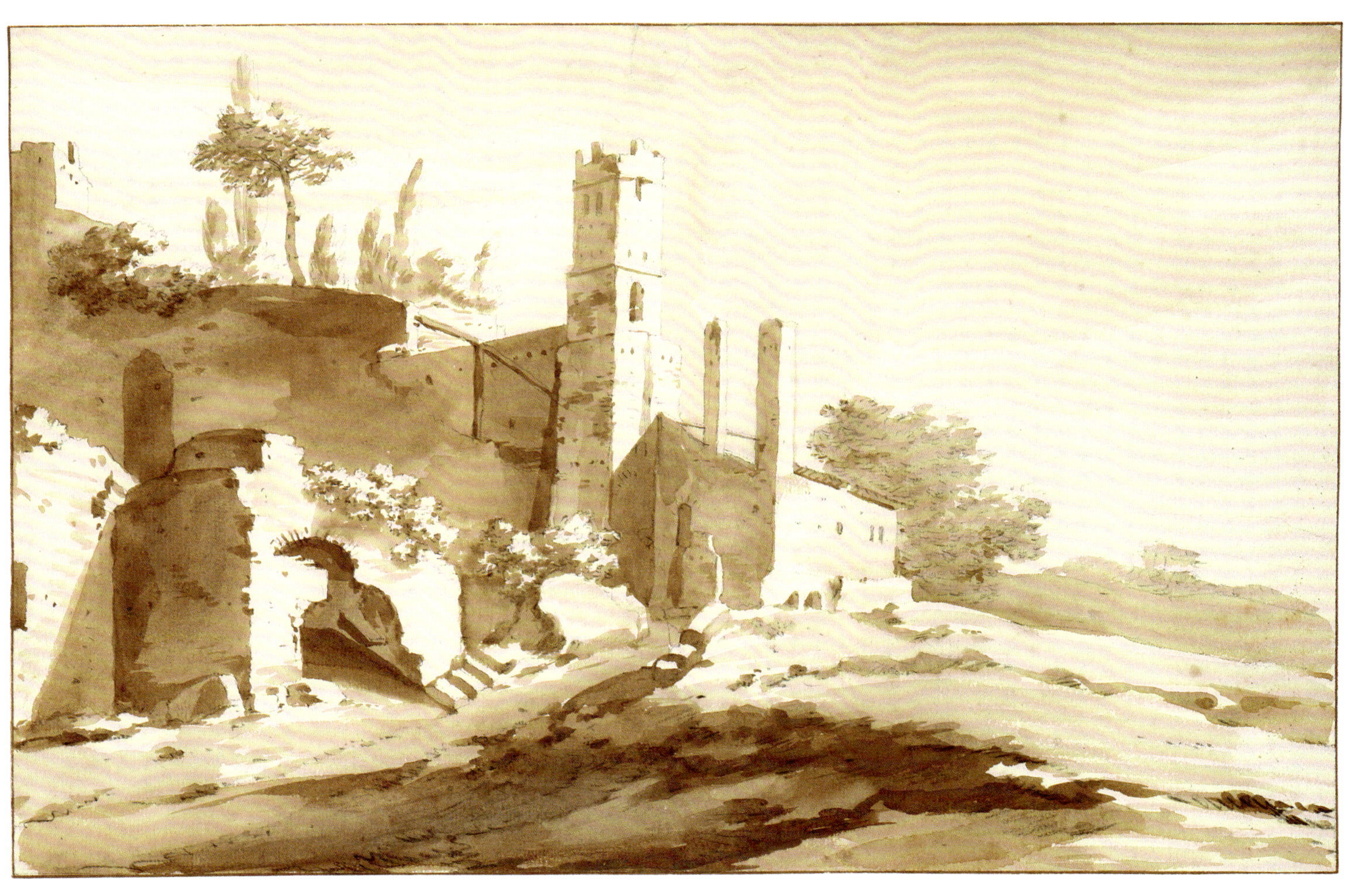

Adriaen van de Velde
Amsterdam 1636–1672 Amsterdam

33 *Shepherds and flocks fording a river*

Brush in gray ink over black chalk; traces of light brown ink framing lines.
139 x 175 mm (5½ x 6⅞ in).

WATERMARK: horn in cartouche with letters DD below, similar to Heawood nos. 2668–71 (c. 1665–80). (R33)

CHAIN LINES: horizontal, 24–25 mm.

INSCRIPTIONS: none.

PROVENANCE: Dionis Muilman (see L. 1420), probably his sale, Amsterdam, de Bosch, Ploos van Amstel, de Winter, 29 March 1773 (and the following days), lot 1119. John Barnard (L. 1419–20 on mount *J:B. N°: 950/ 7x5½/ From the Collection of Mr. Muilman)*, his sale, London, Greenwood, 22 February 1787, lot 55. C. Duits, London. H. R. Bijl, his sale, Amsterdam, Sotheby's, 17 November 1993, lot 58, acquired at the sale.

LITERATURE: none.

EXHIBITIONS: none.

Adriaen van de Velde's paintings are unusual in seventeenth-century art in that they are intensely controlled and calculated; even in relatively small compositions, he analyzes the various elements of the composition, as well as the space and light and shadow, in order to create an aura of order and equilibrium. The end result is a series of paintings of shepherds and peasants in the 1660s and 1670s that managed to recreate in contemporary Dutch terms the timeless Arcadian world of the Italian and French baroque that he saw first-hand when he worked in Rome in 1653–56.

The present drawing is an example of Adriaen's style at its loosest and freshest; using just a few strokes of black chalk as a guide, the artist has defined all the forms by wash, instead of pen. Similar tours de force by Adriaen are in the St. Annen-Museum, Lübeck, and the Michaelis Collection, National Museum, Capetown.

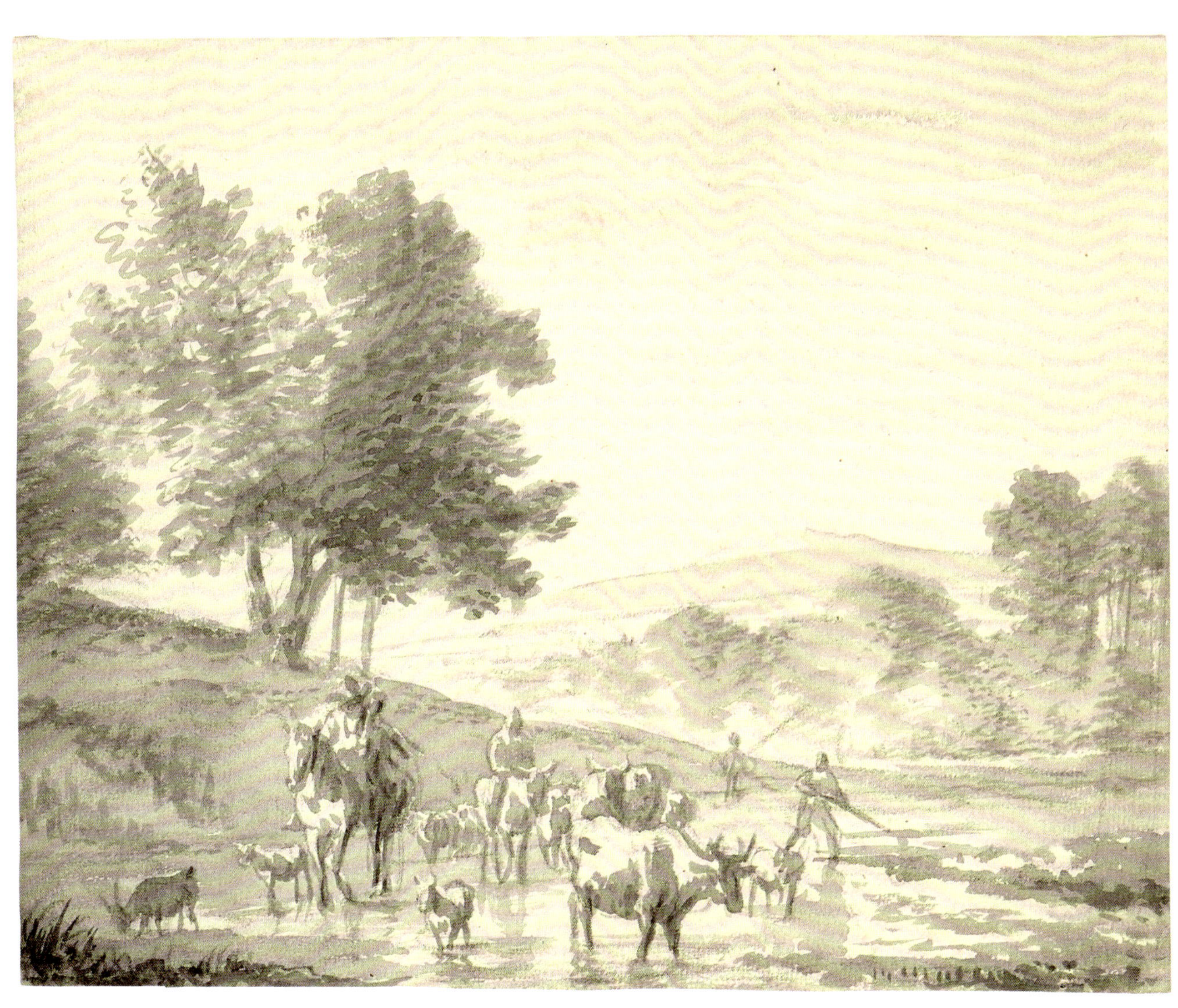

Adriaen van de Velde
Amsterdam 1636–1672 Amsterdam

34 *Sheep hut in the forest*

Brush in gray ink over black chalk; gray ink framing lines. 180 x 276 mm (7⅛ x 10⅞ in).

WATERMARK: two standing lions in a crowned shield above the letters BW, identical to Heawood no. 3167 (London, dated 1672). (R34)

CHAIN LINES: horizontal, 22–25 mm.

INSCRIPTIONS: verso, at lower center *A. van de Velde* (pencil); at lower left */r:v–* (pencil); at upper right *XV* (pencil).

PROVENANCE: Jacob de Vos Sr. (1735-1833), his sale, Amsterdam, de Vries, Roos et al., 30–31 October 1833, Kunstboek W, lot 5. Jacob de Vos Jr. (1803-1878), (L. 1450), his sale, Amsterdam, Roos, Muller & Co., 22–24 May 1883, lot 550. Constant C. Huysman, Breda, and A. J. van Wijngaerdt, Haarlem, their sale, Amsterdam, Muller, 21–22 June 1887, lot 222. August Sträter, Aix-la-Chapelle (L. 787), his sale, Stuttgart, H. G. Gutekunst, 10–14 May 1898, lot 1207. Rudolph P. Goldschmidt, Berlin (L. 2926), his sale, Frankfurt, F. A. C. Prestel, 4–5 October 1917, lot 593. H. C. Valkema Blouw (1883–1953), his sale, Amsterdam, F. Muller, 2–4 March 1954, within lots 725–734. Hans van Leeuwen, Amerongen (L. 2799a), his sale, Amsterdam, Christie's, 24 November 1992, lot 204, acquired at the sale.

LITERATURE: Schatborn 1975, pp. 159–65, plate 6. Robinson 1979, p. 18, cat. no. A-3. Schapelhouman and Schatborn 1987, under no. 69.

EXHIBITIONS: Cat. Utrecht 1959–60, no. 69 Cat. Laren. 1963, no. 113. Cat. Nijmegen 1965, no. 39. Cat. Leeuwarden 1966, no. 31. Cat. Bonn/Saarbrücken/Bochum 1968–9, no. 138. Cat. Rheydt 1971, no. 77. Cat. Amsterdam 1975–6, no. 124. Cat. Bremen/Braunschweig/Stuttgart 1979–80, no. 139. Cat. Amsterdam/Washington 1981–2, p. 117, no. 6.

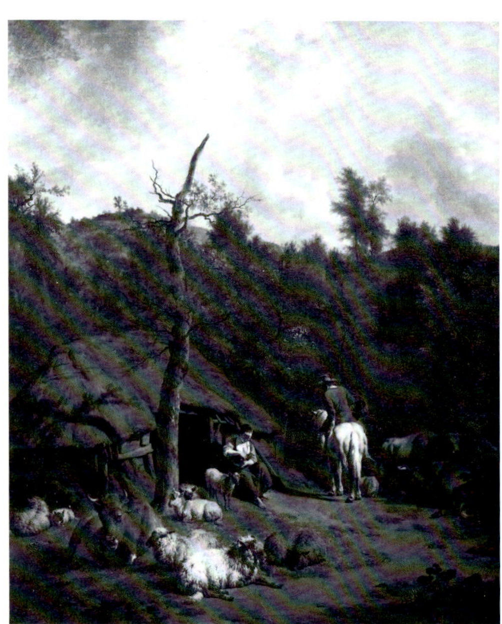

Fig. 1. Adriaen van de Velde, *The Hut*, 1671, oil on canvas. Rijksmuseum, Amsterdam.

Adriaen van de Velde's careful, disciplined creative process is clearly illustrated by this drawing. Jacob Houbraken, the seventeenth-century Dutch artist and art historian, tells us that Adriaen went out into the fields and woods once a week, carrying his artist's equipment with him, to make the studies after nature that would result in his paintings. In this case, he encountered a farmer's hut and made a careful watercolor, now in the Rijksprentenkabinet, Amsterdam.

He then made the present drawing, of a very similar hut. However, there are a few differences from the Amsterdam drawing; the light is now coming from in front of the hut, instead of behind it, and there are slight changes in its structure.

Next, Adriaen turns to the painting (Fig. 1), using the present drawing as a preparatory study; again, there are slight adjustments in this new stage: the tree does not divide into two or three separate limbs, the dog has been left out, and a hill rises behind the hut.

This painting, dated 1671, just a year before he dies at age 36, used this and several other drawings, and even a counterproof of a drawing, to make one of Adriaen's most successful translations of the baroque Arcadia into Dutch dress.

One sign of Adriaen's great popularity in the seventeenth and eighteenth centuries was the fact that this painting or its replica (Sotheby's London, December 9, 1992, no. 202) was copied twice by Dirk van Bergen or another member of the artist's circle (Kurt Goldschmidt, Düsseldorf, 1957, and the Colonna collection, Turin, 1927).

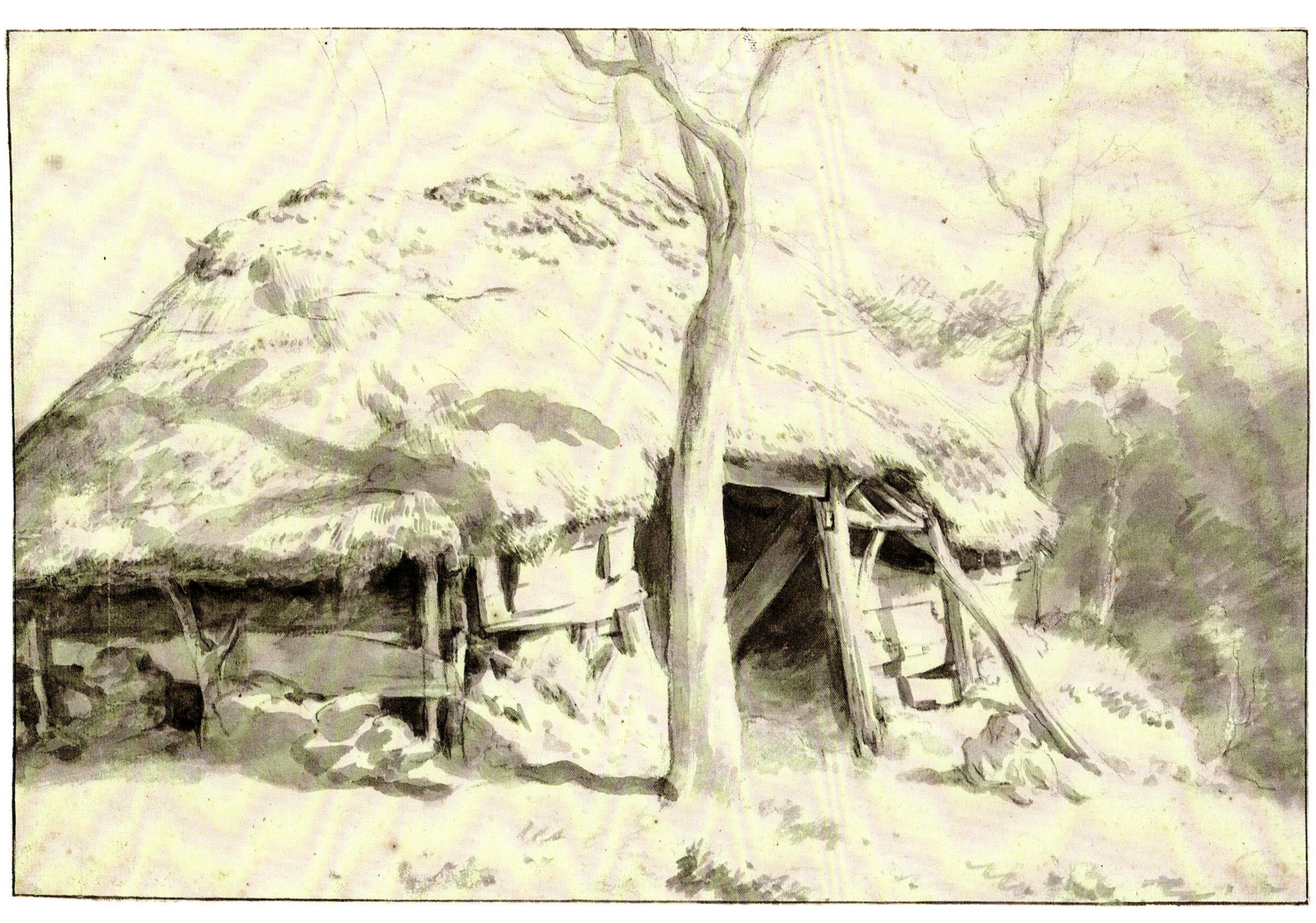

Willem van de Velde the Younger
Leiden 1633–1707 London

35 *Ships and fishing boats off the dunes in a calm sea*

Pen and brush in gray and black ink over traces of graphite; brown ink framing lines.
102 x 318 mm (4 x 12½ in).

WATERMARK: countermark PB, similar to Churchill no. 7 (Arms of Amsterdam, dated 1662); Gaudriault 1995, no. 4233 (Arms of Amsterdam, dated 1662); Robinson 1958–74, vol. 1, pp. 205, 213, no. 8 (Arms of Amsterdam, dated 1665), vol. 2, p. 146 (?1665). (R35)

CHAIN LINES: horizontal, 23–25mm.

INSCRIPTIONS: initialed *W.V.V J* at lower left corner (pen in black ink); verso, at lower left corner vertically *lot 1* (pen in black ink, 19th century?); at center *28* (pencil); at upper left, paraph? (pencil).

PROVENANCE: Sale, London, Christie's, 29 June 1971, lot 282. Sale, New York, Sotheby's, 6 February 1997, lot 18, acquired at the sale.

LITERATURE: none.

EXHIBITIONS: none.

The drawings in this exhibition by Willem van de Velde the Younger, Abraham de Verwer, and Allart van Everdingen are testimony to an intense interest in the sea, and the Dutch relationship to it. For example, van de Velde's father, also a distinguished marine painter, carefully "reported" the Four-Day Sea Battle between England and the Netherlands in 1662, as well as many other events that became familiar to every Dutch adult and child.

This sensitive drawing by Willem the Younger, whose brother Adriaen is also represented in this exhibition, is apparently not a preparatory study for a painting; it is, in fact, similar to many such calm seascapes by Willem. This appears to be a morning scene with a *weyschuit* in the right foreground unfurling its sails and preparing to lift anchor. It is particularly close to a drawing (Fig. 1) of almost the same size (85 x 305 mm), with a sailboat in the left foreground, other boats and larger ships in the right background, with a cloudy sky and the shore just visible in the distance; it is signed in the lower right. In this way, the drawing, in a private collection, England, becomes a virtual pendant to the present drawing, signed in the lower left, and the two sheets, probably made in the studio from Willem's great familiarity with such scenes, were no doubt intended to be sold together.

Further, the paper can be dated to 1662–5, and the drawing can be related to other works by the artist from about 1665 to 1675.

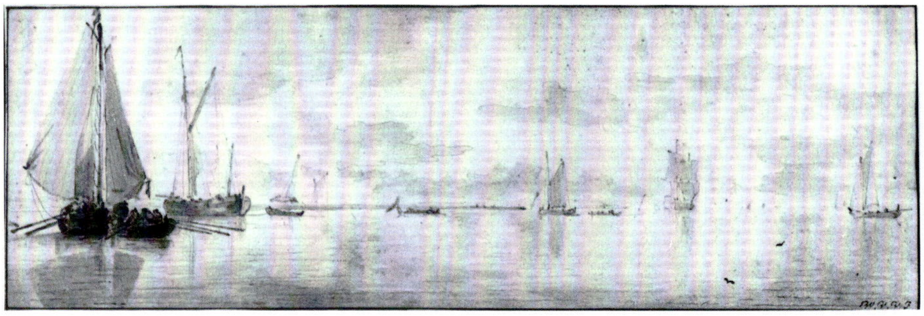

Fig. 1. Willem van de Velde, *Shipping offshore*, pen and ink with washes.
Private Collection: photograph Courtauld Institute of Art, London.

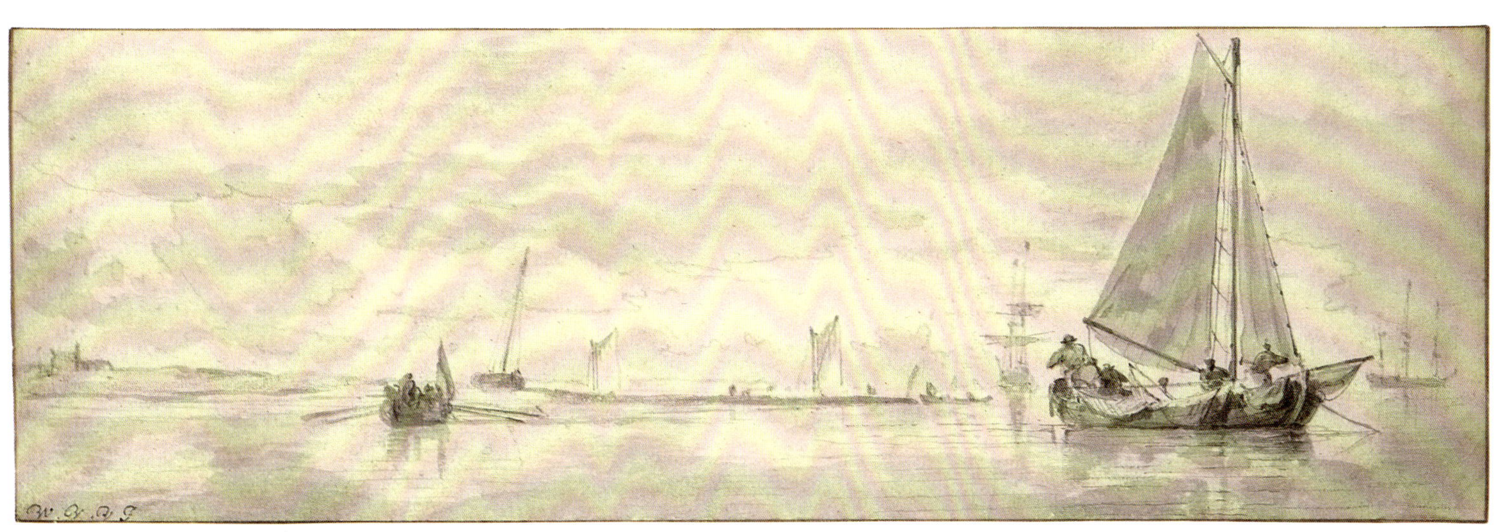

Adriaen Verboom
Rotterdam c. 1628 – c. 1670 Amsterdam

36 *Woods with travelers on a path by a stream*

Brush in gray ink over black chalk on light brown paper; brown ink framing lines. 163 x 204 mm (6⅜ x 8 in).

WATERMARK: none. (R36)

CHAIN LINES: horizontal, 25–27 mm.

INSCRIPTIONS: at lower left *Ruisdael* (graphite, 18th century, Francis Fagel?); verso, at lower left *Greffier Fagels Colln 1799 WE. P4*(crossed out) *55N60x / Old Hackaert* (pen in dark brown ink, in the hand of William Esdaile); at upper left *Cat. 894* (pencil).

PROVENANCE: Francis Fagel (1740–1773) and Hendrik Fagel, Sr. (1706–1790), sale, London, T. Philipe, 20–25 May 1799, probably part of lot 398 or 400. William Esdaile (1758–1837), London (L. 2617), his sale, London, Christie and Manson, 24 June 1840, lot 1180 (one of two, as "Hackaert"). Sale, London, Sotheby's, 10 December 1968, lot 69. Th. Laurentius, Voorschoten, 1969, cat. no. 33. Hans van Leeuwen, Amerongen (L. 2799a), his sale, Amsterdam, Christie's, 24 November 1992, lot 208, acquired at the sale.

LITERATURE: none.

EXHIBITIONS: none.

Adriaen Verboom's landscape drawings are among the most intimate and charming of his time. His work in the 1640s is close to that of the Haarlem amateur Claes van Beresteyn and Cornelis Vroom, and is mainly executed in pen and ink. In the 1650s, he came under the influence of Jacob van Ruisdael, and his drawings then are usually in black chalk and gray wash.

The present drawing is probably from the 1650s; the foreground is lively and animated, lacking the intense, linear calligraphy of his earlier work, and still far from the more sedate, less individual views of the 1660s, as in his drawing of the village of Moordrecht, dated 1663, in the Fondation Custodia, Paris (Van Hasselt 1968, cat. no. 161, fig. 128). The present sheet is close in style to his paintings dated in the 1650s (in the Rijksmuseum, 1653, and the Boymans, Rotterdam, 1657), as well as his superb etching of a landscape with stream, Hollstein 2. I. Q. van Regteren Altena (before 1968) appears to have been the first to attribute this drawing to Verboom.

In this typical work, Verboom's trees seem like miniature, bonsai versions of trees, gnarled yet blossoming, blown up to full size; their long, twisting trunks contrast with the short, stunted branches and sprays of leaves executed in individual short strokes. The trunks seem too big for their branches, and yet the final effect is fresh and unassuming, less muscular and heroic than Ruisdael's conception of nature, intimate instead of intimidating.

On the verso is the sketch of a building, probably not by Verboom.

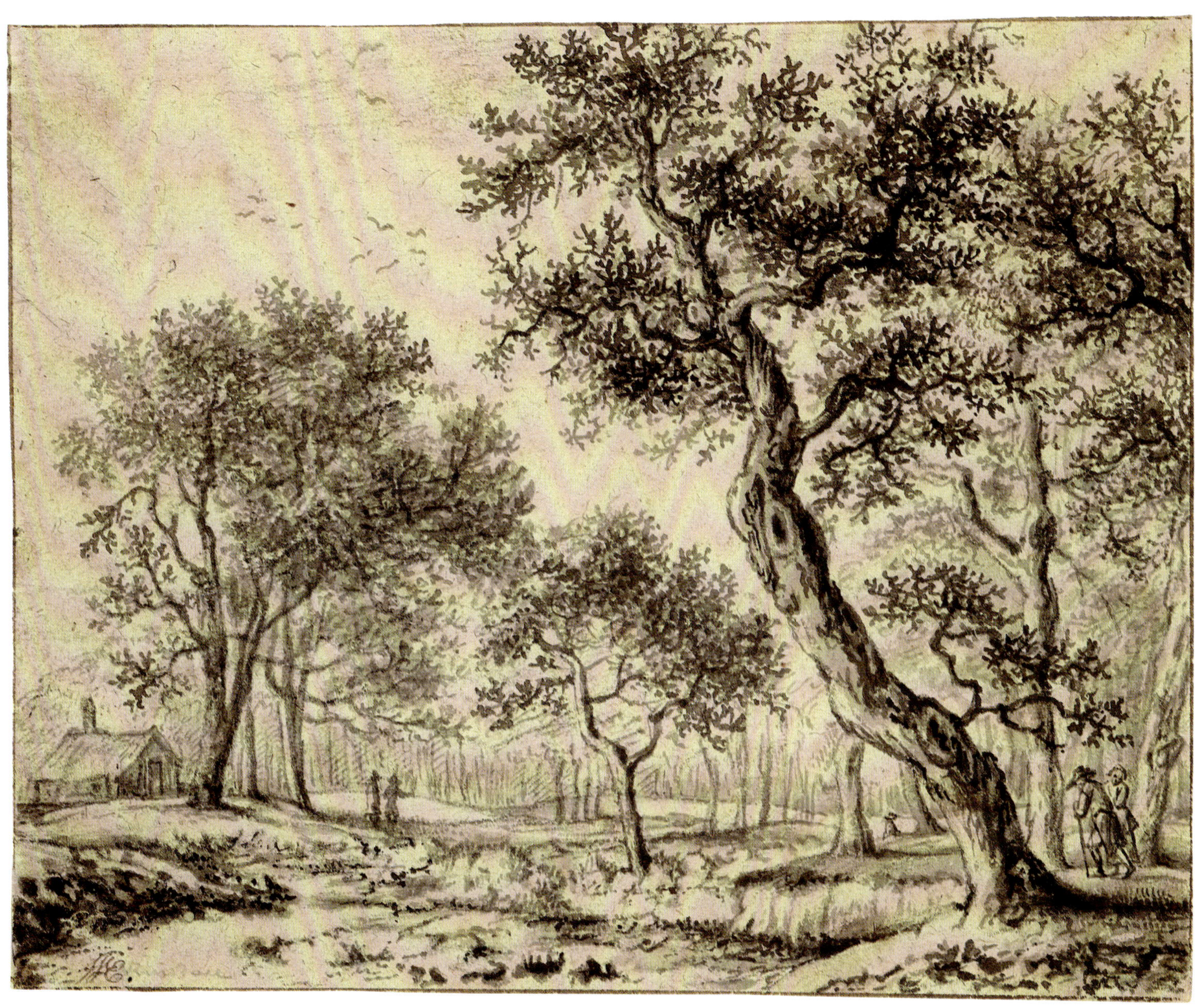

Abraham de Verwer
Amsterdam c. 1585–1650 Amsterdam

37 *Shipping on a calm sea*

Pen in brown ink, brush in brown and gray ink; dark-brown ink framing lines.
151 x 317 mm (5⅞ x 12½ in).

WATERMARK: none. (R37)

CHAIN LINES: horizontal, 27–30 mm.

INSCRIPTIONS: signed *verwer* at lower right (pen in brown ink); verso, at center *A H Verveer, Dordrecht 1646.* (pencil); at upper left *Verwer henry hubert* (pencil); at lower left corner *Verws 2247/ 11* and to the far right *2247* (pencil); at the upper right *N3147/ Rowlandson wash line* (pencil).

PROVENANCE: A. Chariatte, London. Tobias Christ, Basel, his sale, London, Sotheby's, 9 April 1981, lot 47. Robert Noortman, London and Maastricht. Sale, Amsterdam, Christie's, 25 November 1992, lot 614, acquired at the sale.

LITERATURE: Henkel 1931, p. 119, plate 47. Chudzikowski 1957, p. 673, fig. 10.

EXHIBITIONS: none.

This limpid, serene drawing gives a sense of the shifting patterns of light and shadow on the surface of the water, without a ripple, under a high cloudless sky. This work, executed in pen and brown ink and brown wash, with touches of gray wash in the rigging and the distant town, is different in effect from Verwer's sketchy, unwashed landscapes of c. 1637–38, with their sites clearly identified, in the British Museum (Hind 1931, vol. 4, pp. 89–90, plate LIII). This sheet may be slightly later, from the 1640s, given its low horizon, spare, simple composition, and understated tonal range. It is particularly close to a drawing formerly in the Bruce Ingram collection, with two ships off a coastal village, in the same media and of similar size (161 x 298 mm), as well as a painting formerly in the A. Waller collection, Utrecht, a view of Hoorn, and other drawings, in the Teyler Museum, Haarlem, and the Fondation Custodia, Paris.

It is difficult to determine the city or town far in the background. The city profile is similar in a drawing by Verwer inscribed "Vlissingen" in the British Museum; the artist does several other views of that city (Paul Oppé, London; Victoria and Albert Museum; P. de Boer, Amsterdam; and two in the Rijksprentenkabinet, Amsterdam), but there are other candidates, such as Zierikzee.

Verwer's beautiful evocations of the sea near the Dutch shore look forward to similar renderings by Jan van de Cappelle, Lieve Verschuier, and other artists of the second half of the seventeenth century.

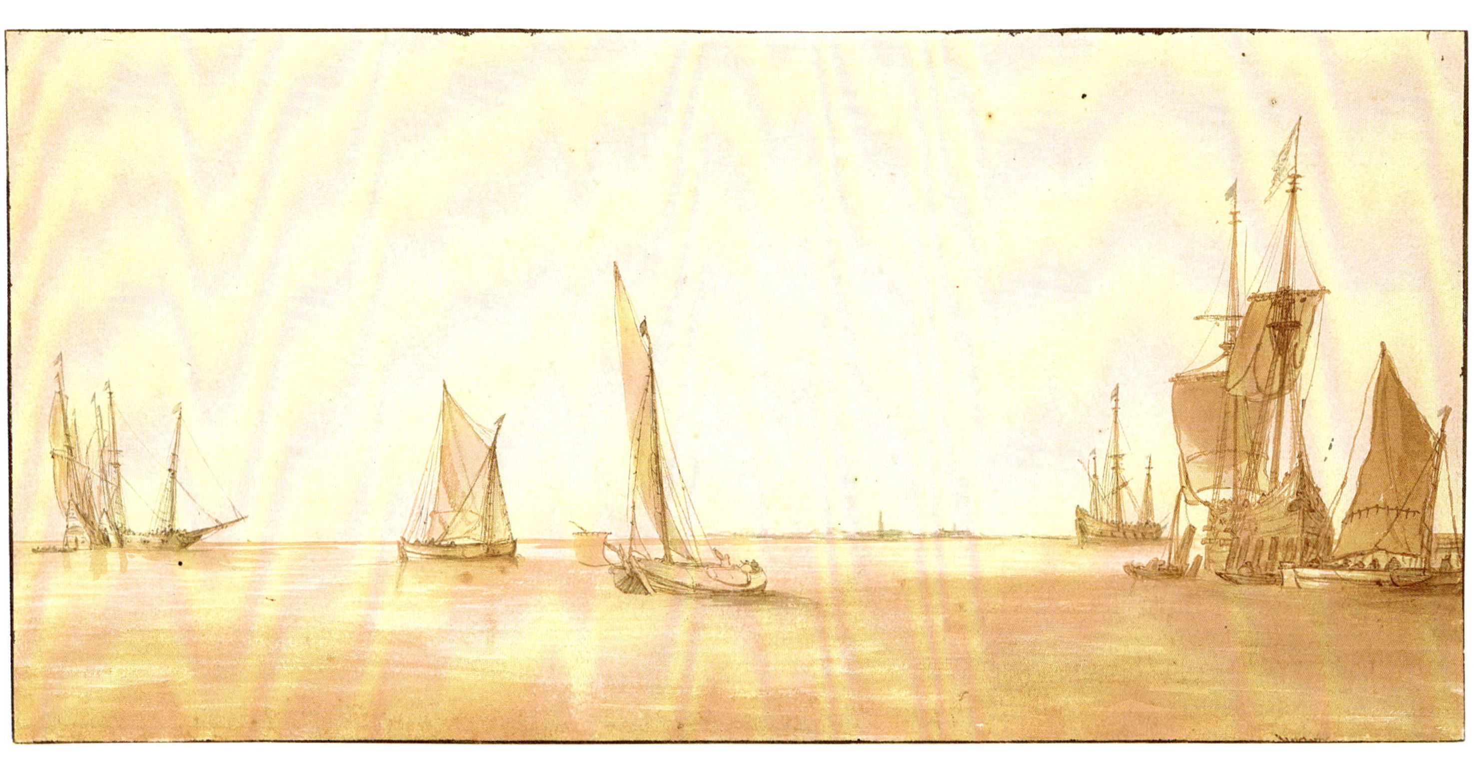

Laurens Vincentsz.
van der Vinne
Haarlem 1658–1729 Haarlem

38 *Two pigs by a high wooden fence*

Black chalk, brush in gray ink; black chalk framing lines.

150 x 194 mm (6 x 7⅝ in).

WATERMARK: fragment, crown of Arms of Amsterdam, at lower center, similar to Churchill nos. 32 (dated 1693) and 34 (dated 1698); Heawood no. 369 (Holland, dated 1697). (R38)

CHAIN LINES: vertical, 23–25 mm.

INSCRIPTIONS: verso, at lower left corner *A.v.d.Velde.465* (in graphite, 19th century?)

PROVENANCE: Th. Laurentius, Voorschoten. F.W.A. Knight, his sale, Amsterdam, Sotheby Mak van Waay, 29 October 1979, lot 24, acquired at the sale.

LITERATURE: none.

EXHIBITIONS: none.

Laurens Vincentsz. van der Vinne was a member of a large family of artists, most of whom seemed to have concentrated on landscapes; the work of at least nine van der Vinnes (some with the first names of their fathers or grandfathers, as well) can be identified. Nevertheless, Laurens, who may have been a pupil of Nicolaes Berchem, has a style all his own, clearly evident in this sensitive drawing.

This work is especially close to a drawing in the Fondation Custodia, Paris (Van Hasselt 1968, cat. no. 164, fig. 135), a farm among trees, near Overveen; the two sheets show the same interest in the construction of simple farm buildings, especially the pattern of boards that make up the walls, and the same treatment of foliage, particularly where the light has struck the leaves, an effect achieved simply by leaving patches of the paper blank, while other trees are indicated by vertical columns of short, staccato strokes piling upwards, as well as touches of gray wash and, here and there, stronger accents created by wetting the tip of the black chalk.

Interestingly, van der Vinne's first version of the fence, still visible, went down to the bottom of the paper; in the final version, the wall stops short of the bottom. Clearly, the artist enjoyed recording the mixture of horizontals and verticals created by the boards of this modest farm house. Pigs were a fairly common subject for Dutch artists, from the sheer pleasure in their depiction in Paulus Potter and Adriaen van Ostade to the moralizing humor of Jan Steen and the remarkable sympathy of Rembrandt's etching.

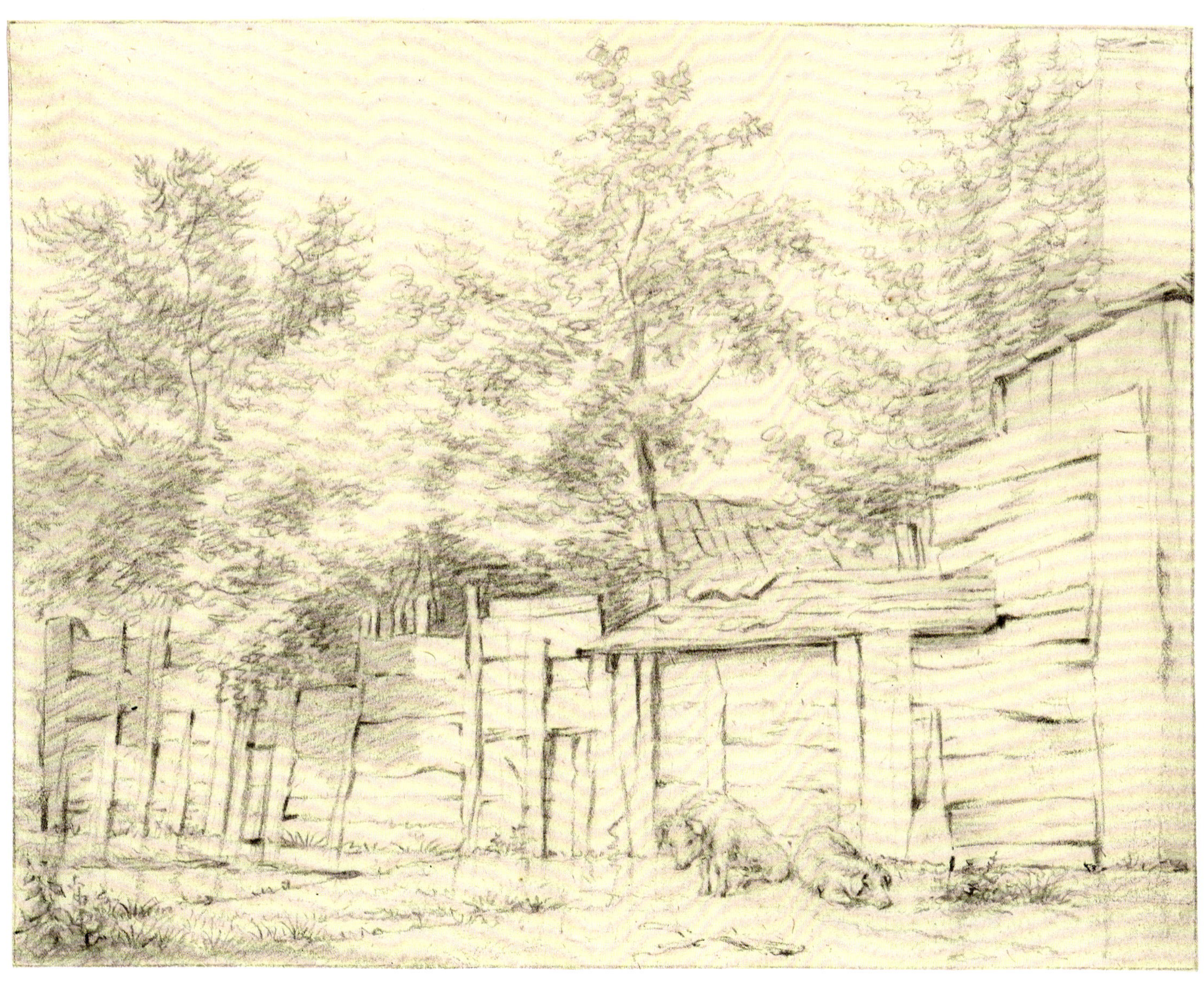

Cornelis Vroom
Haarlem 1591/1592–1661 Haarlem

39 *Ruins of the Temple of Venus Genetrix and the Forum of Nerva*

Pen in brown ink, brush in brown and pink ink; graphite framing lines.
202 x 299 mm (8 x 11¾ in).

WATERMARK: none. (R39)

CHAIN LINES: horizontal, 25–26 mm.

INSCRIPTIONS: verso, at lower left *T. Wyk* (pencil).

PROVENANCE: H. C. Valkema Blouw (1883–1953), his sale, Amsterdam, F. Muller, 2–4 March 1954, within lots 725–734. Sale, Amsterdam, Mak van Waay, 25 November 1971, within lot 687. Hans van Leeuwen, Amerongen (L. 2799a), his sale, Amsterdam, Christie's, 24 November 1992, lot 220, acquired at the sale.

LITERATURE: Keyes 1982, pp. 119–20, plate 10.

EXHIBITIONS: Cat. Utrecht, 1959–60, no. 109. Cat. Fribourg/ Passau/Trier/Aachen/Nuremberg, 1982–4, no. 114. Cat. Rome 1982.

This is an early and unusual drawing by Cornelis Vroom; as George Keyes has pointed out, it shows the Forum of Nerva in Rome and is related to a long tradition of Dutch fascination with Roman ruins, from Jan Gossaert and Maerten van Heemskerck to Paul Bril, Willem van Nieulandt, and many other artists into the nineteenth century. This spacious drawing is especially close in style to van Nieulandt (to whom it was once attributed), for example, in his pen and wash view of the Roman Forum in Dresden. The present work is related to another of overgrown ruins in the Kunstmuseum, Düsseldorf, and is in fact different from what was left of the Forum at this time, suggesting that the artist used an engraving or drawing. As Keyes notes, the shepherd tending his flock and the touches of vegetation growing out of the ruins are important additions that indicate Vroom's use of such a model.

This drawing dates from the second decade of the century. Later, Vroom's drawings take on an intense, linear calligraphy that is close to Adriaen Verboom, Claes van Beresteyn, and the young Jacob van Ruisdael.

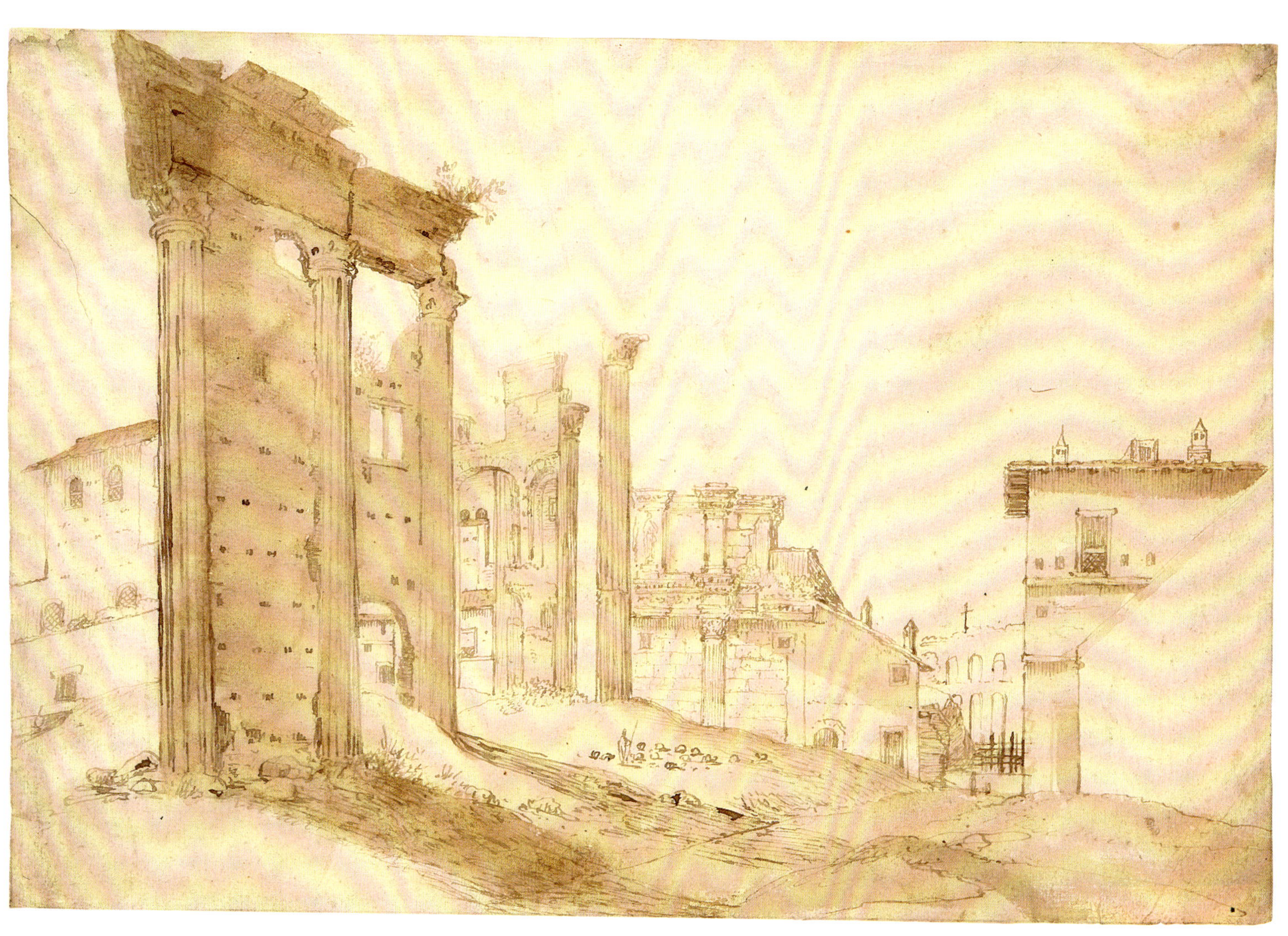

Thomas Wyck
Beverwijk c. 1616–1677 Haarlem

40 *Italian courtyard*

Brush in gray ink, pen in light brown ink, with traces of graphite; brown-gray ink framing lines. 172 x 194 mm (6¾ x 7⅝ in).

WATERMARK: fragment, Strasbourg lily with letters WR below, at upper center, similar to Heawood no. 1730 (Amsterdam, dated 1646); Ash and Fletcher 1998, variant G.c., pp. 185, 205 (dated 1648). (R40)

CHAIN LINES: vertical, 25–26 mm.

INSCRIPTIONS: verso, at lower left *N⁰1473* (pen in black ink, crossed-out) and above *N3998* (pen in black ink, in the hand of J. Goll van Franckenstein Sr.).

PROVENANCE: Jonkheer Johann Goll van Franckenstein Sr., (1722–1785) (L. 2987); his son, Jonkheer Johann Goll van Franckenstein Jr. (1756-1821); his son, Jonkheer Pieter Hendrik Goll van Franckenstein (1787-1832), his sale, Amsterdam, de Vries et al., 1 July 1833, lot D20. W. van Dalfsen (his monogram "WVD" on recto, lower left, not in Lugt). Sale, Amsterdam, Sotheby Mak van Waay, 18 November 1985, lot 44. Sale, Amsterdam, Sotheby's, 12 November 1991, lot 129, acquired at the sale.

LITERATURE: none.

EXHIBITIONS: none.

Thomas Wyck spent most of his life in Haarlem, but traveled to England and Scotland in the 1660s and, before that, to Italy. It was the trip south that changed his artistic vision forever. Although he does a number of paintings of alchemists in their laboratories, his favorite subject is Italy, harbors with "Orientals" on the docks, peasants among ancient ruins, and, above all, scruffy, picturesque courtyards, empty except, on occasion, for a traveler dozing in the late afternoon sunlight.

The present drawing is typical of Wyck in its mixture of architectural elements, the three arches in a row, two filled in, the slits to the right (in a city wall?), and the vegetation growing out of the stonework. The same love of overlapping and juxtaposed arches and curves, verticals, and horizontals, in the doorways, barrels, and lattice, and the fall of light and shadow over them, can be seen in many other of the artist's drawings, for example, in the Rijksprentenkabinet, Amsterdam, and the painting for which it was the preparatory study (formerly A. Schloss, Paris). An unusual aspect of the present drawing is the treatment of the tightly drawn, highly finished figures.

Not only did Wyck himself repeat the same courtyard, for example, in drawings in the Morgan Library, Groningen, Amsterdam, Dijon, Haarlem, and Brussels; other Italianate Dutch artists, such as Willem Schellinks and Jan Asselijn, were attracted to the subject, and Jan Vincentsz. van der Vinne (brother of Laurens) made an etching in 1686 that is very similar in subject to the present drawing.

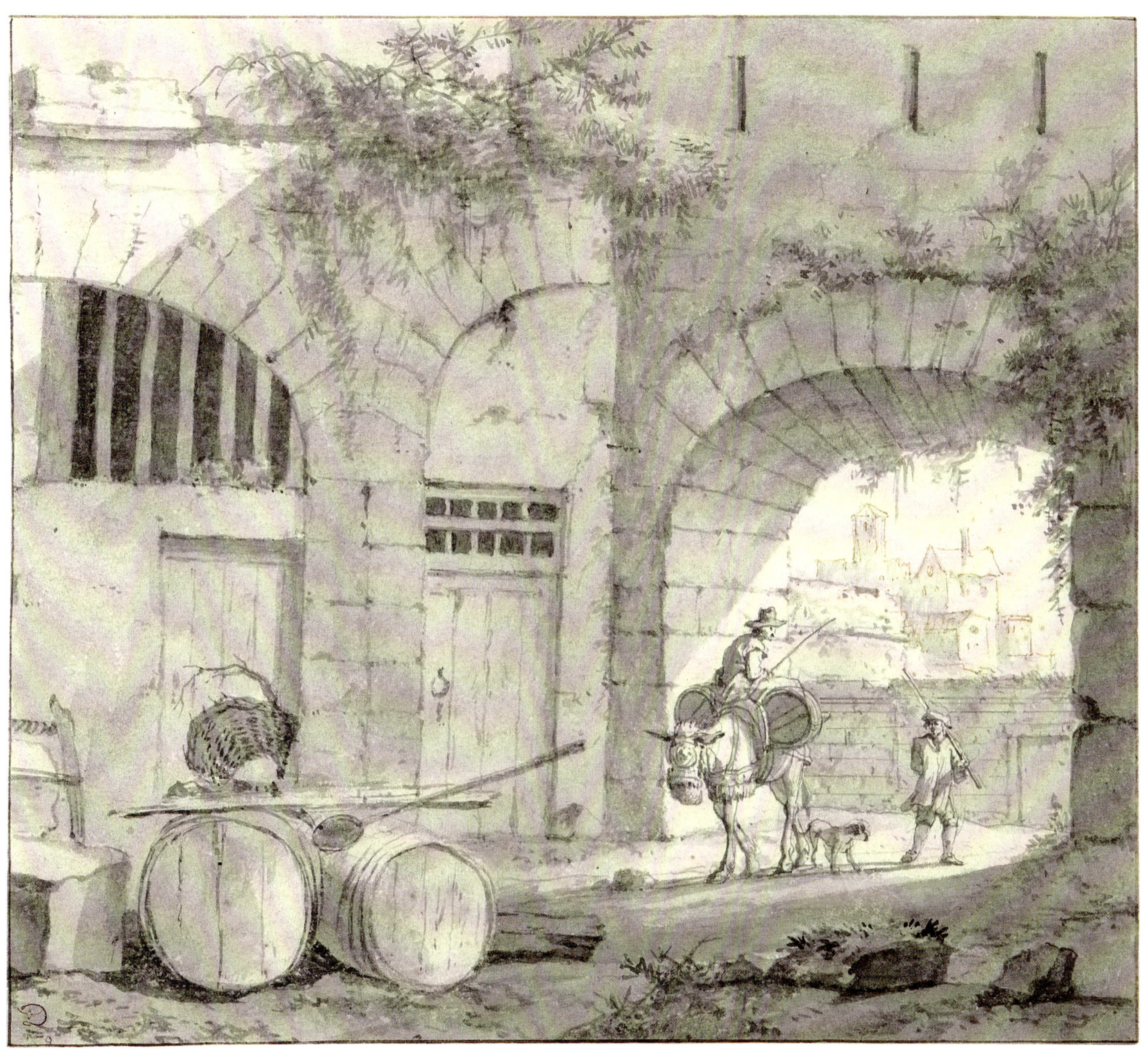

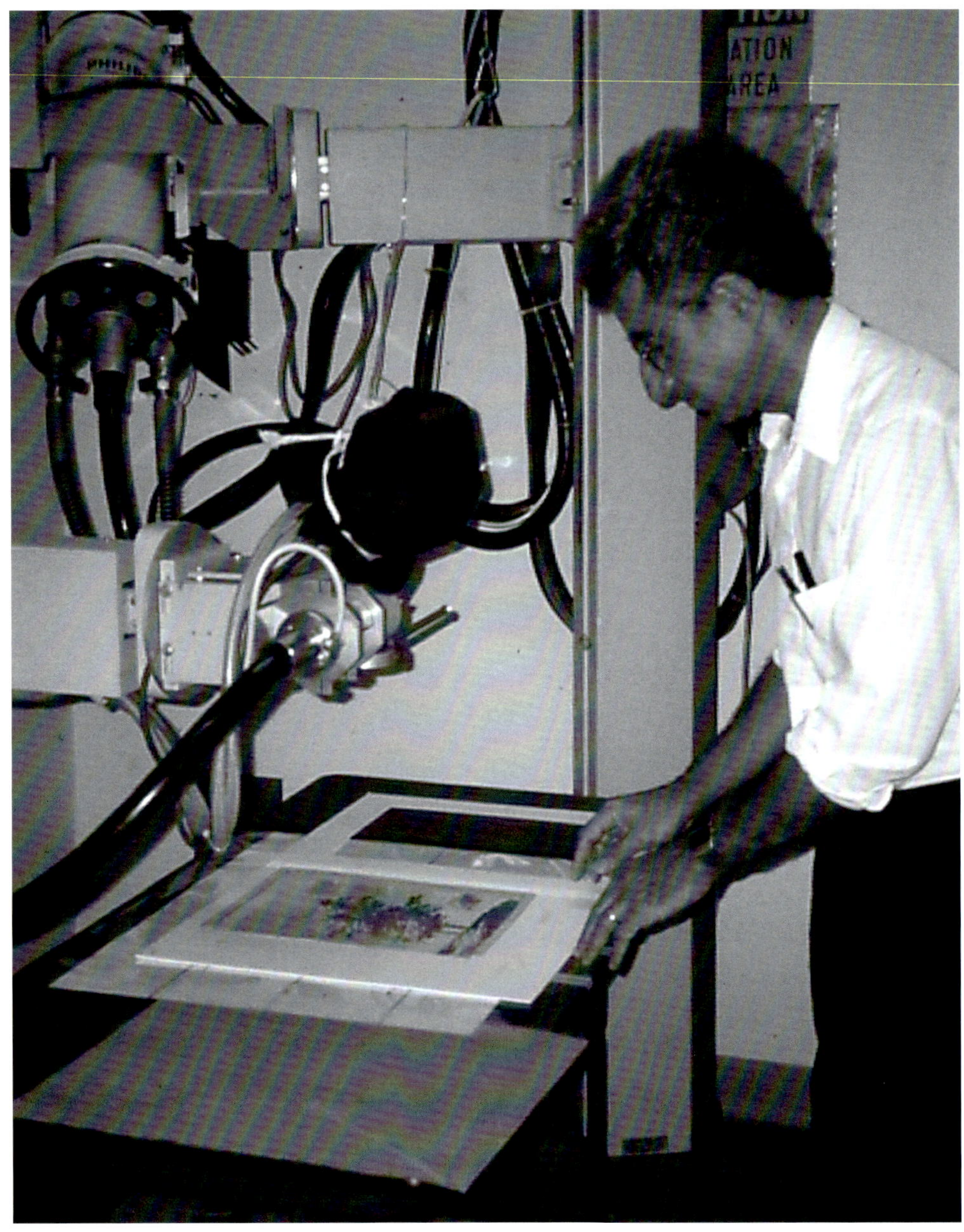

Fig. 1. The author positioning a drawing, Cat. no. 31, Jacob van der Ulft, under the x-ray tube for low-energy (grenz) radiography.

Radiographic Methods Used in the Recording of Structure and Watermarks in Historic Papers

RADIOGRAPHY, the use of x-rays or other ionizing radiation to create images, has for decades been among the most useful techniques for the recording of watermarks and other structural details in historic papers. Its major advantage over methods using visible light, such as tracing, transmitted-light photography, contact printing, and Dylux® recording, is its ability to eliminate printing or other design elements that overlay and visually obscure the watermark or structural information. The success of the technique, however, rests on the proper choice of radiographic method for the material composition of the overlaying inks or paints. There are three radiographic techniques commonly employed. The discussion that follows details each of these, discussing criteria for the choice of the method, procedures and materials used, and advantages and disadvantages relative to the other methods.

Low energy x-radiography or grenz radiography[1]
This technique involves the use of extremely low energy, long wavelength x-rays (also referred to as "soft" x-rays) produced by an x-ray tube at settings below 10 or 15 kilovolts (kV). For comparison, dental radiographs are commonly taken around 70kV. The energy of this x-radiation borders on the upper end of the range of ultraviolet energy, hence the additional term "grenz," German for "border," to describe them. It is the primary technique used for the radiography of all the drawings in this exhibition.

For optimum imaging of watermarks and paper structure, settings from 4kV to 6kV are most desirable because above this energy, image contrast diminishes substantially.[2] The x-ray tube, a standard low-energy industrial unit, has a beryllium window to permit unimpeded passage of low energy radiation out of the tube.[3] The tube also has a relatively small focal spot. The focal spot is the point of origin of the x-ray beam. Since radiographs are essentially shadowgraphs, a smaller focal spot will produce a sharper image.[4]

The film used need not have a special radiographic emulsion; excellent results also can be obtained with high contrast, high-resolution graphic arts films.[5] Working under a photographic safelight, the bare film is positioned on a table surface, emulsion side up.[6] The area of the drawing or print to be recorded is then positioned over the film (Fig.1).[7] Because low-energy x-rays are partially absorbed by air, it is necessary to position the tube closer to the film than in normal radiography, otherwise exposure times will be excessively long, and, of greater importance, contrast will be significantly diminished.[8] (The focal-spot-to-film distance (FFD) used for all the grenz radiographs in this project was 14 inches (356mm), the minimum distance needed to project a beam wide enough to cover adequately the 8 x 10 inch film area and the larger sized watermarks.[9]) The safelights are then turned off to minimize possible fogging caused by excessive safelight exposure, and the film is exposed to the x-ray beam. Exposures in this project were all 15 minutes in duration with the x-ray tube set to 6kV and 12mA (milliamperes).[10] The efficiency of an x-ray tube drops off precipitously and sometimes erratically at the extremes of its kV range, especially the low end. This behavior is often tube dependent; thus initial test exposures are usually essential.

For the imaging of both watermarks and paper structure, grenz radiography has several distinct advantages over beta radiography and electron transmission radiography, the other radiographic methods commonly used for the examination of historic papers. Because the source of "illumination" used to create the shadowgraph is, in essence, a point source, the shadows are extremely sharp and the level of detail recorded, even on the microscopic level, is extremely high, far exceeding that of any other technique.[11] Thus, besides watermarks, even the most delicate details of paper structure, from individual paper fibers to the small particulate metallic inclusions commonly found in historic laid papers, to structural subtleties of the paper mold and watermark wires, all are sharply rendered and well documented. Such details can be valuable supplements to historic paper and attribution studies.

In addition, in terms of the technique's practical advantages, grenz radiography is by far the safest of all the techniques with respect to the handling of the artwork or documents. Unlike the other radiographic techniques, intimate contact between the paper and film is not required (although close contact is desirable). Even when the historic paper is quite cockled, the grenz radiograph never shows areas of blurring that are so commonly observed in beta and electron transmission radiographs. The source of "illumination" used in these other radiographic techniques is diffuse. Intimate contact between the paper and the film is thus essential, necessitating the use of weights or vacuum pressure systems that substantially increase handling risks to the artwork. Yet, despite these measures, perfect contact is rarely achieved and localized areas of blurring are common.

The transmission of the x-ray beam through the paper is affected not only by variations in the physical density of the paper (the paper is thinner in the lines of the watermark; thus, more x-rays pass through causing the film to record a darker line), but also by the kind of atoms making up the artifact. Because of this, a printing or a drawing done with carbon-based pigments or organic inks (e.g., charcoal black, black chalk, carbon black, bistre, sepia) will generally not be recorded in a grenz radiograph, thus revealing any watermark or structural information that may lay beneath. This is because the chemical make-up of both the paper support and the pigment is quite similar; both are composed primarily of carbon and other low atomic weight elements. (This characteristic of x-rays, that they are absorbed more by elements of higher atomic weight, is also the reason that metallic inclusions embedded in the paper structure are so clearly recorded.) If, however, the pigments obscuring the paper are composed of elements of high atomic number, e.g., copper green, vermilion (containing mercury), lead white, or bone (calcium) white, the paper cannot be imaged satisfactorily using grenz radiography because low-energy x-rays can be totally absorbed by such pigments, even if the colors are applied in relatively thin washes (see radiographs R19 and R19a). Iron gall ink, which often has both iron and copper content, may also compromise the image of the paper, especially if heavily applied in washes (see radiographs R22 and R22a). This characteristic can be used to advantage, however, in the examination of drawings as a means of distinguishing iron gall ink from organic inks; these inks are often quite similar in visual appearance.

Beta radiography[12]

As usually practiced, this technique involves the use of a small, thin plastic sheet of poly(methyl methacrylate) (the same as Plexiglas®) which has evenly dispersed within it a radioactive isotope of carbon, ^{14}C.[13] As this isotope decays, it emits high-speed beta (β^-) particles that are, in essence, electrons with "kinetic" energy (energy associated with motion). The energy of these particles is, however, relatively low, sufficient only to allow them to penetrate a maximum of 10 inches of air or 0.28 millimeters of skin, or a sheet of paper.[14]

The technique is carried out under a photographic safelight. A sheet of bare film is placed emulsion side up on a table surface.[15] The area of the paper containing the watermark is positioned over the film, and the β^- source sheet positioned carefully over the watermark. A glass plate is placed on top of the source sheet and, if needed, a weight is placed on top of the glass to insure intimate contact between the paper, the plate, and the film. They are left in contact for the duration of the exposure, generally lasting thirty minutes to an hour depending on the plate output, the film used, and the thickness and density of the paper.[16] To minimize the potential of fogging, the safelight is turned off, or the artifact is covered during exposure.[17] To minimize risk to the artifact and insure proper placement of the film and source sheet, careful preplanning is essential, usually involving the creation of overlays or of guide marks around the perimeter of the setup that can be easily seen under safelight illumination.

β^- particles interact with the paper differently than x-rays; they simply collide with the outside of the electron cloud of the atoms they encounter, and lose a little of their energy (speed) with each collision. In terms of the transmission of the β^- particles through the paper, it is therefore not so much the specific elements, but rather the physical density of atoms in the paper or applied design that is the determining factor. X-rays, on the other hand, interact with the electrons in the cloud; the more electrons there are, the greater the absorption. Since elements of high atomic number have larger electron clouds, they tend to absorb x-rays more than elements of low atomic number. Thus, for β^- radiography, thin applications of inks or paints with pigments containing elements of high atomic number, as long as they are not too thickly applied, do not create significant barriers to the imaging of watermarks they may obscure. This is the primary advantage of beta radiography over grenz radiography.

Beta radiography has, however, numerous disadvantages that should be considered. Primary among them is that, unlike the x-ray tube used in grenz radiography, the ^{14}C sheet is a diffuse imaging source, not a point source. β^- particles are emitted in all directions from the sheet; intimate contact between the film, paper, and source sheet is thus essential or the image will be fuzzy or unreadable. Weights or vacuum pressure systems are required to achieve this contact, and this exposes the artifact to increased handling risk. The diffuse character of the emissions from the source sheet also make it impossible, even under optimum conditions, to record any fine detail in paper structure (although gross structure such as the buildup of fibers around chain lines is recorded),[18] and thicker papers are difficult to image at all.

In terms of practical disadvantages, beta radiography requires significantly longer exposure times than grenz and electron transmission techniques. The radioactive source sheets are also relatively small in size. Large watermarks often require several exposures for full coverage; and proper repositioning of the plate for these separate exposures can also be difficult to accomplish. Nevertheless, beta radiography has remained the most widely used radiographic technique for the imaging of watermarks primarily because of its low purchase and maintenance costs relative to other techniques. Additionally, although its ability to record fine detail is very poor, beta radiography can provide clear high-contrast images of watermark lines that match or exceed the contrast of grenz images.

Electron Transmission Radiography[19]

This technique is similar to beta radiography in that the image is created by a diffuse area-source of energetic electrons. The source of these electrons is, however, not from the radioactive decay process (the electrons are more accurately called beta particles in that case), but from the irradiation of a sheet of lead foil with high energy x-rays. When compared to grenz radiography, it has the same advantages and disadvantages as beta radiography. On the positive side, the electrons – like β^- particles – can penetrate thin applications of ink or paint containing high atomic weight elements (see radiographs R22 and R22a; R19 and R19a); but because both imaging sources are diffuse, both techniques have poor resolution and involve extra handling and weighting of the print, since intimate plate-paper-film contact is required. Electron transmission radiography has, however, two distinct advantages over beta radiography: the area that can be imaged in a single exposure can be quite large (as large as the lead foil and film used); and exposure times are considerably shorter.[20] Its disadvantages relative to beta radiography are: slightly less contrast because the average energy of the emitted electrons is slightly higher than the average energy of the β^- particles emitted by ^{14}C; and the substantial cost of a high energy x-ray unit capable of 200 to 250kV output.

The technique is carried out under a photographic safelight. A sheet of bare film is placed emulsion side up on a table surface.[21] With the design side up, the area of the paper containing the watermark is positioned over the film.[22] Instead of a beta source sheet, an industrial lead foil intensifying screen is placed over the watermark area, lead side down.[23] To insure maximum sharpness in the image, the screen, paper, and film are held in intimate contact with each other through the use of a vacuum envelope or a radiotransparent weight.[24] Using a high-energy industrial x-ray tube, the screen is then irradiated with a heavily filtered 200 to 250kV x-ray beam causing it to emit the electrons that pass through the paper and produce the image.[25] While the x-ray beam also passes through the paper and film, the film is only very slightly fogged by it because the photographic emulsion is far more sensitive to the electrons than to the very high-energy x-ray photons in the beam. Exposure times are quite short; ours generally range from three to six minutes depending on the film used.

In addition to film and exposure factors, the image is optimized in contrast by the proper combination of kV setting and tube filtration. Yet, despite these seemingly rigid parameters, the technique in practice is quite forgiving, efficient, and easily standardized.[26] The literature itself presents a broad range of specifications, all of which can produce successful results.

– Dan Kushel

Notes

1. This application of low-energy, "soft" x-rays or "grenz rays" to the imaging of watermarks is a long established technique dating back at least 60 years. Sheldon Keck, a founding member of the International Institute for Conservation, did extensive work at the Brooklyn Museum in 1939 which he reported in the *Reports of the Museums of the Brooklyn Institute of Arts and Sciences*, January 1, 1939 – June 30, 1940, p. 23, and which he presented at the 1941 meeting of the American Association of Museums in Columbus, Ohio *(The Use of Grenz Rays to Record Watermarks)*. H. F. Sherwood of Eastman Kodak also published on the use of low-energy x-rays for the study of paper, cloth, and similar materials during this time (e.g., "The Radiography of Cloth," *Rayon and Melliand Textile Monthly*, vol. 17, May 1936, pp. 51–53; "Stereoscopic Soft X-ray Examination of Parchment Antiphonaries," *Technical Studies in the Field of the Fine Arts*, vol. 6, no. 4, April 1938, pp. 277–281). Applications to the study of watermarks in stamps was described as early as 1945 by W. H. S. Cheavin ("Photographing Stamps by X-rays," *London Philatelist*, vol. 54, no. 30), followed by several articles in the 1950's by Charles Bridgman and Herbert Pollack discussing both grenz radiography and electron transmission and electron emission radiography for the examination of postage stamp watermarks and inks (e.g., "X-ray Philately," *Seventeenth American Philatelic Congress Book*, Stowell Publishing Company, 1951, pp. 167–171). Bridgman continued to publish extensively in the 1960's, also discussing applications of these radiographic techniques to the study of historic papers (e.g., "The Radiography of Paper," *Studies in Conservation*, vol. 10, no. 1, February 1965, pp. 8–17). Applications of low-energy radiography by the paper industry as a means of analyzing paper structure for manufacturing control is also long established, having been introduced in the 1950's (e.g., J. D. Pelgroms, "A Study of the Structure of Paper by Means of 'Soft' X-Rays," *Paper Trade Journal*, vol. 134, no. 1, January 4, 1952, pp. 25–32). Radiography has, of course, been applied to the examination of artwork and documents almost since the moment of the discovery of x-rays by Röntgen in 1895; today it is a basic tool of the professional conservator. In this profession, low-energy radiographic techniques have had wide application not only in the examination of paper artifacts, but in the examination of parchments, textiles, and ethnographic and archaeological materials such as basketry, bark, beadwork, leather, etc.

2. As an illustration, a test series of radiographs of a sample sheet of sixteenth century paper with a watermark was made at settings of 6kV, 8kV and 10kV. The film used was Kodak Contrast Process Ortho 4154; see note 5 below. Exposures were compensated to produce identical background densities; at a tube-to-film distance (FFD) of 15″ (381mm) and an mA (milliamperage) setting of 12, exposure times were 35 minutes, 125 seconds, and 35 seconds respectively. Densitometric readings were taken to determine the average photographic density of the image of the paper and the average density in the lines of the watermark. The 6kV image showed a contrast difference three times greater than the 8kV image and four times greater than the 10kV image (differences of 0.12, 0.04, and 0.03 density units respectively).

3. The tube used for the radiographs in this project was a Philips MCN 101 with a range of 5 to 100 kV. Low-energy x-ray units are available from nearly all manufacturers of industrial radiographic equipment, as they are used extensively in several major industries, such as electronics, plastics, and paper. Forensic laboratories (in addition to museum conservation laboratories) also make extensive use of this equipment.

4. Tube-to-film distances (FFD) are relatively short in grenz radiography. From the point of view of the film, the focal spot thus appears larger and the shadows cast less sharp than in techniques performed at more standard distances. In this project, the standard 1.5 x 1.5mm focal spot of the Philips tube was used. Although the tube also has a second and smaller focal spot (0.4 x 0.4mm), calculations indicated its use would not provide any substantial improvement in the final image. The "geometric unsharpness" (width of the shadow cast by the edge of any detail) can be calculated using the following formula: [distance between top surfaces of paper and the film / distance between the top surface of the paper and the focal spot (in this case, FFD can be used)] X width of focal spot. At the 356mm FFD used for the radiographs in this study, and assuming an average paper thickness of 0.2mm, the width of the shadow cast by the edge of a paper fiber on the side of the paper away from the film (hence the maximum fuzziness of any shadow) would be .0006mm or one 33rd of the .02mm width of an average fiber of cotton or linen, and well beyond the resolution capabilities of even the high resolution film used (200 lines/mm). Moreover, the shadow sharpness would barely exceed the resolution of the film even if the paper were cockled so that the bottom of the sheet was raised 0.5mm off the surface of the film.

5. The film used in this project was Kodak Contrast Process Ortho 4154, in 8 x 10 inch (203 x 254mm) sheets. It was processed in Kodak D-11 developer for 4 minutes at 68° F (20°C) with constant agitation, followed by 30 seconds in Kodak Indicator Stop Bath, 8 minutes in Kodak Fixer, a two minute water wash, two minute immersion in Kodak Hypo Clearing Agent, and a 30 minute water wash. If radiographic films are used, they must not only be high contrast and high resolution but must also be single emulsion (i.e., emulsion on one side only). Because the low energy radiation will not penetrate the film support easily, the second emulsion layer will primarily contribute only fog thus lowering contrast and possibly diminishing resolution. Kodak Industrex SR, a single emulsion, high-contrast and high-resolution industrial radiographic film, provides excellent imaging for grenz radiography. Its speed is twice that of Contrast Process Ortho, thus halving exposure times; its contrast appears similar to Contrast Process Ortho, although its resolution does not seem to be quite as high. Industrex SR film is processed in Kodak Industrex Developer.

6. It is advantageous to place the long dimension of the film perpendicular to the axis of the x-ray tube so that most of the portion of the beam exhibiting "anode heel" will project beyond the edge of the film. Anode heel is a diminishing of the intensity of the beam in the side of the projected circle of irradiation that is on the same side as the anode end of the tube.

7. The drawing is generally safest if placed face up; face down positioning will have no major effect on the grenz radiograph other than left/right reversals, which can be easily accommodated when viewing the film.

8. At an FFD of 14 inches, for example, 50% of 6keV x-ray photons, the highest energy x-rays emitted at a 6kV setting, are absorbed by the air; while at a 32 inch FFD, 80% of this radiation is absorbed. In terms of contrast, at 14 inches there will be some transmission of x-ray energies down to 2keV, whereas at a 32 inch FFD, transmission below 4keV is negligible, and this relatively monochromatic, or limited range of x-ray energies results in a diminution of contrast in the image. The replacement of the air, or most of it, with a low molecular weight gas such as helium can minimize these attenuation effects. However, this is difficult to accomplish in practice and may involve some additional handling risk to the artifact if extra care is not taken. (Transmission of x-rays through pure helium at an FFD of 14 inches averages over 98% from 1keV to 6keV; as noted above, transmission through air is only 50% for 6keV photons and drops to less than 10% at 4keV and below.)

9. The circle of irradiation at the 14 inch FFD used is 10.25 inches (260mm) in diameter. The tube has an emergent beam angle of 40 degrees; determination of diameter of the projected beam at any given FFD is a simple trigonometric calculation.

10. The common unit for expressing radiographic exposure is "mAS." This unit conveniently combines the two factors determining the total exposure the film receives: "mA," which determines the intensity or "brightness" of the beam; and "S," which is the length of the exposure in seconds. The combined mAS unit is merely the product of the two values (mAS = mA x Seconds). The two factors are thus conveniently reciprocally related so that a setting of 5mA for 60 seconds will produce exactly the same film density or exposure as a setting of 10mA for 30 seconds; both are equal to 300mAS. This allows for much easier translation of exposure recommendations among different x-ray tubes. Exposure for the 6kV radiographs produced for this project at the 14 inch FFD is thus expressed as 10,800mAS. (Note: mA is a measure of the electron flow between the cathode and the anode in the x-ray tube. The impact of these electrons onto a small spot on the anode or "target" creates the x-ray beam. The greater the flow, the greater the intensity of the beam produced. The voltage difference (kV) between the cathode and the anode determines the speed or energy with which these electrons strike the target. The higher the kV setting, the higher the average energy of the x-rays produced by the tube.)

11. For a technical comparative study of the image characteristics of these techniques see: Hiroshi Tomimasu, Daijin Kim, Philip Luner, and Minoo Suk, "Comparison of four paper imaging techniques: β^- radiography, electrography, light transmission, and soft X-radiography," *TAPPI Journal*, vol. 74, no. 7, July 1991, pp. 165–175.

12. The use of beta emitting isotopes for radiography was introduced as early as 1949 (T. Westermark, "Radiography with beta rays, *Nature*, vol. 164, 1949, p. 1086). The technique was first introduced as a means of

quality control for the paperboard manufacturing industry in 1952 (B.W. Atwood, "Examination of Paperboard Formation by Beta Radiography," *British Paper and Board Makers Association Technical Section Proceedings*, vol. 30, pt. 3, December 1952, pp. 659–666). Application to the study of historic watermarks soon followed: e.g., D.P. Erastov, "The Beta-radiographic Technique of Reproducing Watermarks Found in Documents," *Collected Works 1958*, Academy of Sciences of the USSR, Laboratory for the Techniques for Restoring and Preserving Documents and Books (English translation by L.M. Theakstone, Press of the Academy of Sciences of the USSR, Moscow-Leningrad, 1960). Other early work is detailed in: P.A. Tydeman, "A Simple Method for Contact Beta-radiography of Paper," *The Paper Maker*, vol. 153, no. 6, 1967, pp. 42–48; Pamela Hensley, "Contact Beta-radiography of Paper," technical leaflet produced in collaboration with The Minneapolis Institute of Arts, 1 September 1972; and J.L. Boutaine, et al., "La Radiographie dans L'Etude des Manuscrits," *Les Techniques de Laboratoire dans L'Etude des Manuscrits*, Colloques Internationaux du Centre Nationale de Recherche Scientifique, vol. 2, no. 548, September 1972, pp. 159–176.

13. In early studies, other substrates and isotopes were used. Attwood (1952; see note 12), for example, used a stainless steel plate coated with a thin layer of wax in which was dissolved thallous stearate made with the radioactive isotope ^{204}thallium. In 1967 the United Kingdom Atomic Energy Authority's Radio Chemical Centre at Amersham, Buckinghamshire developed the ^{14}C poly(methyl methacrylate) sheet that is used in current practice; these sheets soon became available as a stock item from Amersham/Searle (U.S.) and Amersham UK. In December 1990 the company ceased manufacture of the source sheets as a stock item because of low sales volume. They may still be available, however, as a special-order item from Amersham (now Nycomed Amersham). The Amersham sheet used in our laboratory, Model CFP – 22, is 1mm x 100mm x 100mm in size. It has a nominal specific activity of 500 µCi/g or 1,500,000 disintegrations/minute/cm2. Although the half-life of the isotope is over 5000 years, the plates do have a limited working life; we and others have observed that after about ten years some degradation of the plastic occurs causing the plate to dimple slightly, and making intimate contact between the plate, paper, and film difficult to achieve.

14. The plate may be handled with relative safety held by its edges with surgical gloves. The gloves provide some radiation shielding, as well as mechanical transfer protection. Abrasion of the plate is to be avoided. Before obtaining and using these source sheets, local government radiation regulatory agencies must be consulted; and a program of regular wipe testing to determine any changes in contamination risk as the plate ages should be instituted as soon as the plate is received.

15. As in grenz radiography, a single emulsion film is essential. The energy of beta particles emitted by ^{14}C (0.156 MeV_{max}) is not sufficient to penetrate the film base and reach the second emulsion. The imageless fog of the developed rear emulsion thus will serve only to diminish resolution and contrast. While industrial or direct-exposure radiographic films can be used, a film specially designed for exposure to isotope emissions is far preferable to minimize exposure time and maximize image contrast and quality. These films are readily available, as they are used extensively in the biosciences for autoradiography and electrophoresis studies. Until recently, Kodak SB film was used in our laboratory. In 1997 this film was replaced by a substantially improved material, Kodak Biomax® MR film. MR film has a tabular-grain emulsion thus improving resolution and giving it twice the speed of SB film. It also has a clear film base resulting in improved contrast. Average exposure times with MR film are 30 to 60 minutes rather than the one to two hour exposures required for SB film.

16. These exposure times are for Kodak Biomax® MR film, and assume a source sheet nominal specific activity of approximately 500µCi/g. These times must be at least doubled for Kodak SB and most other industrial or scientific direct-exposure films. The density and thickness of the paper itself also affect exposure times. In practice, the technique is relatively forgiving in terms of exposure so that if, for example, a series of test exposures are made on papers of various thickness and density, simple visual and physical comparisons with the test samples will offer satisfactory exposure recommendations. More precise exposure determinations can be made using a radiation survey meter or Geiger counter to measure transmission of beta radiation through the paper, a suggestion made by Hensley in 1972 (see note 12 above); a more developed description of such an approach is given in Ariane de La Chapelle and André Le Prat, *Les Relevés de Filigranes*, Paris: Musée du Louvre, 1996 (it should be noted that their data are based on the use of Kodak DEF film, a double emulsion film, designed primarily for x-ray diffraction applications).

17. In our laboratory, the beta radiography setup is assembled inside a Solander print storage box. The box provides not only sufficient working room, but a convenient means of allowing the setup to remain in the dark; the box need only be closed and covered with a black cloth to insure there is no light leakage; room lights can then be turned on.

18. Besides paper fibers, metallic inclusions (unless they are extremely large) will not be recorded either; this is not only because of the diffuse character of the source plate emissions, but also because beta radiography does not readily distinguish materials on the basis of atomic number.

19. Also called electron radiography, the technique and its application to the imaging of watermarks was described as far back as 1945 (H.S. Tasker and S. W. Towers, "'Electron Radiography' using Secondary - Radiation from Lead Intensifying Screens," *Nature*, vol. 156, July 14, 1945, pp. 50–51.) Herbert Pollack and Charles Bridgman published extensively on the application of the technique to watermarks in postage stamps beginning as early as 1951, and Bridgman published additionally on applications to fine art prints and drawings (see references in note 1, above.) Excellent detailed descriptions of the technique, with applications to the study of watermarks, are by Arthur I. Berman and James W. Dutli, ("Roentgen-Ray and Electron Radiography of Thin Specimens," *American Journal of Roentgenology*, vol. 74, no. 3, September 1955, pp. 518–525) and by Charles Bridgman ("The Radiography of Paper," *Studies in Conservation*, vol. 10, no. 1, February 1965, pp. 8–17).

20. A third, minor, but interesting advantage is that paper structure or watermarks may be more successfully imaged through thick overlaying applications of ink or pigment provided these inks or pigments contain high atomic weight elements. The high-energy x-ray beam causes not only the lead screen to emit electrons, but also these heavy elements in the pigments. If the artwork is positioned so that the design side is away from the photographic film, the electrons emitted by the pigment can then serve to replace those electrons emitted by the lead screen that are blocked by the pigment.

21. Recommended films for this technique are the same ones used for grenz radiography: Kodak Contrast Process Ortho 4154 and Kodak Industrex SR film. As described in note 5, they are similar in contrast; the Ortho film has slightly higher resolution (not as great a concern in this technique); the SR film has twice the speed, thus halving exposure times.

22. Positioning the ink or painted image away from the film is especially important if the pigments contain high atomic weight elements. The high energy x-rays in the beam will cause these elements to emit electrons just as they do in the lead foil screen. Positioning the artwork so that the design side is up and away from the photographic film is important for two reasons. The first was described in note 21, above. The second is more critical to successful imaging of the paper: if the pigment is placed against the photographic emulsion, the electrons emitted by the pigment will create a pronounced image of the design on the film. Another long-established radiographic technique, however, takes advantage of this phenomenon. It is called electron emission radiography. In this technique, a piece of photographic film is placed in intimate contact with the surface of the subject being radiographed while the subject is irradiated with the same filtered high energy x-ray beam used for electron transmission radiography (the films used and the average exposure times are identical as well). The applications for this technique are wide ranging: from distinguishing metallic inks on stamps or drawings; to producing radiographic images of paintings on radioöpaque or interferential supports (e.g. paintings on copper, panel paintings with thick cradles, frescoes); to the imaging of obscured designs on degraded stained glass, etc.

23. The lead foil screen used in our laboratory, and suggested in most of the literature, is 0.005 inches (0.127mm) in thickness. These inexpensive screens, called lead intensifying screens, are readily available from suppliers of industrial radiographic equipment. They consist of lead foil mounted on a cardboard or plastic backing for ease of handling. It is important to remove any protective plastic film from the foil before use and to keep the screen free from creases and deep scratches. Creases can make good screen-paper-film contact difficult to achieve. Deep scratches may image themselves as fuzzy dark lines. This is because the scratch exposes additional lead surface; thus the emission of electrons per unit area of flat surface is increased along the scratch.

24. In our laboratory, we use a sheet of ½ inch thick Plexiglas® as a weight.

25. The tube used in our laboratory is a Philips MCN322 with a range of 16kV to 320kV. Filtration is 8mm of copper with an additional 5mm of aluminum on the side away from the tube. The copper filtration absorbs nearly all x-ray photons below 110keV (transmission at that energy is only 5%). The aluminum serves to absorb secondary low-energy radiation (Compton scatter) emitted by the irradiated copper; this radiation can cause fogging of the film and a lowering of contrast in the radiograph. Using a 250kV beam, our exposures are standardized at an FFD of 32 inches at 2000mAS (5mA; 6 minutes and 40 seconds) for Contrast Process Ortho 4154 film, and 1000mAS (5mA; 3 minutes and 20 seconds) for Kodak SR film.

26. Inadequate tube filtration results in excessive film fogging, because the film is more sensitive to the lower energy x-rays passed by such a filter; too substantial a filter increases exposure times needlessly. An excessively high kV setting (well above 250kV), even with adequate filtration, results in emitted electron energies that are too high to record differences in paper thickness with satisfactory contrast. Too low a kV setting results in excessively long exposure times; at energy settings under 150 kV the electron output of the screen is nearly negligible. The thickness of the lead foil screen may also affect the process. Use of too thin a screen may result in low intensity of electron emission, and may also result in additional film fogging, as the screen itself must provide some filtration effect. Too thick a screen may also result in low emission and longer exposure times, but because of internal absorption. While FFD might not seem to have much of a bearing on the technique other than affecting exposure time, our experience indicates that distances much above 32 inches may result in the creation of excessive amounts of film-fogging, low-energy secondary radiation caused by the interaction of the beam with the large volume of air. This phenomenon was observed doing electron emission radiography at an FFD of 58 inches; its effect relative to electron transmission radiography has not yet been explored. It is possible that the lead foil screen (which is not used in electron emission radiography) may provide sufficient filtration to eliminate the problem. Unlike grenz or other direct exposure techniques, FFD will, of course, have no bearing on image sharpness as the image is made by the electrons emitted by the lead foil screen, and not by the x-ray beam itself. The minimum distance needed to cover the area of the film with an even x-ray intensity is all that is required, although excessively short FFD's should be avoided as they can result in unevenness in electron output from the effect of anode heel (see note 6, above).

Atlas of Radiographs

Notes and Acknowledgments

The photographs in this atlas represent details from 8-by-10-inch radiographs taken of all 40 drawings in the catalogue. They are reproduced actual size. The radiographs have R[adiograph] numbers corresponding to the catalogue numbers of the drawings. Twenty-six (65 percent) of the drawings are on paper with watermarks. A descriptive analysis of each watermark is included within its drawing's text entry in the catalogue section of this volume. All radiographs, except R19a and R22a, are the products of grenz roentgenology. The two exceptions were made by the electron transmission method.

Professor Dan Kushel performed the radiography at Buffalo State College, Buffalo, New York. We are indebted to Theo Laurentius for his comments on the radiographs. Martin Senn is credited for high-resolution digital photography of the radiographic negatives, and for his application of contrast enhancement techniques through Adobe Photoshop, version 5.0.

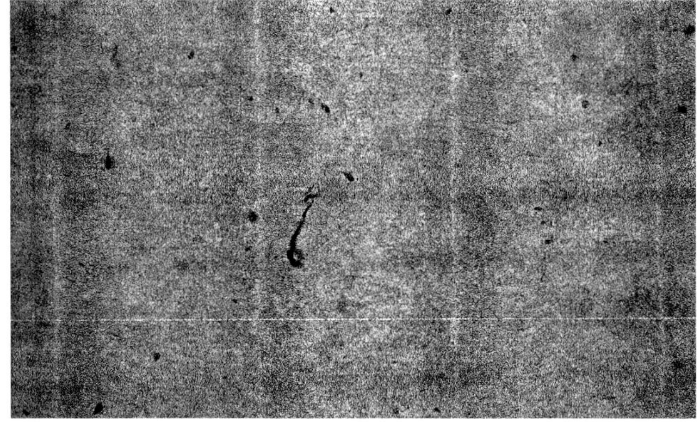
R1

R2

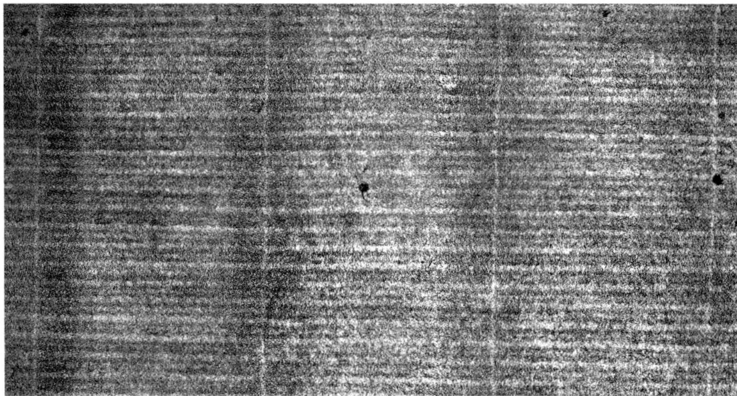
R3

R1
Cat. 1
Bartholomeus Breenbergh

R2
Cat. 2
Bartholomeus Breenbergh
Italian paper, 17th century.

R3
Cat. 3
Bartholomeus Breenbergh
(dated 1657?)
Italian paper, 17th century.

R4
Cat. 4
Michiel Carrée
Thicker wire lines datable after 1690, possibly in the early 18th century, late in the artist's career.

R5
Cat. 5
Guillam Du Bois
Identical to the paper in R6, probably from the same ream.

R6
Cat. 6
Guillam Du Bois
See R5.

R7
Cat. 7
Allart van Everdingen

R8
Cat. 8
Allart van Everdingen

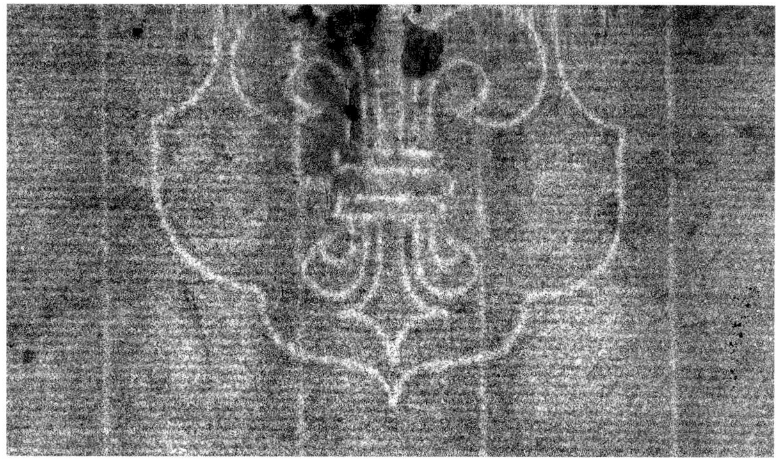
R4

R5

R6

R7

R8

R9
Cat. 9
Allart van Everdingen

R10
Cat. 10
Abraham Furnerius
Paper structure nearly identical to paper with paschal lamb watermark, as used by Rembrandt c.1651 (compare Rembrandt's etching "Clement de Jonghe," B.272, second state, Rijksprentenkabinet, Amsterdam).

R11
Cat. 11
Jan van Goyen (dated 1626)
Radiopaque inclusions indicate low-quality, cheap paper.

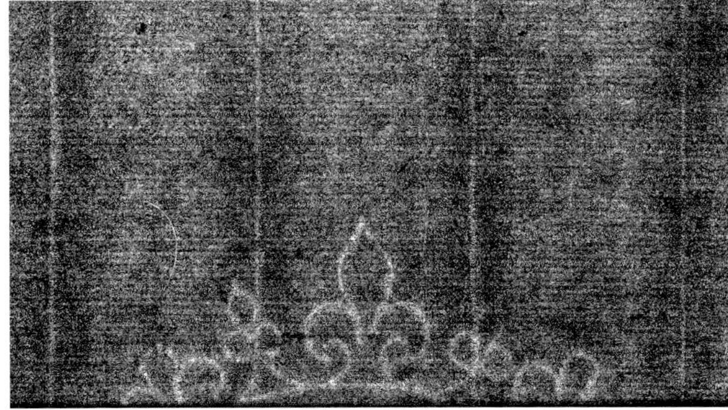
R9

R10

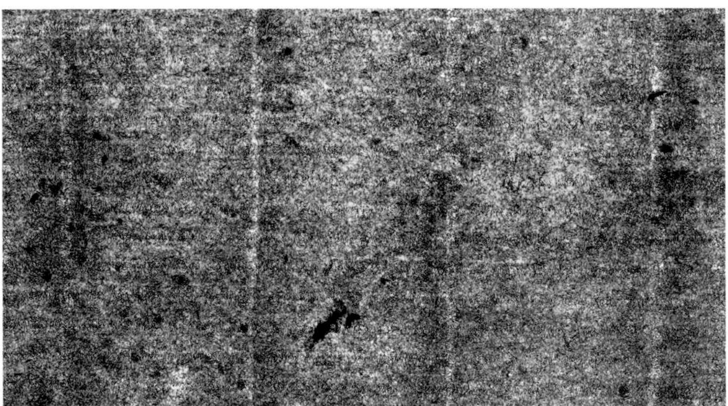
R11

R12

R12
Cat. 12
Jan van Goyen

R13
Cat. 13
Jan van Goyen (dated 1653)
"Three worlds" watermark, probably Italian paper, but copied by paper-makers in Provence, France, and in Catalonia.

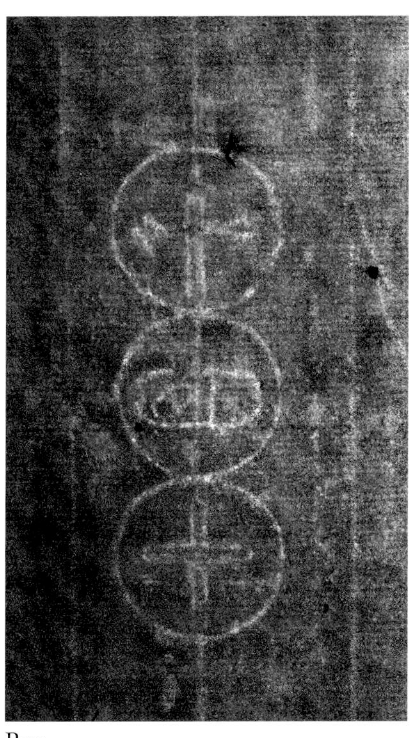

R13

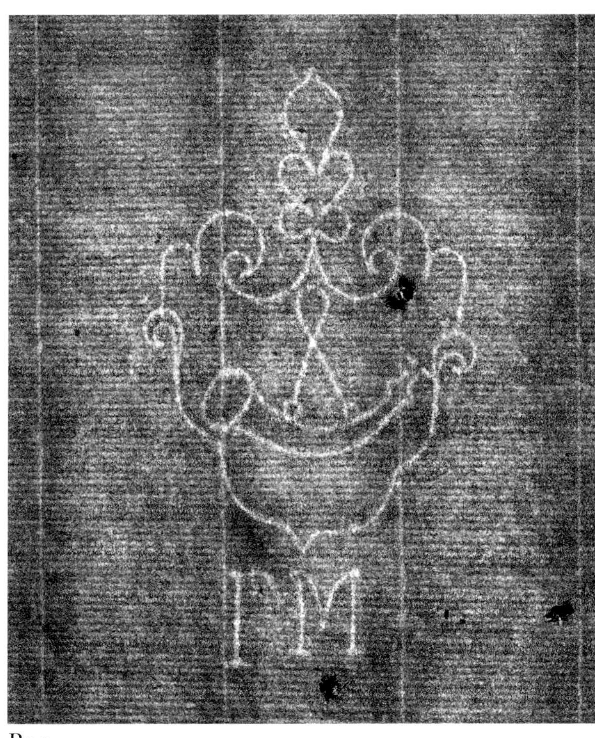

R14

R15

R14
Cat. 14
Jan van Goyen

R15
Cat. 15
Joris van der Haagen

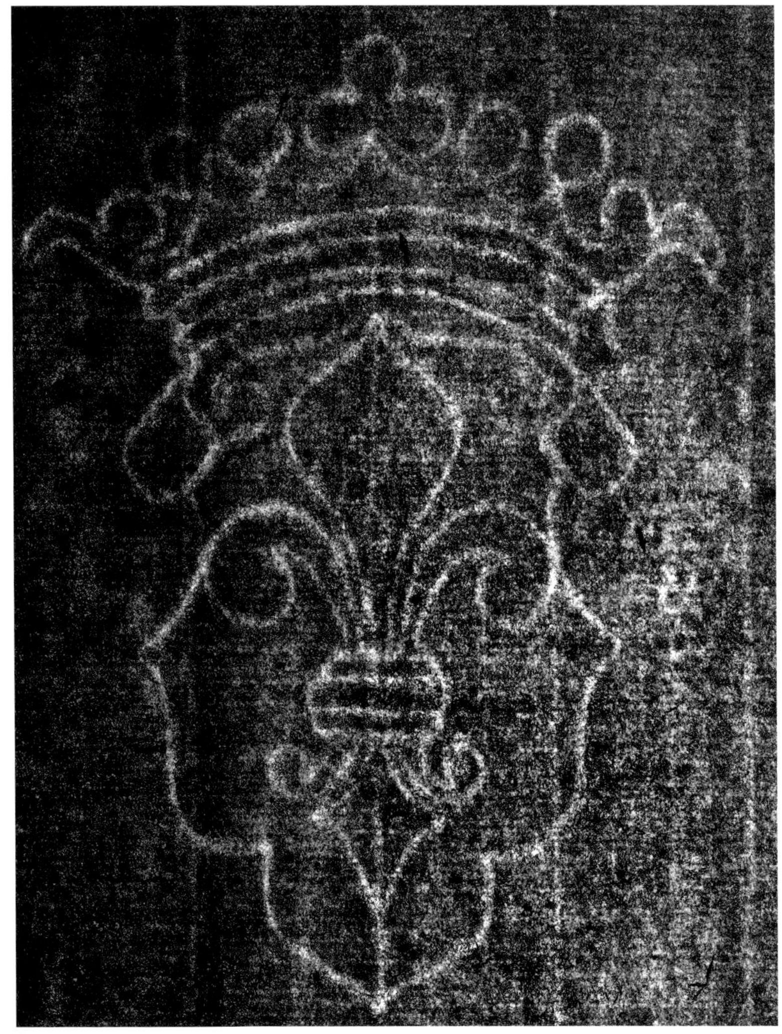

R16

R17

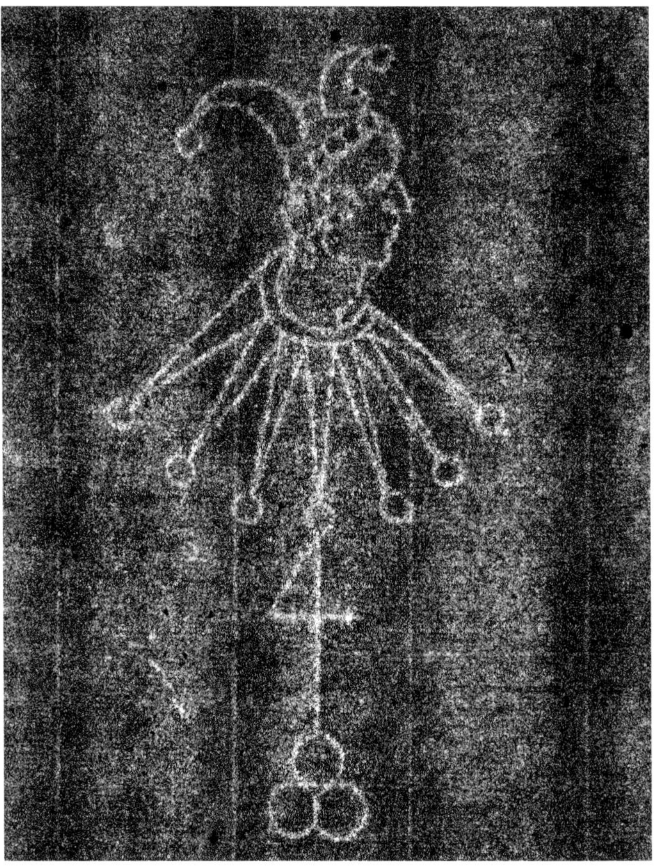

R18

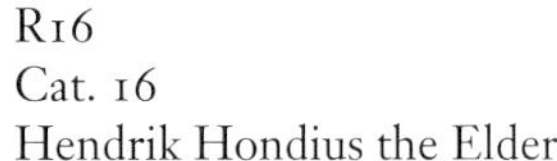

R16
Cat. 16
Hendrik Hondius the Elder

R17
Cat. 17 Jan van Kessel

R18
Cat. 18 Jan Lievens

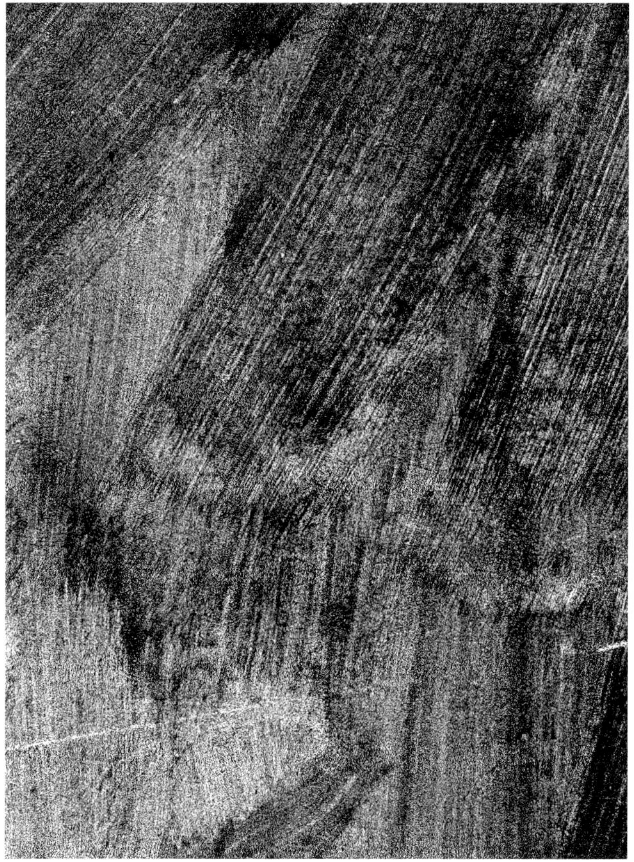

R19

R19
Cat. 19
Pieter Molyn
(dated 1634)
Verso is prepared with brushed-on radiopaque material (pulverized-bone white?), absorbing x-radiation and masking watermark image. Electron transmission radiography is indicated (seeR19a).

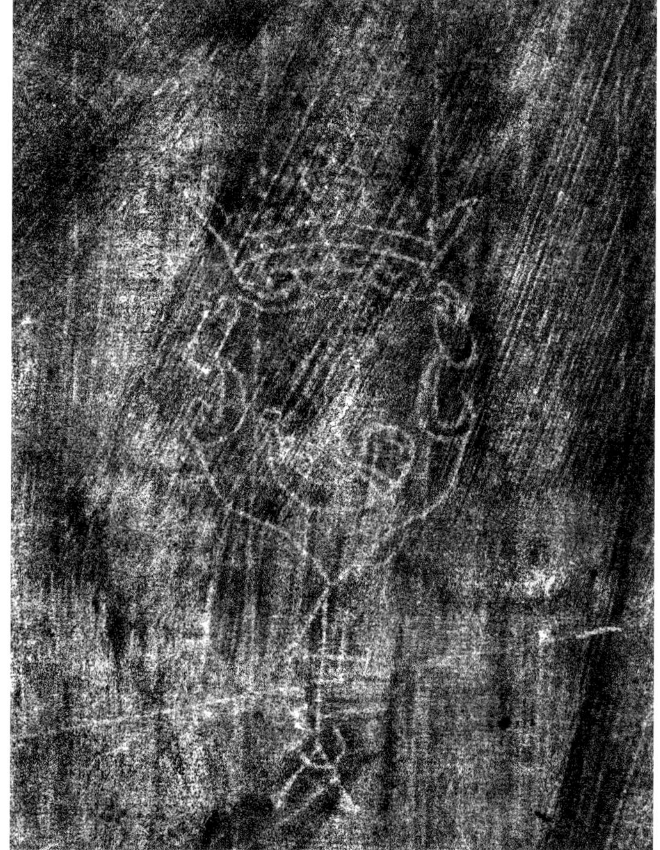

R19a

R19a
Cat. 19
Pieter Molyn
(dated 1634)
electron transmission

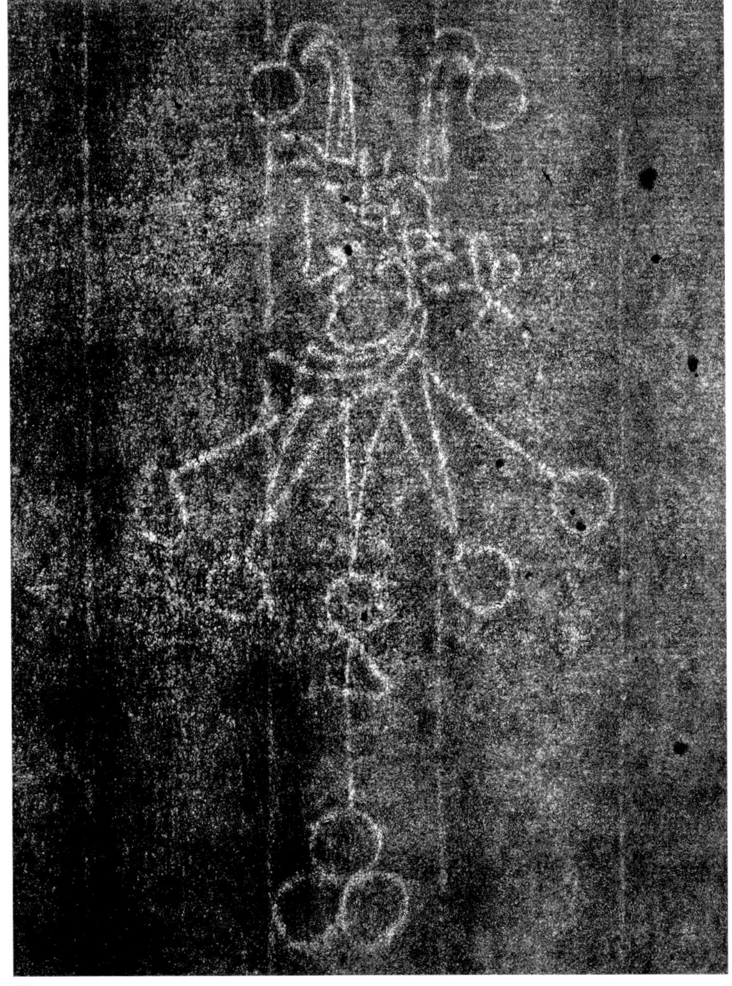
R20

R20
Cat. 20
Pieter Molyn
(dated 1659)

R21
Cat. 21
Herman Naiwincx

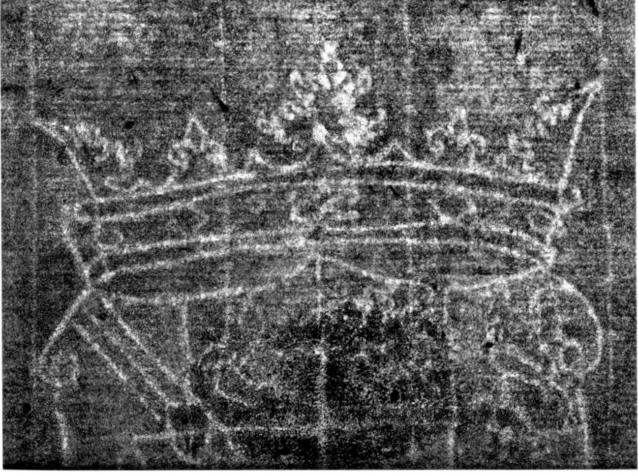
R21

R22
Cat. 22
Rembrandt van Rijn
Ink on recto and verso made from gallnuts containing radiopaque iron compounds, partially obscuring watermark image. Electron transmission radiography is indicated (seeR22a).

R22a
Cat. 22
Rembrandt van Rijn
electron transmission

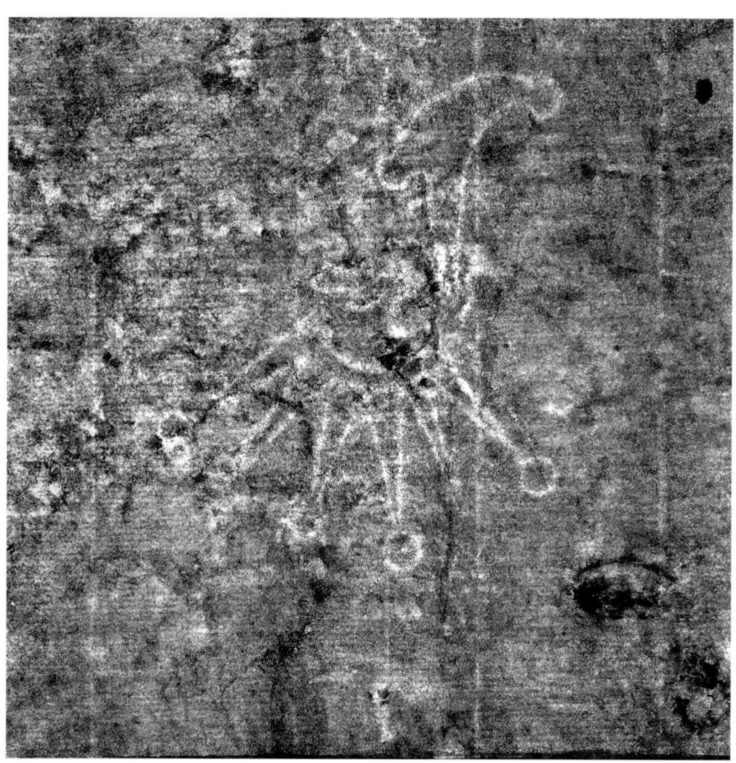
R22

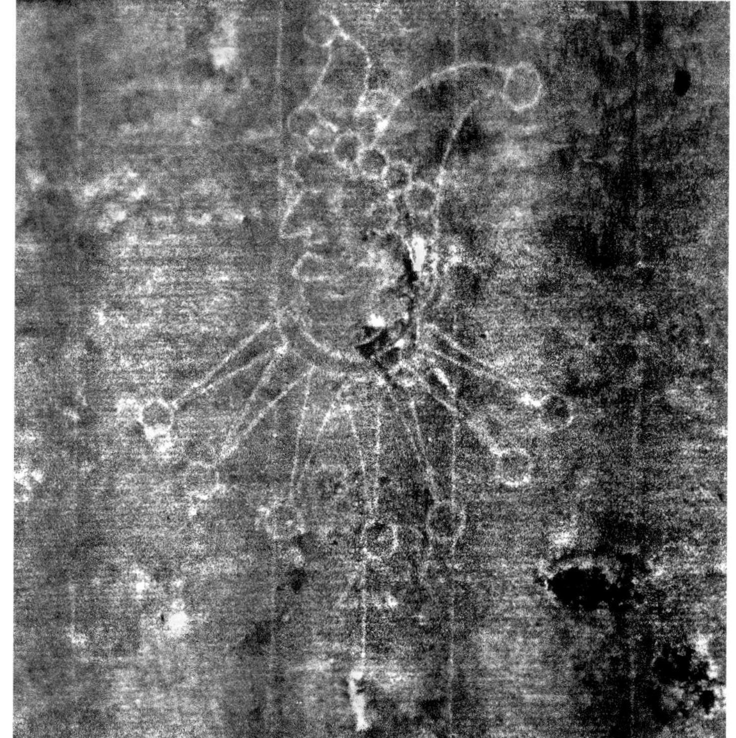
R22a

R23
Cat. 23
Roelant Roghman

R24
Cat. 24
Roelant Roghman

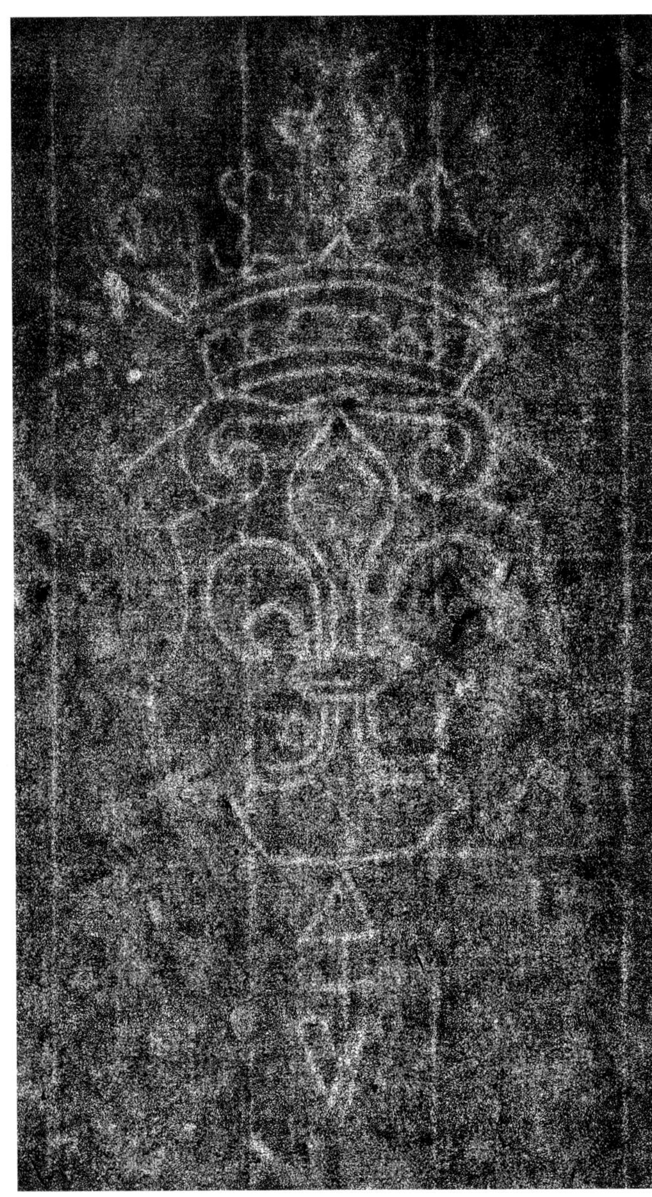
R23

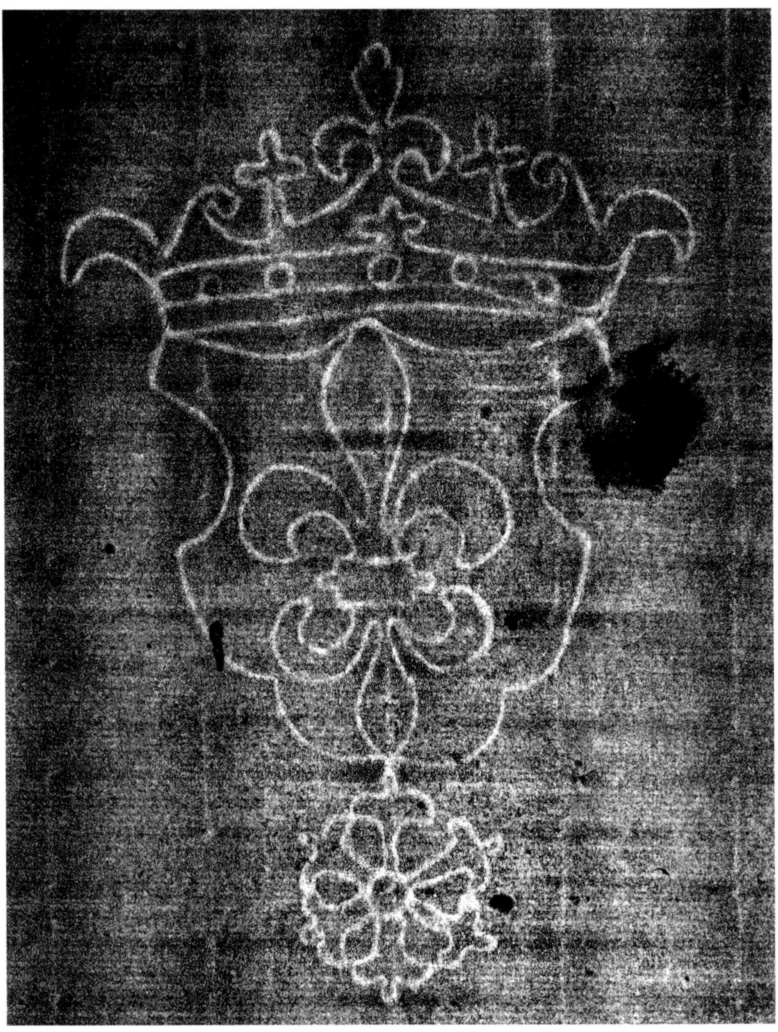
R24

R25
Cat. 25
Willem Romeyn
(dated 1694)

R26
Cat. 26
Jacob van Ruisdael

R27
Cat. 27
Jacob van Ruisdael

R28
Cat. 28
Cornelis Saftleven

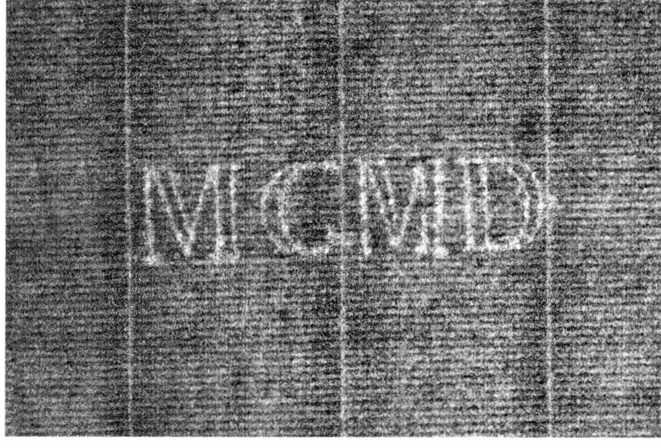

R25

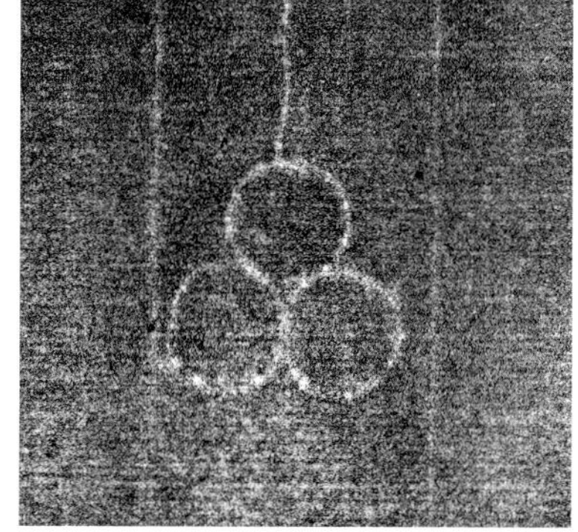
R26

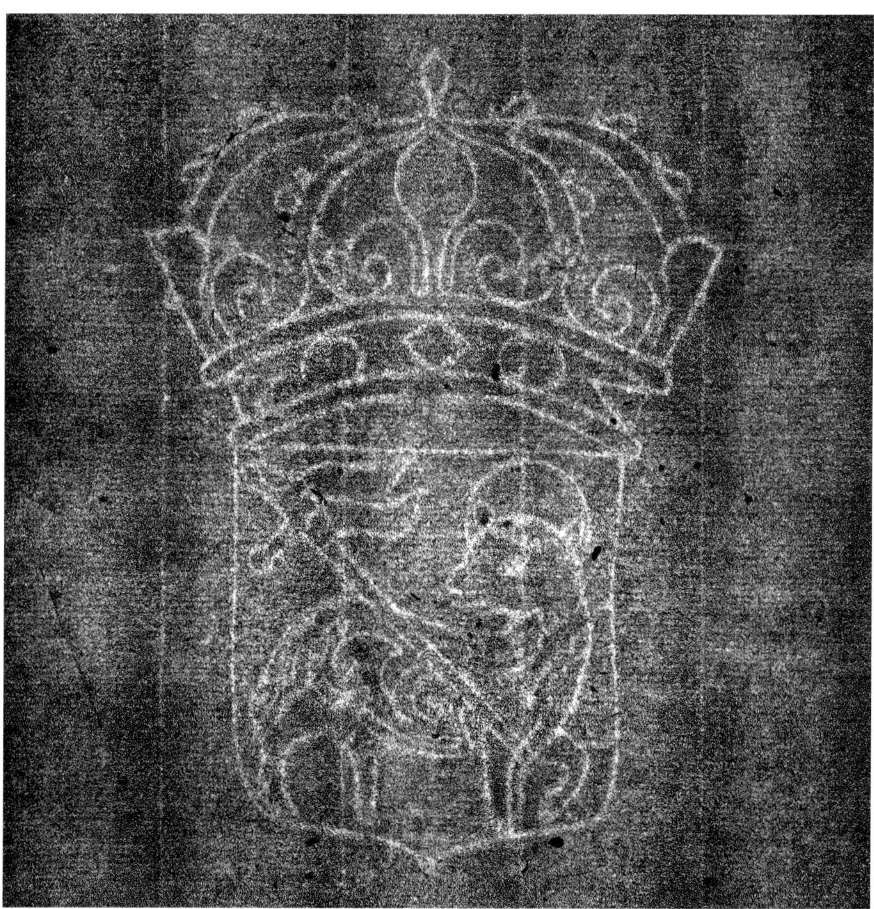
R27

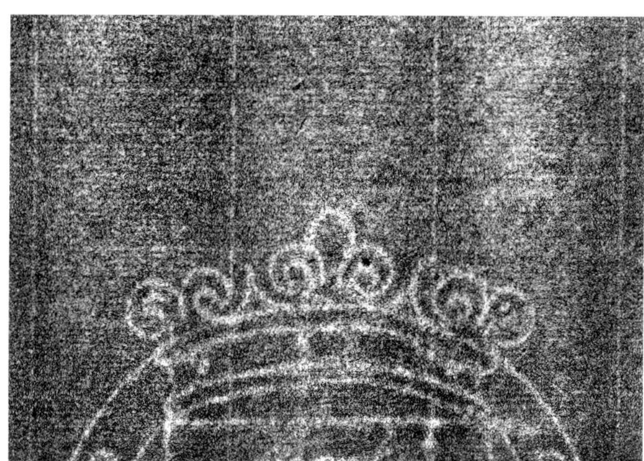
R28

R29

R29
Cat. 29
Herman Saftleven
Probably Italian paper,
17th century.

R30
Cat. 30
Herman Saftleven

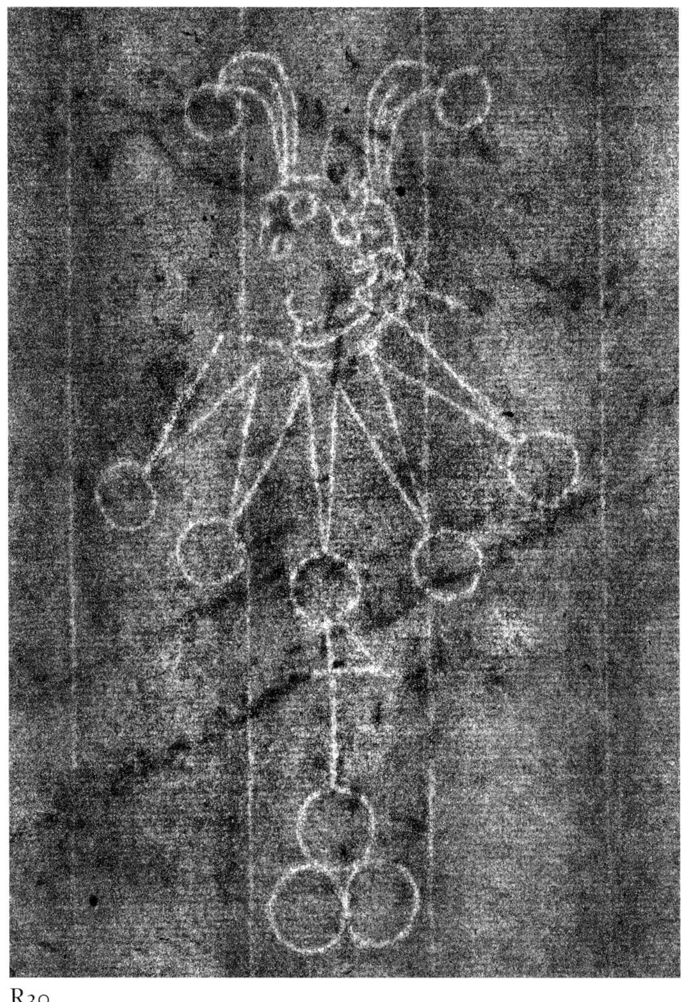
R30

R31
Cat. 31
Jacob van der Ulft

R32
Cat. 32
Jacob van der Ulft

R33
Cat. 33
Adriaen van de Velde

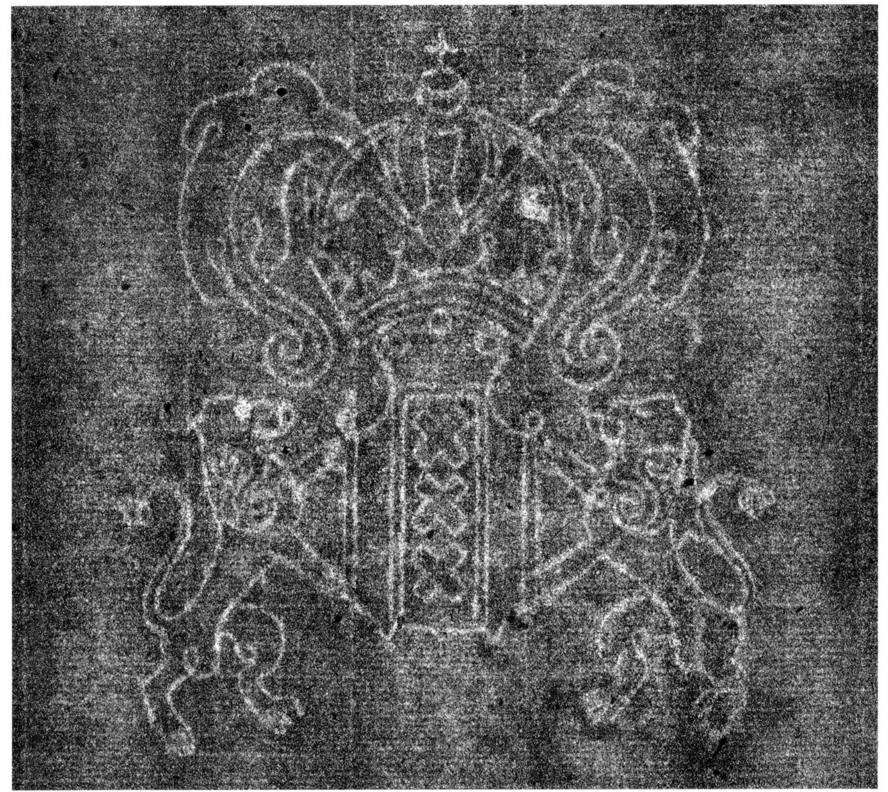

R31

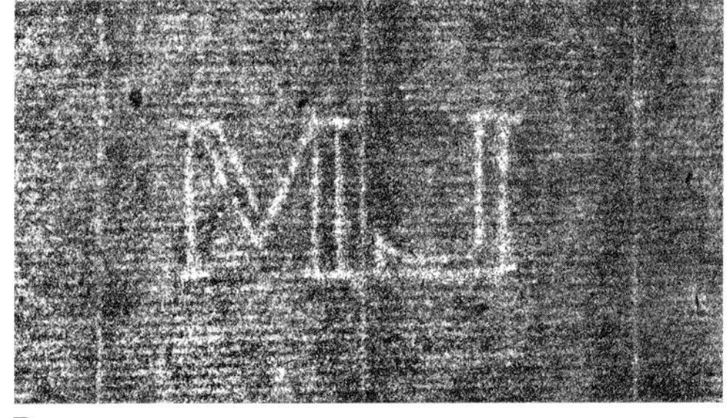

R32

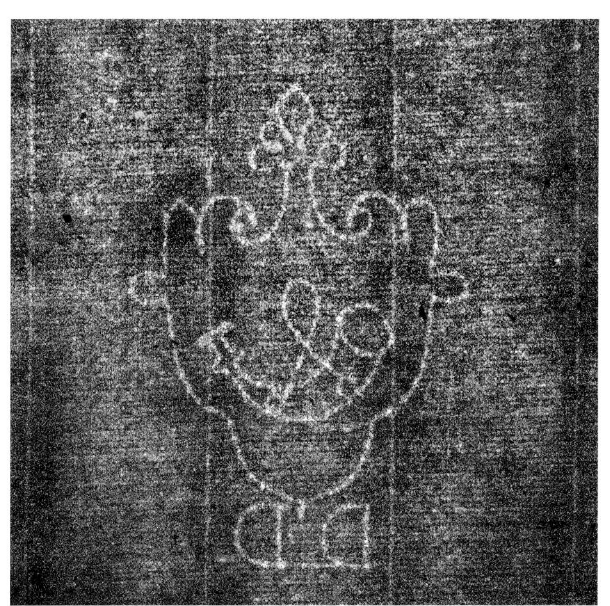

R33

R34
Cat. 34
Adriaen van de Velde

R35
Cat. 35
Willem van de Velde the Younger

R36
Cat. 36
Adriaen Verboom
Radiopaque inclusions indicate low-quality, cheap paper.

R37
Cat. 37
Abraham de Verwer

R38
Cat. 38
Laurens Vincentsz. van der Vinne

R39
Cat. 39
Cornelis Vroom

R40
Cat. 40
Thomas Wyck

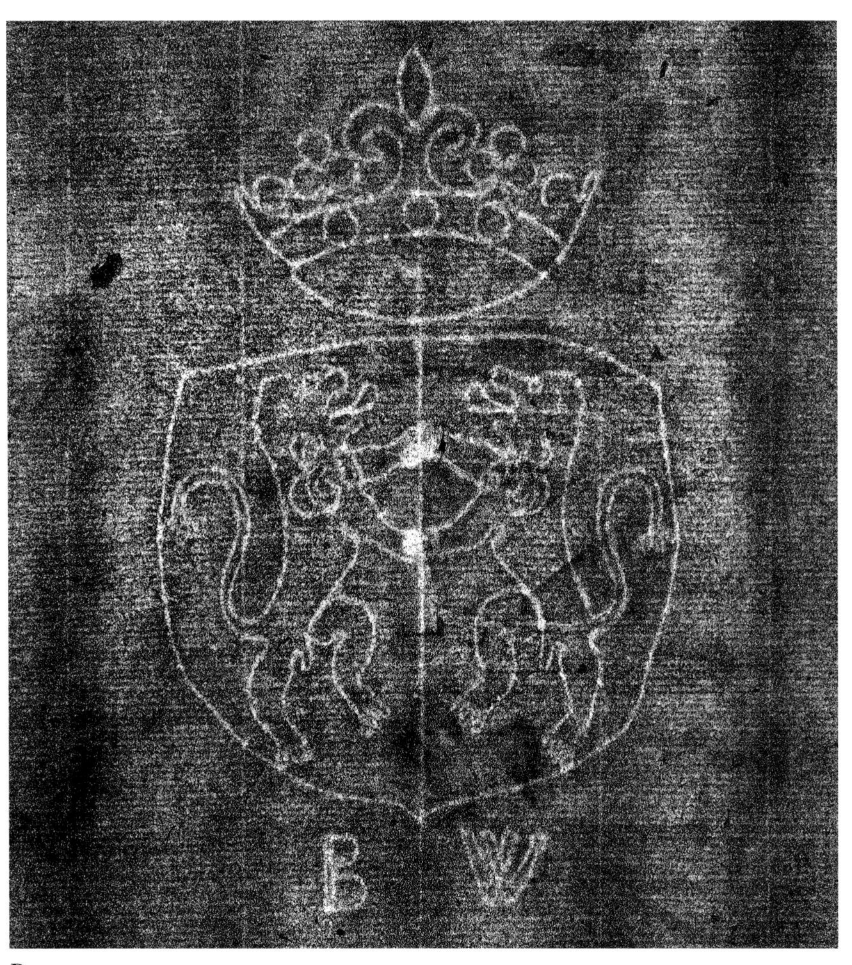

R34

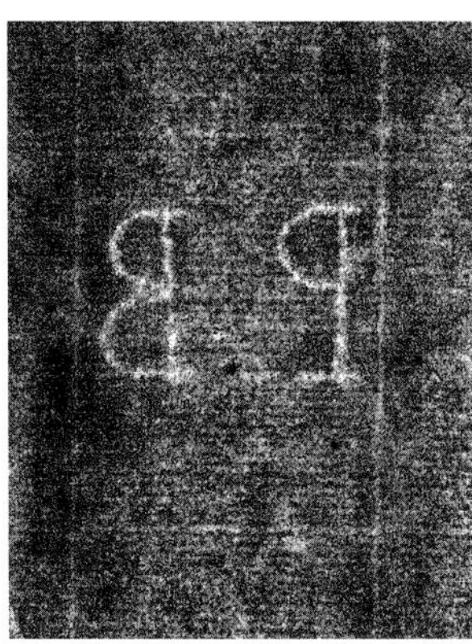

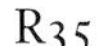

R35

R36

R37

R38

R39

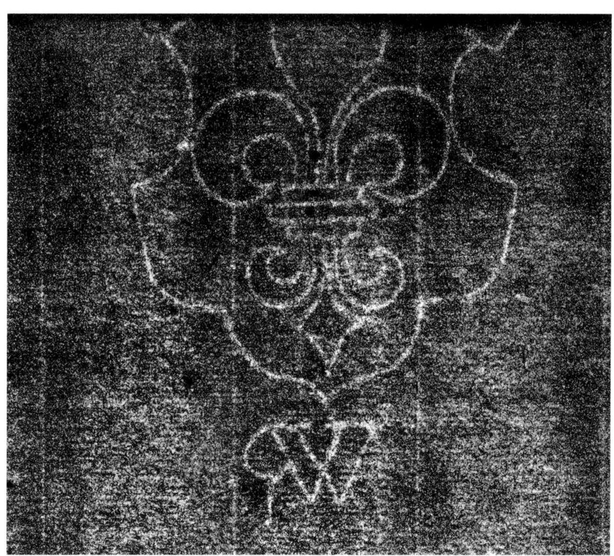
R40

References

Andrews 1985
Keith Andrews, *Catalogue of Netherlandish Drawings in the National Gallery of Scotland*, 2 vols. Edinburgh, 1985.

Ash and Fletcher 1998
Nancy Ash and Shelley Fletcher, *Watermarks in Rembrandt's Prints*, Washington, 1998.

Bartsch 1797
Adam Bartsch, *Catalogue raisonné de toutes les estampes qui forment l'oeuvre de Rembrandt, et ceux de ses principaux imitateurs, composé par les Sieurs Gersaint, Helle, Glomy et P Yver*, 2 vols., Vienna, 1797.

Beck I 1972
Hans-Ulrich Beck, *Jan van Goyen, 1596–1656*, vol. I (Einführung, Katalog der Zeichnungen), Amsterdam, 1972.

Beck III 1987
Hans-Ulrich Beck, *Jan van Goyen, 1596–1656*, vol. III (Ergänzungen zum Katalog der Handzeichnungen und Ergänzungen zum Katalog der Gemälde), Doornspijk, 1987.

Beck 1998
Hans-Ulrich Beck, *Pieter Molyn. Katalog der Handzeichnungen.* Doornspijk, 1998.

Benesch 1935
Otto Benesch, *Rembrandt, Werk und Forschung*, Vienna, 1935.

Benesch 1954–7
Otto Benesch, *The Drawings of Rembrandt*, Complete Edition, 6 vols., London, 1954–7.

Benesch 1973
Otto Benesch, *The Drawings of Rembrandt*, Complete Edition (enlarged and edited by Eva Benesch), 6 vols., London/New York, 1973.

Bol, Keyes and Butôt 1981
Laurens J. Bol, George S. Keyes and Frans C. Butôt, *Netherlandish Paintings and Drawings from the Collection of F. C. Butôt*, London, 1981.

Brandt 1986
Hans Brandt, *De Tekeningen van Joris van der Haagen*, Dissertation, Nijmegen, 1986.

Broos and Schapelhouman 1993
Ben Broos and Marijn Schapelhouman, *Nederlandse tekenaars geboren tussen 1600 en 1660*. Amsterdam, 1993.

Cat[alogue] Amsterdam 1954
Dessins, Amsterdam, Bernard Houthakker, 1954.

Cat. Amsterdam 1956
Exposition de dessins et eaux-fortes de Rembrandt et de son entourage, Amsterdam, Bernard Houthakker, 1956.

Cat. Amsterdam 1961
Master Drawings, Amsterdam, Bernard Houthakker, 1961.

Cat. Amsterdam 1964
J. W. Niemeijer, *De Verzameling van Bernard Houthakker*, Amsterdam, Rijksprentenkabinet, 1964.

Cat. Amsterdam 1965
Master Drawings, Amsterdam, Bernard Houthakker, 1965.

Cat. Amsterdam 1975–6
L. C. J. Frerichs, P. Schatborn, *De Verzameling van H. van Leeuwen*, Amsterdam, Rijksprentenkabinet, 1975–6.

Cat. Amsterdam/Washington 1981–2
Peter Schatborn, *Dutch Figure Drawings from the Seventeenth Century*, Amsterdam, Rijksprentenkabinet, 1981–2; Washington, National Gallery of Art, 1982.

Cat. Arnhem, 1958
Collectie H. van Leeuwen te Amsterdam/Tekeningen van 17e-eeuw, Arnhem, Gemeentemuseum, 1958.

Cat. Austin 1981–2
17th Century Landscape Drawings, Archer M. Huntington Art Gallery, 1981–2.

Cat. Bonn/Saarbrücken/Bochum 1968–9
E. K. J. Reznicek et al., *Niederländische Zeichnungen des 17. bis 19. Jahrhunderts aus der Sammlung Hans van Leeuwen Utrecht*, Bonn, Rheinisches Landesmuseum, 1968; Saarbrücken, Saarländisches Museum, 1968; Bochum, Städtische Kunstgalerie, 1968–69.

Cat. Bremen/Braunschweig/Stuttgart 1979–80
Meisterzeichnungen aus drei Jahrhunderten, Niederländische Handzeichnungen des 17. bis 19. Jahrhunderts aus der Sammlung Hans van Leeuwen, Bremen, Kunsthalle, 1979; Braunschweig, Städtisches Museum, 1980; Stuttgart, Galerie der Stadt Stuttgart, 1980.

Cat. Dresden 1909
Lagerkatalog 39, Dresden, F. Meyer, 1909.

Cat. Düsseldorf 1981
Aus Unseren Mappen, Neue Lagerliste 74, Düsseldorf , C. G. Boerner, 1981.

Cat. Frankfurt 1926
Rembrandt-Ausstellung, Frankfurt, Städelsches Kunstinstitut, 1926.

Cat. Fribourg/Passau/Trier/Aachen/Nuremberg 1982–4
Niederländische Meisterzeichnungen des 17. bis 19. Jahrhunderts aus der Sammlung Hans van Leeuwen, Fribourg, Musée d'Art et d'Histoire, 1982; Passau, Oberhausmuseum, 1982; Trier, Städtisches Museum, 1982; Aachen, Suermondt-Ludwig-Museum, 1983; Nuremberg, Dürerhaus, 1984.

Cat. Laren 1963
Nederlandse Tekeningen, Collectie Hans van Leeuwen, Laren, Singer Museum, 1963.

Cat. Leeuwarden 1966
Tentoonstelling Oude Tekeningen uit Drie Eeuwen, Collectie Hans van Leeuwen, Leeuwarden, Museum Princessehof, 1966.

Cat. London 1988
Master Drawings, London, Adolphe Stein, 1988.

Cat. New York 1991
Marcel G. Roethlisberger, *Bartholomeus Breenbergh*, New York, Richard L. Feigen and Co., 1991.

Cat. New York/Fort Worth 1995
M. Bisanz-Prakken, *Drawings From the Albertina: Landscape in the Age of Rembrandt.* New York, The Drawing Center, 1995; Fort Worth, Kimbell Art Museum, 1995.

Cat. Nijmegen 1965
M. van Boven, *Tekeningen uit de collectie Hans van Leeuwen*, Nijmegen, Waag Museum, 1965.

Cat. Paris 1977
Dessins, Paris, Galerie Julia Kraus, 1977.

Cat. Rheydt 1971
Niederländische Zeichnungen des 17. – 19. Jahrhunderts aus der Sammlung Hans van Leeuwen, Utrecht, Rheydt, Städtisches Museum Schloss Rheydt, 1971.

Cat. Rome 1982
Zicht op Rome 1620–1720, Nederlands Instituut, 1982.

Cat. Stockholm 1953
Dutch and Flemish Drawings in the Nationalmuseum and other Swedish Collections, Stockholm, Nationalmuseum, 1953.

Cat. Utrecht 1959–60
S. H. Levie, *Catalogus der tentoonstelling van tekeningen uit de collectie van de heer Hans van Leeuwen te Amsterdam*, Utrecht, Genootschap Kunstliefde, 1960.

Cat. Utrecht 1978
L. Brozek-Dolezal et al., *Nederlandse Tekeningen uit drie Eeuwen*, Utrecht, Centraal Museum, 1978.

Chudzikowski 1957
A. Chudzikowski, In: *Rocznik Muzeum Narodowego U Warszawie*, Warsaw, vol. 2, 1957.

Churchill
W. A. Churchill, *Watermarks in Paper in Holland, England, France, etc., in the XVII and XVIII Centuries and their Interconnection*, Amsterdam, 1935.

Davies 1972
Alice I. Davies, "Allart van Everdingen's Drawings of the Twelve Months," *The Register of the Museum of Art, University of Kansas*, vol. 4, no. 9, 1972.

Davies 1992
Alice I. Davies, *Jan van Kessel (1641–1680)*, Doornspijk, 1992.

Depauw 1989
Carl Depauw, "Een merkwaardige tekening van Paul Bril in het Antwerps Prentenkabinet," *Delineavit et Sculpsit*, vol. 2, 1989, pp. 20–25.

Fechter 1989
Isabel Fechter, In: *Weltkunst*, vol. 59, no. 12 (June 15), 1989.

Gaudriault 1995
Raymond Gaudriault, *Filigranes et autres caractéristiques des papiers fabriqués en France aux XVIIe et XVIIIe siècle*, Paris, 1995.

Giltaij 1995
Jeroen Giltaij, "Further Additions to Jacob van Ruisdael," In: C. P. Schneider, W. W. Robinson, A. I. Davies, *Shop Talk, Studies in Honor of Seymour Slive*, Cambridge, 1995, pp. 87–8, 312–4.

Giltay 1977
Jeroen Giltay, "Guillam Du Bois als tekenaar," *Oud Holland*, 1977, vol. 91, pp. 144–165.

Van Hasselt 1968
Carlos van Hasselt, *Dessins de Paysagistes Hollandais du XVIIe Siècle de la Collection Particulière Conservée à l'Institut Néerlandais de Paris*, Parts 1–2, Paris, 1968.

Heawood
Edward Heawood, *Watermarks, Mainly of the 17th and 18th Centuries (Monumenta Chartae Papyraceae Historiam Illustrantia I)*, Hilversum, 1950.

Henkel 1931
M.-D. Henkel, *Le Dessin Hollandais des Origines au XVIIe Siècle*, Paris, 1931.

Hind 1915–31
Arthur M. Hind, *Catalogue of Drawings by Dutch and Flemish Artists preserved in the Department of Prints and Drawings in the British Museum*, 4 vols., London, 1915–31.

Hind 1943
Arthur M. Hind, In: *The Connoisseur*, December 1943.

Hollstein
F. W. H. Hollstein, *Dutch and Flemish Etchings, Engravings and Woodcuts ca. 1450–1700*, Amsterdam, 1949–(in progress).

Kettering 1988
Alison M. Kettering, *Drawings from the Ter Borch Studio Estate in the Rijksmuseum*, Amsterdam, 1988.

Keyes 1982
George S. Keyes, "Hendrick and Cornelis Vroom: Addenda," *Master Drawings*, vol. 20, 1982, pp. 115–24.

Kloek 1990
W. Th. Kloek, *De kasteeltekeningen van Roelant Roghman*, Vol. II, Alphen aan den Rijn, 1990.

Laurentius, Niemeijer and Ploos van Amstel 1980
Th. Laurentius, J. W. Niemeijer, and G. Ploos van Amstel, *Cornelis Ploos van Amstel, 1726–1798, Kunstverzamelaar en prentuitgever*, Assen, 1980.

L.
Frits Lugt, *Les Marques de Collections de dessins et d'estampes*, Amsterdam, 1921; *Supplement*, The Hague, 1956.

Plomp 1997
Michiel C. Plomp, *The Dutch Drawings in the Teyler Museum, Volume II, Artists born between 1575 and 1630*, Doornspijk, 1997.

Rademaker 1725
Abraham Rademaker, *Kabinet van Nederlandsche outheden en gezichten*, 2 parts, Amsterdam, 1725.

Robinson 1958–74
M. S. Robinson, *A Catalogue of Drawings in the National Maritime Museum made by the Elder and the Younger Willem van de Velde*, 2 vols., Cambridge, 1958–74.

Robinson 1979
William W. Robinson, "Preparatory Drawings by Adriaen van de Velde," *Master Drawings*, vol. 17, 1979, pp. 3–23.

Roethlisberger 1969
Marcel Roethlisberger, *Bartholomäus Breenbergh, Handzeichnungen*, Berlin, 1969.

Roethlisberger 1991
Marcel G. Roethlisberger, *Bartholomeus Breenbergh*, New York, 1991.

Roethlisberger 1998
Marcel G. Roethlisberger, "Tipologia del Paesaggio," In: *Itinerari Sublimi. Viaggi d'artisti tra il 1750 e il 1850*, Museo Cantonale d'Arte, Lugano, 1998, pp. 320–1.

Royalton-Kisch 1991
Martin Royalton-Kisch, "A Landscape Watercolour by Rembrandt? The use of watercolor in Rembrandt's circle in Amsterdam," *Apollo*, vol. 133, no. 347 (New Series), January 1991, pp. 10–19.

Schapelhouman and Schatborn 1987
Marijn Schapelhouman and Peter Schatborn, *Land & Water, Dutch Drawings from the 17th Century in the Rijksmuseum Print Room*, Amsterdam, 1987.

Schapelhouman and Schatborn 1998
Marijn Schapelhouman and Peter Schatborn, *Dutch Drawings of the Seventeenth Century in the Rijksmuseum, Amsterdam, Artists born between 1580 and 1600*, 2 vols., Amsterdam/London, 1998.

Schatborn 1975
Peter Schatborn, "De Hut van Adriaen van de Velde," *Bulletin van het Rijksmuseum*, vol. 23 (3), 1975, pp. 159–65.

Schneider 1973
Hans Schneider, *Jan Lievens, sein Leben und seine Werke*, Reprinted with supplement by R. E. O. Ekkart, Amsterdam, 1973.

Schulz 1978
Wolfgang Schulz, *Cornelis Saftleven*, Berlin/New York, 1978.

Schulz 1982
Wolfgang Schulz, *Herman Saftleven*, Berlin/New York, 1982.

Schulz (in press)
Wolfgang Schulz, *Herman Saftleven*, 2nd edition, (in press).

Slive 1995
Seymour Slive, "Additions to Jacob van Ruisdael: II," *Burlington Magazine*, vol. 137, July 1995, pp. 452–7.

Stift und Feder 1930
Stift und Feder, "Zeichnungen von Künstlern aller Zeiten und Länder in Nachbildungen," 1930.

Sumowski 1981
Werner Sumowski, *Drawings of the Rembrandt School*, vol. 4, New York, 1981.

Sumowski 1992
Werner Sumowski, *Drawings of the Rembrandt School*, vol. 10, New York, 1992.

Trautscholdt 1973
Eduard Trautscholdt, *Johannes Ruischer, Die Radierungen.* Supplement to: Egbert Haverkamp-Begemann, *Hercules Segers, the Complete Etchings*, The Hague, 1973.

Wegner 1967–8
Wolfgang Wegner, "Bermerkungen zu Zeichnungen Rembrandts und seiner Schule in der Albertina," *Albertina-Studien*, vol. 5–6, 1967–8.

Index of Artists

Artist/Catalogue Number

This book was designed and set in type by
Gilbert Design Associates, Providence, Rhode Island.

It was printed by Meridian Printing
on Potlatch Karma paper
and bound at the Acme Bindery.

The original drawings and radiographs were digitally
copied and separated by Martin Senn.

The typeface is Janson, a design based on fonts
cut by Miklós Kis, Amsterdam, about 1685.

2,500 softcover and 100 casebound copies
on the occasion of the exhibition
August 1999

PM
PM
PM
PM